Taunton's COMPLETE ILLUSTRATED *Guide to*

Finishing

Taunton's **COMPLETE ILLUSTRATED** *Guide to*

Finishing

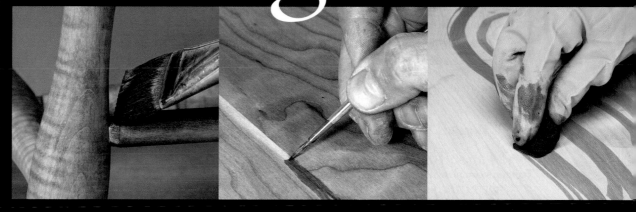

JEFF JEWITT

The Taunton Press

Contents

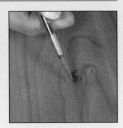

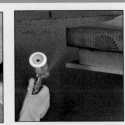

   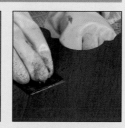

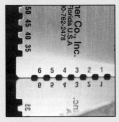

Introduction

FINISHING. It's the aptly named final detail of making furniture. Finishes not only protect wood from stains, water damage, and other mishaps, they also make it look richer and deeper and add dimension and luster. For me, finishing is the most enjoyable part of working wood, because it's where everything comes together. Whether you get a tingly feeling from wiping a coat of oil or shellac on highly figured curly maple or excitement from matching an old finish, you'll find finishing is one of the rewards of making things from wood.

Yet I'll wager that for most of you finishing isn't fun or has been an unpleasant experience. Sadly, most woodworkers find out the hard way that Murphy's Law begins with the introduction of a finish to wood. Just think of the phrases used to describe finishing problems: "fisheye," "wrinkling," "splotching," "bleeding," or "orange peel." You want that on your furniture?

This book will guide you through the finishing process and make it as exciting for you as it is for me. I learned finishing by making mistakes, lots of them, and you probably have neither the time nor the furniture to practice on the way I did. I'll guide you through the tools, the products, and the techniques for gaining control over the process, which is the point at which finishing becomes fun. You won't find a dogmatic style or preachy opinions in these pages; I'll show you proven, classic ways of doing things alongside new techniques using modern materials.

You'll see that almost 30 percent of this book is devoted to surface preparation, techniques not often shown or elaborated on in other finishing books. Proper surface preparation is what makes great finishes heads above others. Then we'll move on to coloring, which is where most finishing problems arise. A full chapter will be devoted to troubleshooting and overcoming staining problems. From there we'll look at how to choose a finish by its physics and chemistry, as well as aesthetic qualities. We'll finally get to applying clear finishes, and you'll learn how to French polish, spray lacquers, and work with water-based products.

Above all, keep an open mind. While there really aren't secrets or tricks to finishing, there is practical advice to get you started, so I'll show you as many options as possible to accomplish the same end, whether it's staining, filling pores, or applying a finish. Hopefully, some of the techniques may spark an idea of your own to try out. Even after 25 years of putting finishes on wood, I'm still learning, so use this book as a reference guide and feel free to experiment a bit and make something your own.

How to Use This Book

FIRST OF ALL, this book is meant to be used, not put on a shelf to gather dust. It's meant to be pulled out and opened on your bench when you need to do a new or unfamiliar technique. So the first way to use this book is to make sure it's near where you do woodworking.

In the pages that follow you'll find a wide variety of methods that cover the important processes of this area of woodworking. Just as in many other practical areas, in woodworking there are often many ways to get to the same result. Why you choose one method over another depends on several factors:

Time. Are you in a hurry or do you have the leisure to enjoy the quiet that comes with hand tools?

Your tooling. Do you have the kind of shop that's the envy of every woodworker or a modest collection of the usual hand and power tools?

Your skill level. Do you prefer simpler methods because you're starting out or are you always looking to challenge yourself and expand your skills?

The project. Is the piece you're making utilitarian or an opportunity to show off your best work?

In this book, we've included a wide variety of techniques to fit these needs.

To find your way around the book, you first need to ask yourself two questions: What result am I trying to achieve? What tools do I want to use to accomplish it?

In some cases, there are many ways and many tools that will accomplish the same result. In others, there are only one or two sensible ways to do it. In all cases, however, we've taken a practical approach; so you may not find your favorite exotic method for doing a particular process. We have included every reasonable method and then a few just to flex your woodworking muscles.

To organize the material, we've broken the subject down to two levels. "Parts" are major divisions of this class of techniques. "Sections" contain related techniques. Within sections, techniques and procedures that create a similar result are grouped together, usually organized from the most common way to do it to methods requiring specialized tools or a larger degree of skill. In some cases, the progression starts with the method requiring the most basic technology and then moves on to alternative methods using other common shop tools and finally to specialized tools.

The first thing you'll see in a part is a group of photos keyed to a page number. Think of this as an illustrated table of contents. Here you'll see a photo representing each section in that part, along with the page on which each section starts.

Each section begins with a similar "visual map," with photos that represent major groupings of techniques or individual techniques. Under each grouping is a list of the step-by-step essays that explain how to do the methods, including the pages on which they can be found.

Sections begin with an "overview," or brief introduction, to the methods described therein. Here's where you'll find important general information on this group of techniques, including any safety issues. You'll also read about specific tools needed for the operations that follow and how to build jigs or fixtures needed for them.

The step-by-step essays are the heart of this book. Here a group of photos represents the key steps in the process. The accompanying text describes the process and guides you through it, referring you back to the photos. Depending on how you learn best, either read the text first or look at the photos and drawings; but remember, they are meant to work together. In cases

The "VISUAL MAP" tells you where to locate the essay that details the operation you wish to do.

A "SECTION" groups related processes together.

The "OVERVIEW" gives you important general information about the group of techniques, tells you how to build jigs and fixtures, and provides advice on tooling and safety.

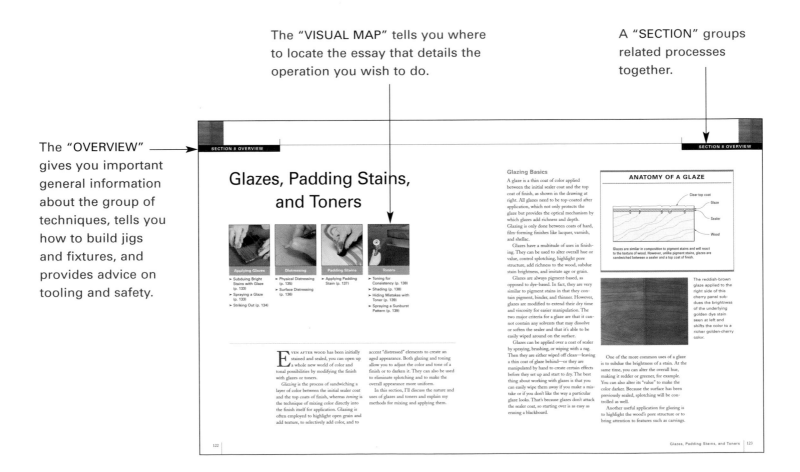

where there is an alternative step, it's called out in the text and the visual material as a "variation."

For efficiency, we've cross-referenced redundant processes or steps described in another related process. You'll see yellow "cross-references" called out frequently in the overviews and step-by-step essays.

When you see this symbol ⚠, make sure you read what follows. The importance of these safety warnings cannot be over-emphasized. Always work safely and use safety devices, including eye and hearing protection. If you feel uncomfortable with a technique, don't do it, try another way.

At the back of the book is an index to help you find what you're looking for in a pinch and Resources to help locate hard-to-find supplies.

Finally, remember to use this book whenever you need to refresh your memory or to learn something new. It's been designed to be an essential reference to help you become a better woodworker. The only way it can do this is if you make it as familiar a workshop tool as your favorite bench chisels.

—The editors

"STEP-BY-STEP ESSAYS" contain photos, drawings, and instructions on how to do the technique.

"CROSS-REFERENCES" tell you where to find a related process or the detailed description of a process in another essay.

The "TEXT" contains keys to the photos and drawings.

"TIPS" show short-cuts and smart ways to work.

"VARIATIONS" show alternatives for doing a step.

"WARNINGS" tell you specific safety concerns for this process and how to address them.

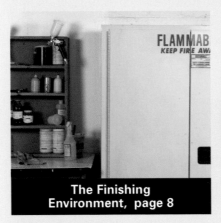

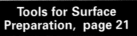

Tools

THE TOOLS USED to prepare wood may not seem as glamorous as table saws or routers, but they are every bit as important. The proper tools can make the difference between a simple, successful job and a nightmarish experience. The two categories used in finishing are surface preparation tools and finish application tools. Surface preparation tools include planes, scrapers, and sanders—all of which have particular applications and which yield different results. Finish application tools range from the humble brush to complex spray systems and have just as dramatic an impact on your works as does your choice of finish.

In addition to the appropriate tools, there are a few other basic necessities you'll need for proper finishing. These include safety gear, storage for your supplies, and a finishing area that is well lighted, ventilated, and heated. This part of the book discusses how to set up a finishing area and which tools and safety equipment might best serve your needs.

The Finishing Environment

Whether you work in a production shop or in your home basement, it's important that your finishing area be clean, ventilated, and well lighted. It's also critical that you're able to heat the area in cold weather. If you work with flammable or hazardous materials, you'll need to provide mechanical ventilation to exhaust fumes and overspray. You'll also want cabinets or shelves to store finishing materials, as well as devices to hold your projects in process.

A Space To Finish

Ideally, you should finish in a dedicated space separate from your machining area. If this isn't practical, at least keep the finishing space as far away as possible. Weather permitting, you may be able to finish outdoors. Here are a few suggestions for working indoors or outside.

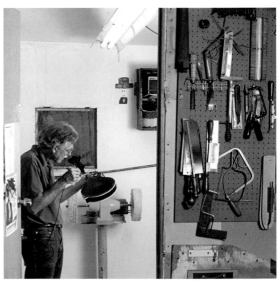

Luthier Don MacRostie creates impeccable mandolin finishes in his dedicated finishing room. Note the white walls and reflectors on the overhead fluorescent lights—both of which help distribute light evenly in the room.

A stout cabinetmaker's bench is a great tool for preparing workpiece surfaces and applying wipe-on finishes. The large, south-facing glass-block windows in the author's shop provide plenty of natural light, which is supplemented by overhead strip fluorescent lights.

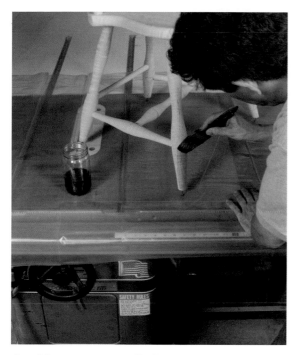

A table saw can easily be converted to a finishing bench by covering it with clear plastic drop cloths. Four drywall screws driven into the feet of this chair raise it up for easier, cleaner finishing of the legs.

Indoors

In a cramped shop, you may find that the only place to finish is on top of a bench or table saw. If so, protect your saw or bench with drop cloths. Plan your work sequence to allow at least 12 hours for the dust to settle after sanding and machining. Using an ambient air cleaner will significantly shorten this time. In mild weather, you can use fans to evacuate the dust outdoors. In cold weather, you may want to avoid this, as your shop heat goes out the window too. When you're forced to finish in your general shop area, it's best to use fast-drying finishes like shellac or oils and varnishes that wipe on. These finishes don't attract dust that ends up creating pimples in the finished surface.

Weather permitting, finishing outside provides great light and ventilation. Just make sure you work in shade. A pair of sawhorses and a piece of particle-board make a great temporary bench.

Outdoors

Another option when working in a cramped shop is to finish outdoors, where you've got plenty of good lighting and natural ventilation. Of course, weather conditions have to cooperate, as you need to avoid cold or extremely hot and humid days. But when the weather is nice, finishing outdoors on a couple of sawhorses is fine. Just work in a shaded area entirely out of direct sunlight. If shade is scarce and you're feeling industrious, you can construct a tent top of canvas or plastic sheeting. For protection against a breeze, you can set up a plywood windbreak against the side of a garage or other structure. When you do finish outdoors, always bring your work inside to dry. Never leave finished items out all night.

Temperature and Humidity

Temperature and humidity are the two hardest things to control in the shop. Finishing products cure best at temperatures ranging from 65°F to 80°F, with a relative humidity of 50 percent or less. Temperatures below 50°F will retard or prevent many finishes

This digital thermometer/hygrometer will tell you when conditions are right for finishing. The temperature and humidity shown here are about as good as it gets.

from curing. Although heat alone doesn't necessarily make for bad finishing conditions, the humidity that often accompanies it can pose a real problem.

To help you gauge temperature and humidity, I suggest investing in an inexpensive digital thermometer/hygrometer available for about $25. (See Resources, p. 287.) Avoid finishing when the relative humidity is over 85 percent unless you can provide good air circulation using fans, which help somewhat—particularly when using water-based finishes. With some finishes, additives are available to improve flow and cure time in extreme humidity.

Don't forget about the moisture content of the wood itself, which should range between 5 percent and 8 percent for furniture making. To accurately detect moisture content in lumber, use a wood moisture meter (available from woodworking tool suppliers). If you don't have a moisture meter, a good rule of thumb is to bring seasoned lumber indoors to acclimate for at least two months before machining and finishing.

Lighting

Natural lighting is ideal for finishing. Its full color spectrum allows you to view the true color of your finish. However, if you don't have a lot of windows in your shop, you'll have to make do with fluorescent and incandescent lighting. I prefer fluorescent lights because they are available in different "color temperatures," rated in Kelvin (K) and with different "color rendering index" (CRI) ratings. A low color temperature of around 3000 K is considered warm and inviting, like

Full-spectrum fluorescent tubes often aren't labeled with their color temperature or CRI rating, but the product name usually includes the number "50," such as "Chroma 50," "Colortone 50," "SPX 50," etc.

candlelight. Higher color temperatures of around 5000 K are considered "cool," but mimic the full spectrum of color found in natural sunlight. For matching colors, a CRI rating of about 90 with a Kelvin rating of 5000 is considered standard. These bulbs are pricey and consume more energy than standard bulbs, so you should only use them in color-critical areas such as a spray booth or staining area. Unfortunately, the Kelvin and CRI ratings aren't always indicated on bulb packaging, so you may have to purchase your lights from a knowledgeable lighting dealer.

To help ambient shop lighting, paint the ceiling flat white and mount overhead strip fixtures for your fluorescent lights. If the ceiling is a dark color, or if you have to suspend the fixtures, use strip fixtures with reflectors to help distribute the light. For task lighting at benches and workstations, I

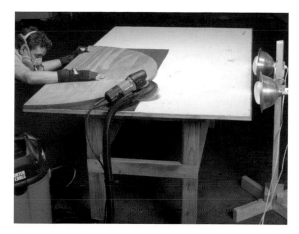

For large, flat tops such as on this mahogany demilune table, the raking light supplied by these two "can" lamps highlights defects that overhead lighting doesn't pick up.

This totally enclosed, gas-powered radiant heater provides plenty of heat for the finishing/spray area of this commercial shop. These units heat fresh air brought in from the outside, radiate the heat from the large pipe, then vent the fumes outside.

use incandescent lights. When I sand at my bench, I use 65-watt portable floodlights placed so the light rakes across the work surface at a low angle to expose defects.

Heating

Finishing during the cold season requires heating your shop. Finishes are best applied at room temperatures of 70°F to 80°F, although you can sometimes get by in temperatures as low as 60°F or as high as 90°F. How you heat your shop is a matter of preference and availability of appliances and utilities. Gas, electric, or wood-burning stoves can all be used, though wood-burning stoves and other appliances with an open flame or glowing heat element pose a hazard around flammable finishing products.

In a commercial shop, you should check local codes to see what heating regulations apply to locations where flammable products are being used. My local code required the use of a totally enclosed system with no open flame. As a result, I opted for a gas-powered infrared tube-type heating system that draws air from the outside, heats it in a totally enclosed chamber, forces it through a tube that radiates the heat downward, then discharges the exhaust outside. It's clean, produces no dirt or soot, and is energy-saving to boot. Totally enclosed gas- or propane-powered heaters that vent to the outside are also a safe alternative.

Ventilation

Almost all finishing products release some type of hazardous solvent into the air during application and curing. The best way to protect your health—besides wearing safety equipment—is to finish in a well-ventilated area. Ideally, you should have cross-ventilation, working near a window fan that is pulling the vapors away from you and the workpiece to the outside. To determine the size of the fan

This open-faced commercial metal booth satisfies all local codes with its explosion-proof fan, motor, lights, and metal walls. Note the fire extinguisher at hand.

you may be able to pick up a used one at an auction for next to nothing.

If you purchase a booth as a complete package, its explosion-proof fan is usually sized to the dimensions of the booth. Be aware that the high-velocity exhaust fans in spray booths will quickly suck out all the available air from inside a building. "Makeup" air devices solve this problem by bringing fresh air in from the outside and putting it in front of the spray booth. While makeup air units are costly, they are worth every penny for a commercial shop.

► BOOTH MAINTENANCE

For optimum performance, it is important to properly maintain a spray booth. Here are a few things you can do to ensure its efficiency and safety:

- Use a removable booth coating on a metal booth. This light-reflective, temporary coating can be peeled off when heavily fouled with overspray.

- Tape temporary, fire-retardant paper covering to the floor to protect it and to help reflect light. The covering can also be taped to booth walls and used as a disposable palette for checking color and spray gun adjustments.

- Change filters—particularly the plenum (back) filters—when they are 50 percent or more restricted with particulate. These filters may be classified as hazardous waste, so check local ordinances before pitching them into a dumpster.

- Frequently vacuum the floor inside and outside the booth.

A metal booth can be coated with a rubbery white paint that can eventually be peeled off when it loads up with finishing materials. The coating can be applied with a spray gun or latex paint roller.

Fire-retardant paper can be used as a temporary floor coating to keep the floor free of overspray and to help reflect lighting upward onto hard-to-see undersides of workpieces.

Indoor spraying of flammable finishes is possible with the right setup. This spray area is outfitted with an explosion-proof exhaust fan and lights. The prefan filter was removed for clarity in this photo.

The author's booth features a door that filters out dust from the shop. The makeup air unit above brings in fresh air from the outside, replacing the exact amount of air that the booth fan exhausts.

Codes require that light fixtures used for the booth be explosion-proof. Installation of the lights, electrical fixtures, and ventilation may require the services of professional, licensed technicians. In addition, building and fire codes require automatic water or dry powder sprinklers. Codes may also stipulate the placement of the exhaust stack. When installing a booth in a commercial building, consult the local fire marshal to ensure that all local ordinances and codes are followed.

Storing and Dispensing Finishing Products

Flammable finishing products should be stored in a metal cabinet for fire safety. In fact, cabinets in commercial shops are required to meet National Fire Protection Association (NFPA) fire-rating codes. I recommend that cabinets in a home shop be made of at least 22-gauge metal.

To work with finishing products, you'll need to measure and transfer liquids, powders, and pastes. I use a variety of simple tools for this. Many can be purchased from mail-order plastics dealers. (See Resources, p. 287.) However, I also routinely look for

This fire-rated metal cabinet meets the approval of the author's local fire marshal. The cabinet sits conveniently next to the spray gun table, an old Hoosier cabinet with an easily cleanable porcelain top.

Antifatigue mats provide great protection against scuffing work-in-process against floors and work surfaces. You can also use moving blankets for this, but they're more difficult to keep clean. I find blankets are better for covering pieces before and after finishing and during delivery.

Finishing boards hold work during and after finish application. They're particularly helpful when dealing with a lot of different parts, like drawers, doors, and shelves. Also called "nail boards," the best finishing boards support the workpiece on nail or

screw points. This way, you can apply the finish to the "nonshow" side first, then place that side on the points while you finish the "show" side.

Nail boards are easy to make. One strategy is to drive four drywall screws though a piece of plywood. Alternatively, you can take the "bed of nails" approach, in which you drive staples through a board in a 4-in. grid. This distributes workpiece weight evenly, minimizing any marks in the finish. Of the two designs, precisely placed drywall screws with their sharp points are best for painted finishes. The blunt end of a staple can leave a visible mark on paint but is hardly visible on clear finishes.

Drying racks provide a consolidated space to put your finishing boards while the finish cures. The best drying rack design that I've seen is one that can be wheeled around

Rubber antifatigue floor mats provide a soft platform to protect parts during sanding. These mats are much easier to keep clean than carpet or fabric mats.

A "bed of nails" will nicely support a panel to be sprayed with stains or clear finishes . The nail board is made from ½-in.-thick oriented strand board or plywood with 1-in.-long staples driven through the board in a 4-in. grid. To prevent marks on painted surfaces, use drywall screws instead of staples.

The arms on this mobile drying rack are adjustable to suit workpieces. It was designed for kitchen cabinet parts.

This mobile turntable is outfitted with casters and weighted with sand to prevent tipping. Various tops can be connected to the base by attaching 1¼-in.-diameter pipes of different lengths that simply slide inside the 2-in.-diameter base pipe.

when it's full. Another option is to simply bolt to a wall a couple of 4x4s that have been drilled every 5 in. to accommodate 1-in.-diameter dowels or PVC pipe.

Finishing turntables are essential for spraying many projects. A simple finishing turntable can be made by attaching a plywood panel to a lazy susan-type swivel plate, then fastening the unit to a table. However, a more effective and versatile design is a freestanding turntable/dolly unit. The base is outfitted with casters for mobility and weighted with sand to prevent tipping. Use 2-in. floor flanges to connect the pipes to the top and bottom.

An ABC-type fire extinguisher is the best all-purpose kind for a finishing shop. Make sure it's serviced regularly.

Fire and Disposal Safety

Most finishing products contain materials that are flammable or hazardous to the environment. First and foremost, you should have at least one ABC-type fire extinguisher near your finishing area, which will handle the three common types of potential shop fires. These, of course, are mandatory in commercial shops. One of the most common dangers is spontaneous combustion caused by improper disposal of finish-soaked rags. More finishing-related fires have probably been caused by this than by any other reason. Dispose of used rags properly! (See the sidebar on p. 20.)

You can "clean" used solvents by decanting the liquid until the debris settles. After it does, pour off the clear liquid at the top for cleaning brushes and work surfaces.

▶ SAFE RAG DISPOSAL

Rags used to apply oil finishes can spontaneously combust if not handled correctly. Rags should be soaked in water, then spread or hung out to dry without wadding or folding them. When they're dry, you can dispose of them in the trash.

Take care to properly dispose of finishing wastes. Never pour them down the drain, even water-based products (which contain hazardous chemicals). Many municipalities have a paint and solvent recycling program, and welcome drop-offs of these materials. Commercial shops will have to pay for hazardous waste services and/or invest in a solvent-recovery system. Solvent-recovery systems are often a cost-effective option if you generate more than 5 gallons of solvent waste per month.

You can easily recycle and reuse solvents like used mineral spirits and lacquer thinner by storing them in containers until the solids settle to the bottom. Then you can pour off the clear solvent for reuse in work surface cleanup and preliminary brush washing.

If hazardous waste disposal isn't available in your area, the best thing to do is to let the product evaporate outside. However, do not mix oil-based finishes with sawdust, as this poses a risk of fire. Place the waste product outside in a shallow pan until it evaporates enough to become a dry paste that you can then dispose of in your regular trash.

The best defense against product hazards is knowledge of the ingredients and the health and safety precautions, all of which can be found on the packaging label. So read the label! For industrial products, federal law mandates that Material Safety Data Sheets (MSDS) be made available to workers who use the products. An MSDS is obtainable from the manufacturer for any product—consumer or industrial—whether it contains hazardous ingredients or not.

Tools for Surface Preparation

Sharpening

A GOOD FINISH JOB depends largely on a well-prepared surface. Before you apply a finish, wood must be clean and smooth. Mill marks from planers, jointers, and saws must be removed, as well as any stray wood fibers. And flat surfaces must be truly flat, especially if they'll be treated with a reflective finish that will highlight a wavy surface. Don't expect stains and finishes to hide defects; they'll often highlight them instead.

Surface preparation tools for finishing can be broken down into two basic categories: cutting tools and sanding tools. Cutting tools include planes, scrapers, and files. Sanding tools range from simple sheet sandpaper through large stationary drum and belt sanders. Cutting tools and sanding tools are often used in combination to prepare surfaces.

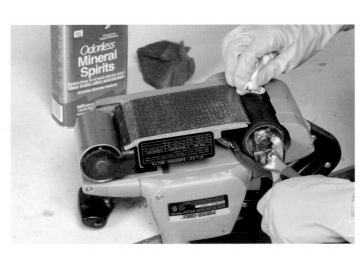

Power tools like this belt sander perform the bulk of flattening operations. Cleaning the platen and rollers with mineral spirits ensures peak performance.

Cutting Tools

Although I use power sanders for the bulk of my surface preparation, planes and scrapers also play a big part, depending on the job. These tools can remove wood much quicker than sandpaper and allow you to keep your head out of the dust clouds. On many types of wood, a finely tuned hand plane can remove milling marks and at the same time create a finish-ready surface that requires little or no follow-up finish sanding. For troublesome woods that tend to tear out, I reach for a scraper or sandpaper.

Planes

Hand planing can be the most efficient way to a flat, smooth surface, especially one that suffers from heavy milling marks or planer snipe. And planes can't be beat when it comes to producing the look of a vintage piece that displays subtle tool marks.

I regularly use three planes: a jack plane, a smoothing plane, and a block plane. I use the jack plane for removing milling marks from tops, legs, aprons, and other long parts. The jack plane's long body makes it particularly useful for the initial flattening of tabletops and other large panels. I use the shorter smoothing plane for general smoothing and to follow up the jack plane on large surfaces. The block plane is useful for cleaning up saw marks on edges and for trimming end grain.

To work correctly, a plane must be properly tuned, and its sole must be dead flat. To check the sole, make sure the blade is clamped in place as usual, then lay a good straightedge across the sole. If the sole isn't flat, true it by lapping it on 120-grit wet/dry sandpaper fixed to a sheet of thick glass or other known flat surface like a table saw or jointer table. The plane blade must also be razor-sharp, or you're asking for tearout. (See *"Sharpening a Plane Blade"* on p. 38.)

However, woods with gnarly grain can be a problem even with a sharp blade in a well-tuned plane. That's where scrapers come in.

Scrapers

Scrapers take a different approach to smoothing wood. Unlike a plane iron, whose tip slices through the wood, a scraper does its work using a sharpened, turned edge, as shown in the drawing below. A scraper's cutting action minimizes tearout, although the resulting surface won't be cut as cleanly as with a well-tuned plane.

The author's three favorite planes for surface preparation tasks are (from left) a no. 6 jack plane, a no. 4 smoothing plane, and a low-angle block plane.

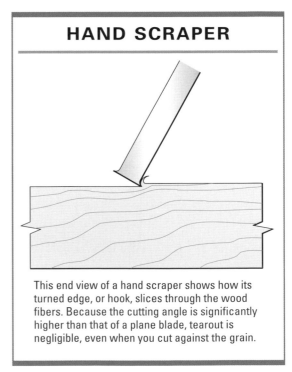

HAND SCRAPER

This end view of a hand scraper shows how its turned edge, or hook, slices through the wood fibers. Because the cutting angle is significantly higher than that of a plane blade, tearout is negligible, even when you cut against the grain.

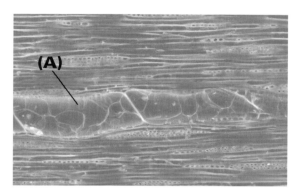

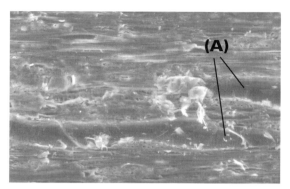

A plane cuts the cellular surface of this walnut cleanly, as you can see from this photomicrograph. The large opening emanating from the center (A) is a pore. Note the clarity of the cellular structure. This surface appears shiny, even without a finish.

A scraper tears the cellular material more than a plane, as you can see from the area surrounding the two large pores (A) in this photomicrograph of scraped walnut. The cellular structure is also less clear than on a planed surface.

Scrapers are my favorite surface preparation tools. Like planes, they're worthless until you get comfortable sharpening them, but once you do, you'll wonder how you did without them. Scrapers come in two basic types: hand scrapers and cabinet scrapers.

Hand scrapers are nothing more than hard, flat pieces of steel. They offer great control and can get into corners and other places that a plane or sandpaper can't. Also called "card" scrapers, they excel at smoothing both curved and flat work and allow you to remove tool marks on complicated shapes like legs. Hand scrapers are available in a variety of shapes. Square scrapers will take care of 90 percent of your work, but curved scrapers can be very useful for removing router-bit or shaper chatter on curved surfaces. Once you learn to sharpen a curved scraper, you'll find no better tool for smoothing cove moldings or the complex curves on cabriole legs.

Cabinet scrapers, sometimes called "scraper planes," use the same cutting principle, although the metal scraper is fixed into a body for better control when you're smoothing flat surfaces. I usually reach for a cabinet scraper when I need to smooth panels or tabletops, particularly if aggressive scraping is required or I'm working with difficult woods. I typically follow up cabinet scraping with hand scraping for the final smoothing.

These scrapers, the most useful for surface preparation, are (clockwise from bottom) a gooseneck hand scraper, a curved hand scraper, a straight hand scraper, a small cabinet scraper, and a no. 80 Stanley™ cabinet scraper.

▶ GRADING ABRASIVES

There are three main systems of grading grit for sandpaper: CAMI, FEPA, and micron. The most common one in the U.S. is the CAMI system, named after the Coated Abrasives Manufacturers Institute.

The FEPA system—in which the letter "P" precedes the grit designation—is equivalent to the CAMI system up to about 220 grit. After that, the FEPA numbers are higher than those for equivalent grits in the CAMI system. The micron system—designated by the symbol "M"—applies to grits 220 and finer.

The CAMI system is the least tolerant of grit-size inconsistencies, whereas the FEPA and micron systems adhere to stricter standards. Grit inconsistency doesn't matter much when you're sanding bare wood. However, when sanding finishes, you'll appreciate the closer tolerances the FEPA and micron systems provide.

Grits 36 to 80 are generally used for shaping, while grits 100 to 220 are used for leveling and smoothing. For general sanding of bare wood by machine or hand, aluminum oxide in 100- through 240-grit with an antiload coating can't be beat. For dry sanding between coats of finish, 320- through 600-grit antiloading paper is best. You should also have silicon carbide wet/dry paper in 400 to 1200 grit for wet sanding.

Sandpaper Grit Comparison

CAMI	FEPA	MICRON	GENERIC
1500		3	Microfine
		5	
		6	
1200			
		9	
1000			
800	p2000		Ultrafine
	p1500	15	
600	p1200		
500	p1000		
	p1000		
400	p800		Superfine
		25	
360	p600		
		30	
320	p400	35	Extrafine
		40	
	p360		
280		45	
		50	
240	p280		
		55	
		60	
220	p220	65	
180	p180		
150	p150		
120	p120		
100	p100		
80	p80		
60	p60		
30	p36		

Film is the most expensive backing and is typically used only for premium products such as 3M's Imperial Microfinishing abrasives. Although you can use these abrasives for sanding bare wood, they're primarily designed for sanding and polishing finishes.

[TIP] **Many specialized sandpaper products like no-load, ceramic, and the ultra- and microfine papers aren't commonly available at your local home supply or hardware store. You'll probably have to mail-order many of these specialized items from the Resources listed on p. 28.**

Sandpaper Products

Sandpaper is available in an array of forms for use by hand or with many different machines. It comes in sheets, disks, belts, drums, and other configurations for special purposes.

Sheets are sold in standard 9-in. by 11-in. sizes, which can be cut into smaller sizes for either hand or machine sanding. A-weight paper is useful for hand-sanding curves and complicated shapes, while the stiffer C- and D-weight papers are good for leveling flat surfaces.

Disks are available in a dizzying multitude of grits, backings, and bonds, either as individual disks or on a roll. Disks attach to their sander pads by either a pressure-sensitive-adhesive (PSA) or a two-part hook-and-loop system (think Velcro™). For production work where the abrasive will be used until it wears out, PSA is best. Hook-and-loop is better for intermittent usage, and I like it for contour sanding because its cushioned back conforms better to curves.

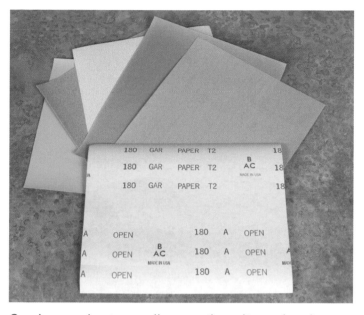

Sandpaper sheets usually carry the grit number, but don't always state the type of grit or whether it's open- or closed-coat. The gold and whitish-gray papers shown here are stearated.

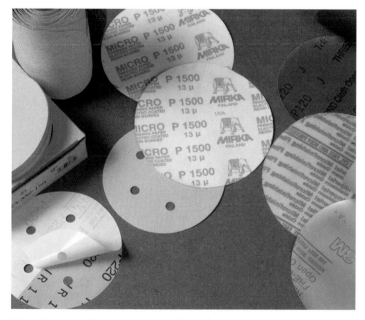

Sandpaper disks are made in a multitude of grits, backings, and bonds. The holes in the disks match up to the holes in the sander pads that allow dust extraction.

The grit on belts and drum sleeves is typically aluminum oxide, ceramic, or a blend of both. The backing is usually cloth, although paper is used for some wide belts. Drum sleeves tend to have thicker, more rigid backings.

Foam pads and blocks are used primarily for contour sanding. Some can be used either wet or dry; some are used only wet. These washable pads are made by gluing silicon carbide or aluminum oxide to open- or closed-cell foam.

Steel wool and synthetic steel wool are sold as individual pads or on a roll. The products I find the most useful are 000 and 0000 steel wool, as well as very fine (maroon) and ultrafine (gray) synthetic abrasive pads.

Belts and drum sleeves typically sport aluminum oxide, ceramic, or a combination of the two. Belts and sleeves usually have a cloth backing, although less-expensive paper belts are available for some wide-belt sanders. Belt-type sandpaper is also available in rolls for wrapping the drums in many small-shop drum sanders.

Sleeves are used on oscillating spindle sanders or soft, air-filled pneumatic drums for sanding contours and profiles.

Foam pads and *blocks* are used primarily for wet or dry contour sanding. Usually made of silicon carbide or aluminum oxide glued to open- or closed-cell foam, they are often waterproof and washable.

Steel wool is a fine abrasive consisting of a stranded network of fine steel wires. Its nasty tendency to shed bits of steel makes it unsuitable for use on bare wood or between coats of finish, so it's typically used only for rubbing out finishes. Instead of steel wool, I use synthetic abrasive pads. Sold under brand names such as Scotch-Brite™, Bear Tex™, and Mirlon™, this material is made by fabricating a random network of plastic fibers that is then impregnated with an abrasive grit-and-glue slurry. The pads are available in various grades equivalent to the common grades of steel wool.

Flutter sheet wheels are strips of sandpaper slashed at the ends and connected to a central arbor. They can be mounted on a drill, in a drill press, or on a bench grinder. They are great for production sanding of curved shapes and molded edges.

Flutter sanders are made of strips of sandpaper slashed at the ends and attached to an arbor. They can be mounted in a drill press or stacked on a drill arbor. They are great for production sanding of curved, shaped, and molded edges.

▶ OPEN COAT VERSUS CLOSED COAT

The grit distribution on sandpaper is applied in different densities. "Open coat" means that the grit covers 40 to 70 percent of the backing, while a "closed coat" indicates 100 percent coverage. Open coatings are used in situations where the material being sanded would clog the paper and are always used to sand bare wood. Closed coatings are suited to wet sanding.

Hand-Sanding Tools

While the bulk of sanding is done with power tools, hand-sanding is still important because it allows more control, especially when you're smoothing complicated surfaces on moldings and carvings. You also need that control when scuff sanding a finish between coats and when hand-sanding as the final pass over a machine-sanded surface.

Hand-sanding doesn't require a lot of tools. The main tool is the sandpaper itself, often backed up by an appropriate block, as I'll discuss in Sections 4 and 5. The only other methods you'll need involve cutting and storing the sandpaper.

You can cut or tear sheet sandpaper into the size you want. I mounted an old hacksaw blade on the edge of my workbench for quickly tearing sandpaper sheets to size.

An old hacksaw blade on the side of a bench allows you to quickly tear sandpaper sheets to size. To avoid driving screws into my bench, I attach the blade using double-sided tape.

Store your sandpaper flat in shop-made bins, preferably in a closed cabinet to keep the paper clean and dry.

Belt sanders are the most aggressive portable sanding tools. Large, heavy, 4-in. x 24-in. sanders (right) excel at leveling, while a lightweight 3-in. x 21-in. model (left) is better for tasks that require greater maneuverability.

Sheet sandpaper needs to be organized and stored flat, and a storage bin provides the best solution to this. If possible, keep the paper cool and dry. Storing the bin inside a cabinet will help with this and will keep shop dust and debris from the paper. If your shop is damp, you can place desiccant inside the cabinet and weigh down the sandpaper with something to prevent curling.

Portable Sanders

Most sanding is done with power equipment, and there are many choices of power sanders. Some excel at leveling and removing defects, while others are best for getting into tight corners and sanding delicate details. The four common categories of portable power sanders are belt sanders, orbital sanders, random orbit sanders, and detail/profile sanders.

Belt sanders are the best tool for heavy-duty work like leveling and initial smoothing of solid wood tops, sides, and other wide stock. Smaller, more lightweight versions can be used for fairing curves, sanding end grain, and other tasks that require great tool maneuverability. Heavier 4-in. by 24-in. sanders are best for leveling panels because of their weight, platen size, and aggressiveness. For general belt sanding, a 3-in. by 21-in. machine will serve well.

Orbital sanders are also known as "jitterbug" or vibrator sanders. These tools are available as either quarter-sheet or half-sheet sanders, based on the size of a standard sheet of sandpaper. In operation, these sander pads orbit in a repetitive curlycue motion. Compared to random orbit sanders, jitterbug sanders are far easier to control on a flat surface or when they're sanding flat edges. Their straight pad edges also allow you to easily sand right up to obstructions, such as on case dividers and drawer sides. These sanders are first-rate for controlled sanding where rapid stock removal is unim-

Most orbital or "jitterbug" pad sanders are sized to accept quarter- or half-sized sheets of sandpaper. A model with a vinyl pad for attaching PSA paper allows quick paper changeover. Vinyl replacement pads are available for older-model sanders.

Random orbit sanders are manufactured in palm, pistol, and barrel styles (from left). Most models have ports for attaching a vacuum hose.

portant, as when leveling inlays and complicated veneer assemblies.

Random orbit sanders are the most popular sanders today for both production and hobby work. A random orbit sander combines the orbital action of a jitterbug sander with the spinning action of a disk sander. This results in more aggressive cutting as well as a random scratch pattern that is less noticeable than jitterbug scratches.

Random orbit sanders are available with various grips and different diameter pads—usually 5 in., 6 in., and 8 in. Palm and pistol-grip-style sanders orient the motor in line with the shaft, resulting in a very controlled "feel" to the sander. These sanders typically sport either 5-in. or 6-in. pads. On the other hand, a barrel-grip sander orients its higher amperage motor at a right angle to the shaft. Barrel-grip sanders tend to be more aggressive, while still providing good control.

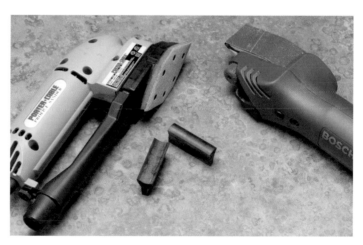

Detail sanders eliminate tedious hand-sanding. The model on the left is a combination detail/profile sander with interchangeable heads for sanding different profiles.

Detail sanders and profile sanders were designed to handle specialized tasks in small areas. Detail sanders have a thin, triangular, oscillating head for getting into small, tight areas. By contrast, profile sanders employ a back-and-forth "in-line" motion. Profile sanders can be outfitted with various concave and convex heads for sanding moldings but will also accept a triangular pad for flat detail work. Belt detail sanders are small, compact units that incorporate a projecting pulley for getting into tight curves and contours.

Stationary Sanders

Years ago, stationary sanding equipment was too large and expensive for many shops. However, manufacturers now offer scaled-down versions of many of these machines, including drum sanders, oscillating spindle sanders, and edge sanders.

Stationary Belt and Disk Sanders

These relatively small machines are extremely useful for shaping small parts, when it's easier to present the work to the tool rather than the other way around. The platens on stationary belt sanders are mounted either vertically or horizontally to the tool table, and some models will convert to either position. Belts are available in various sizes. Disk sanders are large, vertically mounted, spin-

ning disks that are used to true up miters, shape small workpieces, and sand convex edges. Combination belt/disk sanders are very popular machines in both large and small shops.

Wide-Belt Sanders and Stroke Sanders

When it comes to flattening panels and sanding flat workpieces, it's hard to beat a wide-belt sander or stroke sander. These machines both employ a wide, continuous loop of sandpaper that is pressed down against a workpiece by a backing platen. In the case of the wide-belt sander, panels travel on a conveyer through the machine while an adjustable platen inside presses the spinning sandpaper down against the workpiece. With a stroke sander, the operator manually or mechanically presses the platen down against the workpiece. Both of these machines are expensive but can sand very aggressively and quickly.

Stationary Drum Sanders

Stationary drum sanders bridge the gap between the cost of a wide-belt sander and the needs of the small shop. Where a wide-belt sander can quickly hog off a fair amount of material with each pass, drum sanders remove only a marginal amount each time, and their feed rates are slower. Still, they will flatten wide boards and are first-rate at sanding thin panels and small parts.

Edge Sanders

Basically a long, vertically mounted belt sander, an edge sander is used to trim and smooth the edges of doors and panels. This is a great machine for sanding end grain and trimming miters. It's particularly good for

A combination belt/disk sander is handy for trueing up miters, shaping small workpieces, and sanding convex curves.

Drum sanders excel at sanding face frames and wide panels. They spew very little dust when hooked up to a dust-collection system. Some models have two drums for different grits of paper.

An edge sander is great for cleaning up edges and trimming doors and drawer fronts to fit their openings.

trimming panel edges to be fit into frame-and-panel doors. You can also shape concave curves against the belt pulley on the outboard end.

Oscillating Spindle Sanders

An oscillating spindle sander is designed to sand curved edges. Its spinning drum rides up and down to promote clean sanding without burning. The tables on some models tilt for sanding beveled edges. Benchtop models can be quite affordable.

An oscillating spindle sander is the best tool for smoothing curved edges. Smaller benchtop versions of this floor model work just as well.

Through-the-pad dust extraction is one of the great features of random orbit sanders. A "tool-triggered" shop vac that is activated by the sander switch is a great companion.

A downdraft table collects dust at the source. On this model, a fan inside the table daws dust through holes in the top, which doubles as a workbench with an end vise and bench dogs.

Dust Collection Tools

Breathing wood dust is hazardous to your health. Simply providing ventilation in a room while you're sanding wood isn't enough. For effective protection, you need to employ a two-pronged approach that addresses both point-of-source capture and respiratory protection. Point-of-source capture, which I'll discuss here, involves dust collection at the tool. I'll discuss respiratory protection in Section 3.

Dust collection can be accomplished several ways. The simplest and most efficient approach is to hook up a vacuum to the sanding tool to suck dust away before it has a chance to get into the air. Most stationary machines typically include a port for attaching a dust collector or vacuum hose, and the bag on most portable sanders can be removed to attach a vacuum hose. Unfortunately, some of the fine dust still escapes into the air, and the vacuum hose on portable sanders can be cumbersome.

For workpieces that aren't very large, a better solution is to use a downdraft table, which sucks the sanding dust downward through the tabletop. Filters inside the table capture the dust before exhausting the air back into the room. Some downdraft tables sport thick tops with end vises for holding workpieces. Although a downdraft table may seem like a luxury, manufacturers have affordable models geared to the small shop.

Ambient air cleaners are also a great investment to filter the fine dust that tends to hang forever suspended in the air (or at least until you apply that final coat of varnish).

Pneumatic Tools

Many sanders used in surface preparation have pneumatic (air-powered) counterparts. Running these sanders requires a compressor. Of course, a compressor is also required for applying finishes with conventional spray equipment, as I'll discuss in later sections. For now, I'll focus on pneumatic sanders and the compressors needed to run them.

Sanders

The most common pneumatic sanders are random orbit sanders, jitterbug sanders, and flutter sanders. The joy of using pneumatic sanders is that they are much more compact and lightweight than their electric counterparts. They're also usually less expensive and less prone to vibration. It's hard to go back to electric sanders once you've switched. The downsides are that air sanders usually require large stationary compressors, so they may be out of the range of smaller shops and home users.

There are two drawbacks to pneumatic sanders: The first—a minor concern—is that they require regular oiling, but automatic oilers can be installed for that purpose. The major drawback is that you need a large compressor to run these air-hungry tools.

Compressor Basics

A compressor works on the principle that when air is compressed above atmospheric pressure, it contains stored energy. When this stored energy is released as moving air, it can be used to drive machinery. What a compressor does is threefold: It drives a *pump* that compresses the air from low to high pressure; it stores the compressed air in a *receiver tank*; then it releases the air in a

Pneumatic sanders are available in models similar to their electric counterparts. Shown here (from left) are a random orbit sander, a third-sheet orbital pad sander, and a rotary air tool fitted with sanding stars for smoothing profiles.

This two-stage 80-gallon compressor powers a shop that uses spray equipment and air tools at the same time. It can deliver about 26 cfm at 100 psi.

controlled fashion through an *air regulator* for powering machinery or spray guns.

Most compressors used in finishing shops are either single-stage or two-stage, which refers to the number of times the air is com-

► CHOOSING AN AIR COMPRESSOR

When looking for a compressor, don't be misled by horse-power ratings. The most important criteria is the volume of air (cubic feet per minute, or cfm) that the compressor produces at a specific pressure (pounds per square inch, or psi). Before shopping for a compressor, calculate the air requirements of the tools you intend to operate. If you intend to run two or more tools simultaneously using one compressor, add up the total cfm requirements. In most cases however, tools are run intermittently, so a general rule is to add up the total cfm requirements of all the tools, then divide that by two if each tool will be running only about half the time.

You'll also have to choose between oil-lubricated and oil-less models. Oil-lubricated models are generally more expensive but are quieter and cooler. Oil-less models are a bit noisier and hotter. A big benefit of an oil-less compressor is that it eliminates the possibility of oil contaminating your air supply and fouling sprayed finishes.

pressed by the motor piston(s). Two-stage compressors are more efficient and run cooler. Portable compressors are typically single-stage units, while stationary compressors are two-stage units.

To gauge a compressor's capacity, you need to understand two terms: *cfm* and *psi*. Air volume is measured in cfm (cubic feet per minute), and air pressure is expressed as psi (pounds per square inch). A compressor's capacity—as well as the air requirements for any pneumatic tool—is always stated as a combination of these two terms.

For example, a brad nailer may require 2 cfm at 90 psi. Because it uses quick bursts

of air to drive its nail, it doesn't require a large volume of air, but that air needs to be delivered at high pressure. For comparison, a conventional spray gun uses 10 to 12 cfm at 40 to 50 psi, while a continuously running sander gulps an enormous 16 to 19 cfm at 90 psi.

Air Lines

Air tools can be installed directly to threaded fittings on a hose, but it's more convenient to use spring-loaded quick-disconnect fittings. When all you do run is a spray gun from a portable compressor, you can just run a rubber air hose from the compressor to the gun and control the air pressure using the regulator on the compressor. On the other hand, if you have a large compressor and shop, you should consider piping air from your compressor to your workstations, eliminating long air hoses snaking across the floor. As an added benefit, piping acts as an auxiliary receiver tank to increase air storage. It's best to run pipe high on the wall, installing drop lines where necessary for hookups.

When you use compressed air in only one location, simply run pipe from the compressor to that area. However, if you use air at different locations, run the pipe in a loop around the shop. When installing pipe, slant it toward the compressor so moisture will drain back into the tank or into a leg of pipe for easy draining. To prevent air-pressure drop, use large-diameter pipe, installing it in hairpin-turn fashion where it drops down the wall to the work area.

The best pipe to use is either black-iron or galvanized pipe. Because pipe is difficult to cut and thread without specialized tools,

You can easily solder threaded pipe fittings for air lines to copper pipe using a propane torch.

Air pipes should slant downward toward the compressor, allowing the water inside the pipes to drain back into the receiver tank or into a leg on the pipe system for easy removal.

This automatic drain for eliminating compressor moisture is activated whenever the compressor cycles on and off.

many shops contract this out to a plumber. *(If you install pipe yourself, you may be tempted to install plastic or PVC pipe.* **DON'T DO IT!** *Plastic pipe was not designed to hold compressed air!)* Instead, you can use copper pipe, which is easy to cut and solder. Use type-L copper pipe and solder threaded pipe fittings at the end to match up with your air-line fittings. The danger with using copper pipe is that solder can melt in a fire, causing expelled air to feed the flames. Because of this, copper may not be allowed in a commercial shop or in areas with high fire risk.

Filters

Compressed air is laden with moisture that can affect tools and foul finishes. To prevent moisture damage, you can install a moisture

filter between the air hose and the tool, or you can permanently attach filters to your pipe system. Oil-lubricated compressors may require in-line oil (coalescing) filters, as they can spew small oil particles into the air lines, which can also contaminate finishes.

Filters are available in various configurations. Combination filter/regulator units allow you to conveniently regulate the air pressure at your workstation rather than at the compressor. Filter groups are available that include an oil filter and a moisture filter, as well as desiccants to remove water vapor. To minimize moisture throughout the system, make sure to drain the compressor tank regularly. Alternatively, you can install automatic drains.

A

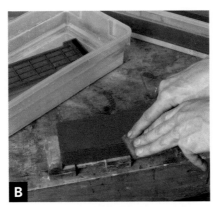

B

C

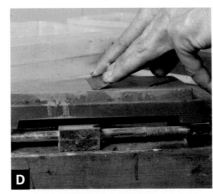

D

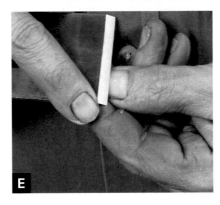

E

Sharpening a Plane Blade

Using a slow-speed (1725 rpm) grinder equipped with white aluminum oxide wheels, grind a primary bevel of roughly 25 degrees on the plane blade **(A)**. Then hone the blade on a 1200-grit waterstone **(B)**. To establish the proper angle for honing, slowly rock the bevel angle on the stone until you feel its tip and heel stabilize on the stone. Then move the blade over the stone, keeping your forearms and wrists locked to avoid rocking the blade. Work the right and left edges of the blade a bit more than the center. This will help keep the corners of the blade from digging in as you plane. It's not necessary or desirable to hone past the point where you've created a 1/32-in.-wide flat at the leading edge of the bevel.

Now switch to a 6000-grit waterstone. Use a Nagura stone to create a fine slurry on the waterstone, then polish the back of the blade **(C)**. When the back is shiny, turn the blade over and register its bevel on the stone as you did before. Then tip the blade forward about 5 degrees and lock your forearms and wrists. Working in a small circular motion, hone the tip of the bevel to create a polished "microbevel" **(D)**. As before, work the right and left edges a bit more.

The blade is sharp when you can slice little curls off your thumbnail **(E)**. Note how the polished microbevel and heel are shinier than the rest of the bevel, which is duller from the coarse grinding-wheel scratches.

Sharpening a Hand Scraper

The first step in sharpening a card or hand scraper is to file the edges flat. The simplest approach is to run the edges of the scraper over a single-cut mill bastard file whose tang is butted against a clamp or bench dog **(A)**. To protect my hands and to provide a better grip, I wear garden gloves with rubberized coating on the fingertips. When the edge is filed completely flat, it will reflect light evenly across its length.

Next, hone the edges on a 1200-grit waterstone, flexing the scraper so it stands upright on the stone **(B)**. Push the scraper back and forth in a little semicircle to remove the coarse file marks. Then hone both faces of the scraper on the stone to remove the burrs.

Lay the scraper on your bench about ½ in. from its edge. Lubricate it with a drop or two of kerosene or lightweight oil, then draw a burnisher across the scraper face several times using moderate pressure while keeping the burnisher parallel to the scraper face. For the final strokes, angle the burnisher downward about 10 degrees **(C)**.

> [TIP] To gauge the proper amount of pressure necessary for burnishing the edge of a scraper, practice by applying 20 pounds of pressure on a bathroom scale.

Clamp the center of the scraper in a metal vise so you don't mar its edges. Holding the burnisher at a 90-degree angle to the face of the scraper, draw it several times along the edge with 20 pounds of downward pressure **(D)**. Then tip the burnisher about 5 degrees down and take two or three more swipes using the same amount of pressure. Finish by tipping the burnisher about 12 degrees downward **(E)**.

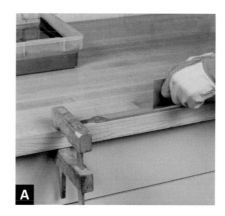

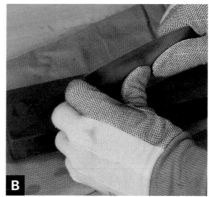

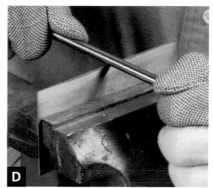

Finishing Tools

Brushes

➤ The Care and Feeding of Brushes (p. 51)

➤ Reviving a Hardened Brush (p. 52)

Spray Equipment

➤ Configuring a Basic Pressure-Pot System (p. 53)

➤ Cleaning and Maintaining Spray Guns (p. 54)

➤ Adjusting a Spray Gun (p. 55)

➤ Using Turbine-Driven Guns (p. 56)

➤ Using HVLP Conversion Guns (p. 57)

FINISH APPLICATION TOOLS are divided into three categories: rags, brushes, and spray guns. Wipe-on and brushable finishes are economical to use but can be tedious to apply, whereas spraying is faster but more wasteful of finish. Spraying doesn't necessarily ensure a flawless finish, so don't feel sheepish about brushing or wiping on finishes. In this section we'll take a look at these finish application tools.

Hand Application Tools

Finishing is uncomplicated if you decide to go the hand-application route. Basically, you can choose from rags, paper towels, and brushes.

Rags, Cloths, and Pads

Almost any clean absorbent cotton cloth will work for applying finishes. I recommend bleached, 100 percent cotton T-shirt material. Paper towels are also handy for applying wiping varnishes. I prefer a nontextured type of paper towel such as Viva™ or Scott™ towels. Linen, 100 percent wool, and muslin (found at fabric stores) are used in some finishing procedures such as French polishing. Padding cloth for applying shellac and padding lacquers is available from specialty finish suppliers. Tack cloth (sold at paint and hardware stores) is used for cleaning debris and dust from sanding between coats. Lamb's-wool applicators and short-nap rectangular pads work well for applying finishes to large surfaces like floors and walls. Brush-style foam pads are suitable for most varnishes and water-based finishes.

Clockwise from top left, T-shirt-type cloth and paper towels can be used for general staining and glazing. The fine-textured, lint-free padding cloth (center) is better for finish application and polishing. Tack cloths (bottom right) lift sanding dust, burlap is used for scrubbing paste wood filler, and muslin is used in French polishing.

Brushes

Brushes are available in a large selection of bristle types, shapes, and prices, but they all fall into two general categories: natural or synthetic. Natural-bristle brushes are commonly made from hog hair (China bristle) and can be used with oil-based products, varnish, shellac, and lacquer. Synthetic bristle is made from man-made fibers like nylon or polyester. Synthetic-bristle brushes are used for applying water-based products as well as most other finishes. The key features of a brush are the shape and profile of its bristle. Round, fat brushes hold more finish, while sharp, chiseled-edge brushes cut into corners and crevices better.

Square-tipped brushes sport a squared-off top. These inexpensive brushes are fine for general-purpose, noncritical work. Chisel-tip brushes are handmade with shorter bristle lengths on the outside and longer bristles in the center. The chisel tip does a better job of laying down a smooth finish than nonchiseled brushes. Many brushes are available with rectangular or round profiles. Round-profile brushes contain approximately double the amount of bristle and are preferred by some because they hold so much more finish.

Brushes are divided into two basic categories. Synthetics (top) include foam brushes and short-nap synthetic pads as well as synthetic-bristle (filament) brushes. Natural-bristle brushes are usually made from hog bristle. The bottom brush is hog bristle dyed to simulate a real badger-hair brush, like the one shown third from the bottom.

A Taklon brush (left) gets into corners but doesn't hold much finish. The oval varnish brush (right) holds more finish and wraps around moldings and other profiles. An imitation-badger brush (center) combines both qualities.

► BRUSH ANATOMY

Brush bristles are set into an epoxy setting that anchors the bristles and attaches them to the handle. A metal ferrule wraps around the plug, attaching to the handle with rivets. A wooden divider in the plug creates a reservoir to hold the finish. When you're dipping the brush, capillary action pulls the finish up into the reservoir, where it's held until the bristles contact the wood to dispense the finish.

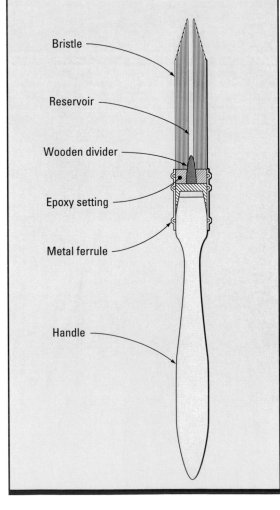

Bristle

Reservoir

Wooden divider

Epoxy setting

Metal ferrule

Handle

Basic Inventory

Following is a basic inventory of brushes for various finishing tasks.

Two good-quality rectangular, chisel-cut bristle brushes for applying clear finishes. A 2½-in.-wide brush is a good all-around size for large areas, while a smaller 1-in. brush is better for detail work. Cost: $30 to $40 for a decent 2- or 2½-in. brush.

Several inexpensive, round or square, average-quality bristle brushes for applying stains and glazes. Cost: $10 or less.

At least one good-quality 2-in.-wide synthetic-bristle brush for applying water-based finishes. Cost: $12 to $35.

Several artist's brushes, including a no. 1 and a no. 4 for touch-up and detail work. Cost: $5 to $6 each.

An expanded inventory would include a few fine-nylon artist's brushes (generic name: Taklon), as well as several 1 in.- to 2½-in.-wide chisel-cut round brushes for creative effects like softening and blending glazes, antiquing, and highlighting.

Spray Guns

A spray gun uses compressed air to atomize liquid finish for delivery to the workpiece. The past 25 years have seen enormous developments in spraying technology. Designers have been working hard to improve the *transfer efficiency*, which represents the amount of finish that actually lands on the workpiece, as opposed to the amount wasted as overspray. The main factor in determining the transfer efficiency is the method of *atomization*, or the way in which the liquid finish is converted into tiny droplets. There are three basic ways to atom-

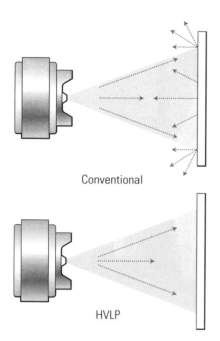

Conventional

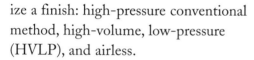

HVLP

Turbine-driven high-volume, low-pressure (HVLP) guns are typically sold as part of a package that includes the gun, turbine, and large-diameter air hose required to deliver the high volume of air.

HVLP conversion guns convert high-pressure air from a compressor into high volume/low-pressure air by restricting the air inside the gun body. Note the smaller-diameter air hose and smaller gun body.

ize a finish: high-pressure conventional method, high-volume, low-pressure (HVLP), and airless.

Conventional

Conventional guns—which have been around the longest—employ air pressure from a compressor to atomize the finish. This technology can produce an extremely fine finish but is wasteful. The high-velocity atomization causes much of the finish to bounce off and away from the workpiece, a condition called "overspray."

HVLP

HVLP guns operate like conventional guns, but with much greater transfer efficiency. As its name indicates, an HVLP gun delivers the finish in greater volume, but at low pressure, producing much less overspray. There are two types of HVLP guns: *turbine-driven* and *conversion*. Each is determined by its type of air-delivery system.

Turbine-driven guns receive high volumes of air from a turbine, which usually comes as part of an HVLP system. These perform well and are suited to folks who want to spray without investing in a large, standard air compressor. Systems range from $300 to $1,000, with good mid-priced systems costing about $600.

Conversion guns are driven by a typical air compressor. Through air restriction, the gun decompresses or "converts" the high-pressure operating air to low pressure within the gun, which increases the volume. The first generation of conversion guns required

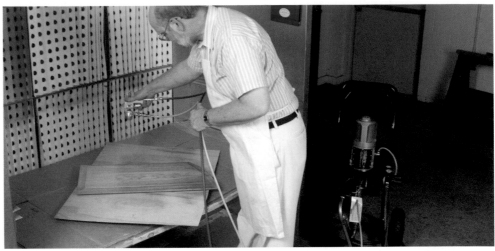

The air cap for a low-volume, low-pressure (LVLP) gun (left) has smaller orifices than an HVLP conversion gun cap (right). While an LVLP gun can't produce the wide fan patterns and fluid delivery of a standard HVLP conversion gun, an LVLP gun requires less air volume, allowing use of a smaller compressor.

enormous amounts of air from a large stationary compressor. Since then, designers have developed hybrid forms of conversion guns, called low-volume, low-pressure guns. These guns work as well, but typically require less than 10 cfm of air, which is well within the range of smaller compressors. Prices for conversion guns range from $100 for cheap imports to $500 for industrial-grade models.

Airless and Air-Assisted Guns

Airless guns are powered by a high-pressure piston pump. The finish is driven through a cat's-eye slit in the gun nozzle at pressures ranging from 2000 to 6000 psi. Airless sprayers are suited for thick utility paints where a fast but perfectly smooth finish is *not* required, such as when painting walls. *Air-assisted airless* employs the same principle but at lower pressures, using a special air cap to further atomize the finish. At prices starting around $2,000, airless technology is suited to production finishing where speed and low overspray are the primary concerns.

Air-assisted airless pumps are becoming increasingly popular due to their great transfer efficiency and speed. The finish is forced through a tiny orifice in the gun by a high-pressure pump (right).

Spray Gun Basics

When using any spray gun, the idea is to deliver a finely atomized, uniform finish that flows out well when it hits the workpiece. Your success will depend on the viscosity of the finish and the settings of the gun controls.

Try to spray a finish without thinning first. However, if the material is too thick, the finish won't flow out correctly and will sputter from the gun. If your unthinned finish doesn't spray well, switch to a larger needle/nozzle combination or add thinner in increments of 1 oz. per quart of finish until you're getting a fine, even spray pattern. Due to environmental concerns, many finish manufacturers discourage thinning solvent-based products these days. For water-based products, they typically recommend thinning no more than 5 to 10 percent with water. If you're unsure about thinning, contact the finish manufacturer.

► ANATOMY OF A SPRAY GUN

Most spray guns operate on the same basic working principles, as shown in the drawing here of a compressor-driven gun. Turbine-driven guns may differ slightly, but the main components are the same. Air (green) from the compressor enters the air inlet (A). Some guns have a "cheater" valve (B) that can open or shut off the air supply internally. Pulling the trigger (C) depresses a plunger rod (D), opening a valve that lets air flow through the gun body and out through the middle of the air cap[1]. (E) As you pull the trigger back further, it engages the spring-loaded needle (F), pulling it backward from the fluid-tip orifice and releasing the finish (black) to be atomized at the air cap.

The fluid-delivery valve (G) limits the needle retraction to control the amount of finish released. When the fan width control valve (H) is closed, air is directed only through the center and small outer holes of the air cap[2], resulting in a small, round pattern. Backing off the fan-width control allows air (blue) into the outer horns of the air cap, flattening the round pattern into an oval.

[1] On turbine "bleeder" -style guns, this air valve and plunger assembly are omitted as air from the turbine flows constantly out from the air cap once the turbine is switched on.

[2] On many turbine guns, the fan width is changed by turning the air cap to different positions.

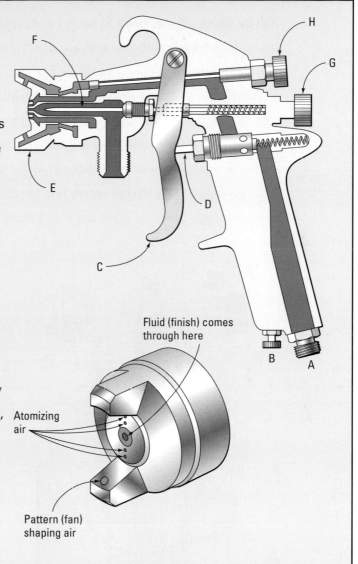

Fluid (finish) comes through here

Atomizing air

Pattern (fan) shaping air

Safety Equipment

Most finishing materials contain hazardous chemicals, so it's important to protect your skin, eyes, and lungs. (See Resources, p. 287.)

Gloves

Use good, chemical-resistant gloves when working with solvents and finishes. Thin vinyl and latex-type gloves won't protect your skin for long, so use heavy-duty gloves instead. For general finishing, I've found nitrile gloves to be excellent, especially the flock-lined versions that absorb sweat from

Reviving a Hardened Brush

If you find that one of your expensive brushes is rock-hard from improper or overlooked cleaning, you can usually bring it back to life. First, soak the brush in an NMP (N-Methyl Pyrrolidone)-based stripper like Citristrip™.

NMP is gentler on bristles than methylene chloride-based stripper. Leave the brush in the stripper for about four hours and then work the stripper into the bristles with gloved hands **(A)**. Hold the brush over the edge of a bench and use a stiff wire brush to clean out the softened finish. Bear down hard on the bristles, particularly near the ferrule **(B)**. Clean away the stripper/finish residue by washing it well in warm water and grease-cutting dishwashing detergent **(C)**. Use a brush comb to straighten out the bristles and remove any last hunks of finish. Finish up by rinsing with plenty of warm water. Wrap the brush for storage as shown in the previous section on brush care.

Configuring a Basic Pressure-Pot System

To set up a remote pressure-pot system that holds finish in a separate container, fill the pot halfway with finish, then replace the top on the pot. Connect the air line to the pot's air regulator output and the fluid line to its fluid output. Connect the air fitting to your gun's air inlet and the fluid fitting to its fluid inlet **(A)**. Tighten the connections, and use plastic cable ties to tie the lines together. Hook up an air line to the air regulator on the pot. The regulator's job is to divert some air pressure to the pot to pressurize it, while allowing the rest to power your spray gun.

To set the correct operating pressure, adjust the pressure-pot regulator to about 5 psi for clear finishes and up to 10 psi for thick paint. Turn off the air to the gun, then depress the trigger until the gun emits a stream of finish. Adjust the pressure-pot regulator until the stream shoots out straight 12 in. to 15 in. before arcing downward **(B)**. This typically creates a good working pressure, although you can increase or decrease the pot pressure for faster or slower delivery.

To clean the system after finishing, you need to back-flush the gun and fluid lines. Shut off your air supply, depressurize the pot, then loosen the top and suspend it over the pot. Reattach the air line, place your finger over the gun nozzle, and depress the trigger. Finish will flow back into the pot **(C)**. (Finish up by running solvent through the system. Fill the pot halfway with solvent, pressurize the pot as before, and squirt the solvent back into a holding container **(D)**.

A

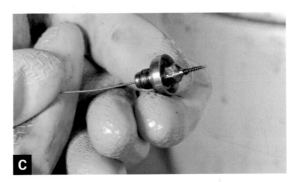

B

C

D

Cleaning and Maintaining Spray Guns

Dirty or damaged air caps, needles, and nozzles cause most spray problems and should be cleaned regularly. Maintenance kits containing the necessary brushes and needles are available from spray gun suppliers. (See Resources on p. 287.) Remove the air cap, needle, and nozzle from the gun and place them in the appropriate solvent. (Never put the gun body in solvent.) Wipe the needle with a clean rag and clean the air cap with a soft bristle brush **(A)**. Insert a wire needle in from the back of the air cap through the annular airholes **(B)**. Clean the center hole of the air cap, then push a small bristle brush through the nozzle opening **(C)**. Wipe off all residue and inspect the parts inside and out. Reassemble the gun, always installing the nozzle before the needle. Then apply petroleum jelly or gun lubricant to the needle using a small brush, and lubricate the trigger pivot screws.

If you'll be using the gun again in a few hours, you don't have to perform such a thorough cleaning. Instead, do this: Drain finish from the gun body by holding it above the cup while you depress the trigger, and run a bristle brush through the siphon tube.

Remove the air cap and drop it in a small jar of acetone **(D)**. This keeps finish from hardening in the small airholes. Before reinstalling the air cap, make sure the acetone has evaporated.

Adjusting a Spray Gun

Here's a quick, reliable way to check the setup of any spray gun for an even distribution of finish: First, set up a piece of wood in a vertical position, then rotate the gun's air cap to spray a horizontal pattern. Hold the gun away from the wood the distance recommended by the manufacturer, then spray until the finish starts to sag. If the resulting drips are somewhat evenly spaced, the spray pattern is fine **(A)**. If not, recheck your air setup, switch to a different nozzle/air-cap combination, or clean the parts.

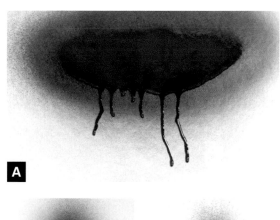

Shooting black paint onto white kraft paper also helps identify setup problems. When the setup is just right, and the air cap set for a vertical pattern, it should produce an oval-shaped pattern with uniform droplet size across the entire spray pattern **(B)**. Large drops indicate insufficient air pressure or too thick a finish **(C)**. Adjust the air pressure or thin the finish as necessary.

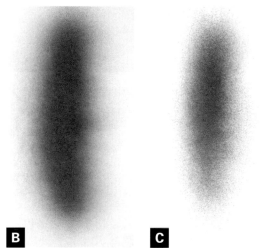

When spraying your workpieces, hold a conventional gun about 8 to 10 in. away from the work and an HVLP gun 6 to 8 in. away. Hold the gun off to the side of the workpiece and depress the trigger. Move across the workpiece, laying down a wet swath of finish without arcing your arm. The finish should not puddle as you spray. Release the trigger only after leaving the other end of the work surface. As you take the next stroke, overlap the first by half its width. Complete the rest of the surface in the same manner. It's wise to start with the area closest to you and move the gun in successive passes away from you to prevent dry overspray from creating a rough finish **(D)**. When spraying vertical surfaces, move the gun quickly enough to prevent sagging. The proper gun adjustments and travel should result in a coat of finish that appears smooth and does not feel rough when dry.

Preparing Flat Surfaces, page 60

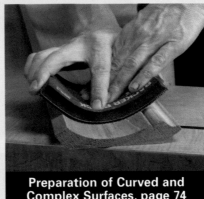

Preparation of Curved and Complex Surfaces, page 74

Fixing Defects, page 86

PART TWO

Surface Preparation

THE ROUGH MACHINING MARKS left by tablesaws, routers, jointers, and planers all need to be removed before a finish is applied. Even the most carefully executed finish will not cover up an improperly prepared wood surface. It's not unrealistic to spend 33 percent to 50 percent of your total finishing time in preparing the surface. Therefore, it's important to understand the proper techniques so you can proceed in an orderly and efficient manner without wasting a lot of time and creating an awful lot of unnecessary sawdust. In this part, I'll show you the best ways to prepare the wood correctly using both hand and machine tools. You'll learn which techniques, cutting tools, and abrasives work best for preparing flat and complicated surfaces. Finally, you'll discover how to correct mistakes and defects that can't be removed by sanding or scraping.

A good sanding table should be at a comfortable height. The author works at a waist-high table when sanding panels. Portable work lights allow good backlighting for detecting scratches.

A drum sander provides a great way to sand thin stock that might otherwise be difficult to secure to a benchtop.

clamped on a post and positioned at workbench height will highlight scratches and surface defects on the workpiece.

Planning your Approach

A properly prepared flat surface should be flat indeed, smooth, and free of dents and other surface defects. The amount of preparation that a piece needs will depend largely on its condition after milling on the planer, jointer, and saw. Narrow pieces such as frames and table aprons will usually be suitably flat after milling and will require only smoothing to remove milling marks. On the other hand, tabletops and door panels that have been glued up from multiple boards will require flattening before smoothing.

Whenever possible, flatten and smooth your individual project parts before assembly. It's much easier to handle them that way. Leave only the very final finish sanding until after the project is assembled.

When tackling flat surfaces, you have a lot of choices of tools to use. Straight-grained, single-board aprons, legs, drawer

fronts, etc., can be easily leveled and smoothed with a couple of swipes with a hand plane. Gnarly grained or highly figured boards are best prepared using abrasives or else scrapers followed by abrasives. Stationary drum sanders do a great job of smoothing thin stock that would be difficult to secure on a workbench. Typically, you'll get the best results if you use a mix of machine and hand tools suited to the type of wood at hand.

Power Sanding

Fortunately, there are a lot of power tools to help you with your sanding chores. Many portable power tools, such as belt sanders, vibrator sanders, and random orbit sanders are relatively inexpensive and widely available.

Portable Belt Sanders

I've used a belt sander extensively for most of my woodworking, finishing, and refinishing career. I suppose that wearing out eight machines over the years makes me somewhat of a "black belt" at belt sanders. It's

➤ GOING AGAINST THE GRAIN

Every woodworker is taught to sand "with the grain" so that the sanding scratches blend in with the morphology and orientation of the wood grain and texture. However, there are times when sanding across the grain is more advantageous. When you sand cross-grain, the grit slices across the cell bundles, removing a greater amount of material. This is helpful when you need to remove a lot of wood, such as when leveling panels. (See "Flattening with a Portable Belt Sander" on p. 68.)

When sanding cross-grain or when using vibrator or random orbit sanders, don't skip grits. I usually start at no coarser than 100 grit, and follow up with 120-, 150-, 180-, and finally 220-grit

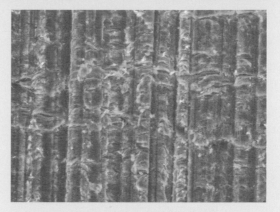

Taken at 100x magnification, the north/south 180-grit scratches shown here are clearly visible as deep furrows running across the grain.

paper. After machine sanding, I hand-sand with the grain to remove any residual cross-grain or circular scratches left by the machines. I begin hand-sanding with the finest grit I used on the machine.

hard to beat these machines when it comes to surfacing tabletops and other panels for a minimal investment of money. For flattening panels, get the heaviest, largest beast you can afford. A 4-in.-by-24-in. model is my favorite for this because the machine's weight and large platen make quick work of flattening large panels. For best performance, replace the stock metal platen with a graphite version. These are often listed as accessories in the tool's manual. For belt

To improve the performance of a belt sander, replace its stock metal platen with a graphite platen like the one shown here.

▶ MAXIMIZING SANDPAPER

Here are a few tips for getting the most from your sandpaper:

1. Before sanding, scrape workpieces clean of any excess glue or veneer tape.

2. Periodically clean clogged sanding belts and disks using rubbery crepe cleaning sticks manufactured for the purpose.

3. Occasionally remove sawdust from sheet paper by swiping the sandpaper across a gray synthetic abrasive pad or a piece of stiff-fiber carpet.

Commercial rubber cleaning sticks can be used to unclog machine belts and disks, extending their usable life.

"finish sanders," they typically do their work with 150-grit through 220-grit sandpaper. I've found stearated aluminum oxide the all-around best paper for these machines.

Stationary Sanders

If you work with a lot of flat panels, consider getting a drum or wide-belt sander. Both of these stationary machines can produce a consistently sanded surface that's hard to match with hand tools. A number of reasonably priced drum sanders are available for the small shop. Large or custom shops should take a serious look at wide-belt sanders, as they are typically more aggressive than drum sanders.

Hand-Sanding

With so many power sanders available these days, hand-sanding may seem anachronistic. But sanding by hand affords great control and allows you to smooth away the swirly scratches left by random orbit and vibrator sanders.

When sanding flat surfaces by hand with sheet sandpaper, use a suitable backer block. Many commercial sanding blocks are made from rubber, which is flat and rigid but which flexes enough to prevent the abrasive particles from breaking off prematurely. If you use wood sanding blocks, it's wise to glue a layer of cork to one face for the same reason.

I often like to use garnet paper for hand-sanding because it has a unique "bite" that leaves a great finished surface. Hand-sanding is usually done with the grain, in which case it's okay to skip intermediate grits. You can safely jump from 100-grit paper to 150-grit to 220-grit.

sanders (as well as drum sanders), I prefer the durability of ceramic aluminum grits. My hands-down favorites are Purple Regalite™ belts made by 3M.

[TIP] Don't forget to protect yourself from wood dust even when running a machine with dust extraction.

Vibrator and Random Orbit Sanders

After belt sanding, I usually reach for a random orbit sander or vibrator sander to further smooth surfaces. They're often the first tools I'll use when sanding veneers. Called

Planing a Panel

Planes are great for flattening straight-grained, single-board workpieces. Secure the piece to the workbench between bench dogs or place it against a stop. If the panel is cupped, place it concave side down and shim any high corners so the panel doesn't rock. Starting with a sharp jack plane set for a fairly aggressive cut, plane diagonally to the grain **(A)**. After a few passes, plane diagonally in the opposite direction, occasionally checking your progress with a straightedge **(B)**. When the panel is flat, plane parallel to the grain to smooth out the diagonal cuts **(C)**. Then switch to a smoothing plane set for a finer cut **(D)**. If you like the resulting surface quality, you can stop at this point. Alternatively, you can smooth remaining irregularities with a card scraper **(E)** followed up with 240-grit sandpaper.

[TIP] **Lubricating the bottom of a hand plane with a swipe of beeswax will greatly reduce planing friction.**

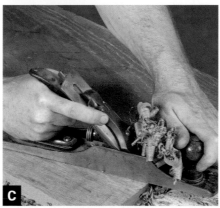

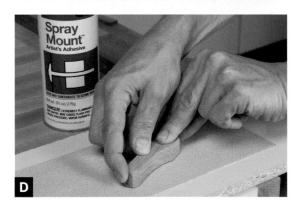

Hand-Sanding

Tear a sheet of 9-by-11 sandpaper into quarters, and wrap it around a rubber or cork-faced sanding block. Moving back and forth along the grain using moderate pressure, sand from one end of the workpiece to the other (A). To maximize your effort, sand at a slight bias of about 7 to10 degrees to the grain, which cuts the wood fibers more effectively than sanding directly parallel to the grain. With each stroke, overlap the previous one by about half (B). Periodically remove the sawdust from your paper by swiping it across a gray synthetic abrasive pad or a piece of stiff-fiber carpet. Pay attention to the "bite" of the sandpaper as you work. Don't try to overuse the paper; when it starts slipping, toss it out.

When sanding small chamfers, use your left thumb and right forefinger to register the sanding block flat on the face of the chamfer (C). Position your left-hand forefinger under the bottom edge to steady the block. Afterward, ease the edges of the chamfer using 220-grit sandpaper on a sanding block.

Sanding small parts can be challenging because it's almost impossible to sand parts flat without rounding them over if you bring the sandpaper or tool to the piece. It's also extremely difficult to hold small parts, so it's best that you bring the part to the paper. The best way to sand small parts flat is to make a sanding board. Take a piece of sandpaper and glue it to a piece of melamine or plywood with contact adhesive. Then move the part back and forth on the sanding board to sand it (D).

[TIP] **It doesn't make much difference if you sand past 220 grit. However, if you plan on using a water-based finish product, sanding to 320 will minimize grain-raising.**

Scraping

When using a card scraper on flat surfaces, I typically combine three approaches: pushing the scraper, pulling it, and "sweeping" with it. Each approach requires a different hand position.

I usually begin by pushing the scraper. I wrap its edges with my fingers while using my thumbs to flex it slightly at its center to prevent the corners from digging into the workpiece **(A)**. I can easily push off the far edge of the workpiece in this position. However, it's difficult to begin a push stroke at the forward edge without digging in slightly. So to scrape the edge closest to me, I change to a pull position, drawing the scraper off the edge toward me **(B)**. When doing this, I slide my thumbs toward the ends of the scraper and move my fingers to the center of the rear face, applying enough pressure there to flex the scraper slightly. For the final step, I sweep the scraper across the surface, grabbing it at opposite ends and flexing it so the corners don't dig in **(C)**.

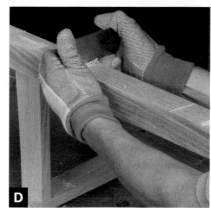

[TIP] **Scrapers are available in different thicknesses. Thinner scrapers flex more easily without heavy pressure and provide more "scoop" when you need to target a smaller area. A scraper can get pretty hot during use, so I wear garden gloves with rubberized fingers that block the heat and allow a good grip.**

When you're scraping legs and other narrow surfaces, it can be awkward to flex the scraper. In these cases, it is easier to first run sandpaper on edges slightly with 220-grit sandpaper before scraping, which prevents the scraper from tearing the sharp edges. When scraping narrow legs, position your middle, ring, and little fingers under the scraper, pressing them against the sides of the leg to cradle the scraper and register it flat **(D)**. You can also use just a portion of the scraper edge to get into tight places, like areas adjacent to a projecting tenon **(E)**.

Flattening and Smoothing with a Portable Belt Sander

In my opinion, a portable belt sander is the best tool for the money for flattening a panel glued up from several boards. Using the cross-hatching technique described here will help ensure that the surface will end up flat and even.

Before beginning, remove as much glue residue as possible from the panel using a cabinet scraper, which levels any edge-joint misalignments at the same time **(A)**. Make sure the sander is tuned up, and that its platen is clean and flat. Then mount a 100-grit belt on the sander.

[**TIP**] **Anti-vibration gloves like the ones shown here minimize hand fatigue.**

After securing the panel to your bench, begin by running the sander four or five times fully across the panel diagonal to the grain **(B)**. Next, work diagonally in the opposite direction until you see a consistent pattern of scratches appear across the whole board **(C)**. At this point, any shiny areas will indicate low spots, in which case you'll have to repeat both directions. When the board shows a uniform scratch pattern, sand parallel to the grain to remove the cross-grain scratches **(D)**. (Wiping the board with solvent will help highlight subtle scratches.) When all the cross-grain scratches are gone, switch to a 120-grit belt and sand parallel to the grain. Follow up by sanding with a 150-grit belt, again sanding parallel to the grain.

At this point, the panel should be flat and need only smoothing. Start with 150-grit paper and move up through successive grits, stopping at 220 grit.

Flattening and Smoothing with a Random Orbit Sander

Although not as effective as a belt sander, a random orbit sander can be used to flatten a panel. Theoretically it doesn't matter which direction you move the tool because the large circular scratches from the spinning pad are cancelled out by the shorter "looping" scratches produced by the eccentric orbit **(A)**. However, using the same cross-hatching technique described for belt sanding helps ensure a more consistent surface. Most random orbit sanders have either a 5-in.-dia. pad or a 6-in.-dia. pad. I prefer a 6-in.-dia. pad because of its larger surface area.

After scraping any glue residue from the panel, outfit the sander with 100-grit paper or finer. Start by moving the sander at one angle **(B)**, then switch to the opposite **(C)**. After you reach your final grit, sand with that same grit by hand **(D)** to remove the cross-grain scratches.

One drawback to a random orbit sander is that its round pad won't reach well into corners and intersections. (For those purposes, try a vibrator sander, as described in the next photo-essay.)

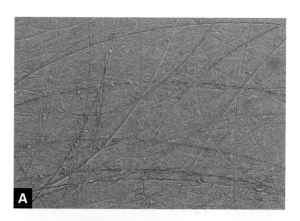

Smoothing with a Vibrator Sander

A vibrator sander doesn't do as fast a job at flattening a panel as a belt sander or random orbit sander. However, it excels at sanding into corners and against intersecting panels because the sides of the pad will ride up against a case divider or face frame. When sanding a bookcase with a face frame, for example, start where the case side meets the top and bottom **(A)**. Then rotate the sander 90 degrees and use its long edge to sand right up to the inside of the face frame **(B)**. Afterward, blend all the sanding strokes together, keeping the front edge of the pad away from the face frame to keep it from banging **(C)**. Finish up by hand-sanding to remove any swirl marks.

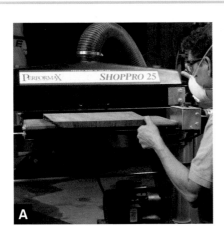

Flattening with a Drum Sander

To use a drum sander for flattening a board, use 80-grit paper and drop the conveyor table down ¼ in. more than the thickness of the board. With the machine off, insert the board under the sanding drum **(A)**. Power up the drum but not the conveyor. Then raise the conveyor table until the spinning drum contacts the wood. Next switch on the conveyor and run the stock through the machine, grabbing it as it exits **(B)**.

Continue to make repeated passes in this fashion, raising the table in small increments for each subsequent pass. After you've sanded the entire surface to 80 grit, you can switch to 120- or 150-grit paper for your final passes **(C)**. Because a drum sander won't produce a finish-quality surface, follow up by finish-sanding with a random orbit sander, beginning with paper that's one grit coarser than the final drum grit you used.

Smoothing Veneer

Begin by scraping away as much of the veneer tape as possible **(A)**. If you used veneer on the edge, sand its top edge flush to the tabletop to prevent tearing the edge veneer. Use 120-grit paper on a sanding block and work inward toward the center of the table **(B)**.

When you're sanding veneer with a power tool, hand position is important. Grasp the machine firmly with both hands to keep it flat. Tie the vacuum hose and electric cord together with hook-and-loop cable fasteners, then drape them your arm to keep them out of the way **(C)**. Starting with 120-grit paper, sand the perimeter first, then move toward the center, blending your strokes. When the panel looks and feels flat, wipe it with solvent to make sure the glue and tape residue is removed **(D)**. Follow with 150, 180, and then 220 grits.

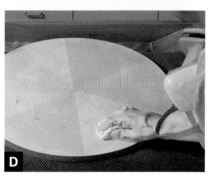

Leveling Solid Wood to Veneer

Whether it's an inlaid border (as shown here) or solid wood lipping, leveling a solid wood piece of trim flush to veneer can be tricky. The scraper works best for the wenge inlay here, but a block plane could be used for wider solid-wood lipping. To avoid digging into the veneer, note how I'm holding the scraper just a hair above the veneer surface with my left hand. My right hand is cupping the bottom while my knuckles ride on the bench **(A)**. After leveling the inlay, I finish up pushing the scraper toward the edge **(B)**, pivoting it sideways at the last second to sweep it across the inlay for the final leveling **(C)**.

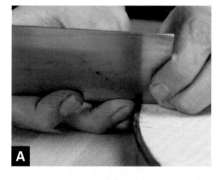

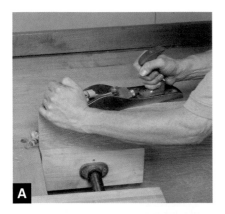

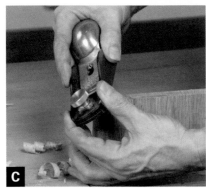

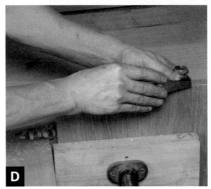

Planing Edges

Hand planes can quickly and efficiently smooth edges. If you plane in the direction of the grain while using a razor-sharp plane iron, the resulting surface will need little or no further smoothing. I find that a low-angle jack plane, like the one in the photo, works best when I'm planing hard wood like this plainsawn white oak **(A)**.

Although the same low-angle jack plane could be used on end grain, it's more common to use a low-angle block plane for this **(B)**. If you plane straight across the end grain, you'll chip out the opposite edge. The solution is to plane a slight chamfer on the trailing end first **(C)**. Alternatively, you could just plane inward from both ends toward the center of the board **(D)**. A couple of quick swipes with the same block plane puts a nice chamfer on edges **(E)**.

You can also use a scraper on the end grain but it won't be very smooth. You'll have to sand it afterwards with 180- or 220-grit sandpaper **(F)**.

Sanding Edges with a Vibrator Sander

When it comes to power sanding edges, it's hard to beat a vibrator sander. As opposed to that of a random orbit sander, a vibrator sander's pad registers flat against an edge. With the power off, place the pad of the vibrator sander against the workpiece edge and rock it a bit side to side until you can feel that it's riding flat on the edge **(A)**. Then switch it on and start sanding by moving the sander up and down a bit or at an angle so you don't wear the sandpaper in only one spot **(B)**. A vibrator sander works well on both long-grain and end-grain edges **(C)**.

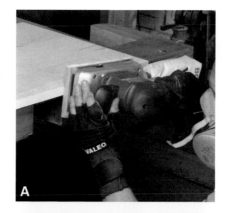

Sanding Edges with a Belt Sander

A small 3-in.-by-21-in. variable-speed belt sander can also be used on edges, provided you run it at its slowest speed and support the workpiece well. Use a shoulder vise and an adjustable bench slave to hold a large workpiece like a tabletop at a comfortable working height **(A)**. To help stabilize the sander, use the fingers of your forward hand to reach down and touch the workpiece. This technique is first-rate for sanding end grain as well, using the tail vise to hold the piece **(B)**. You can check your progress with a square if necessary **(C)**.

Preparation of Curved and Complex Surfaces

Simple Profiles

➤ Smoothing an Edge Roundover (p. 79)

➤ Fairing and Sanding a Curve by Hand (p. 79)

➤ Sanding Curves with Power Tools (p. 80)

Moldings and Carvings

➤ Sanding Molded Edges by Hand (p. 81)

➤ Using a Power Detail Sander (p. 82)

➤ Sanding Carved Moldings (p. 82)

Sanding Moldings

➤ Sanding Complicated Moldings (p. 83)

➤ Making a Custom Sanding Block (p. 84)

Turnings and Shapes

➤ Sanding on the Lathe (p. 85)

➤ Sanding Complicated Parts After Glue-Up (p. 85)

SELDOM DOES FURNITURE consist entirely of flat, straight surfaces. You often need to smooth curves, profiles, and complex surfaces, like intricate moldings and cabriole legs. As with flat surfaces, you'll first need to remove defects, irregularities, and milling marks before working the surfaces to final smoothness.

For the most part, the basic smoothing techniques explained in the previous section apply for curved surfaces. However, leveling most flat surfaces requires the use of a rigid sanding block, while curved work requires a different approach. In this section, I'll discuss the appropriate sanding blocks and techniques used for preparing various "non-flat" shapes for finishing.

Begin with Clean Cuts

There are a few preliminary steps you can take to reduce the amount of work involved in surface preparation. First of all, use sharp tools for the initial shaping. A dull router bit or shaper cutter can burn and tear out wood, requiring tedious sanding to remove the burns and refine the shape. Before cutting profiles on edges, make sure all surfaces are flat and straight. Otherwise, a bearing-guided cutter will follow irregularities on the edge and produce a similarly irregular profile. To minimize router-bit or shaper-cutter chatter, use as slow a feed rate as possible without burning the wood.

When using a bandsaw to cut curves, saw a bit shy of your cut line, leaving it as a reference for the final smoothing of the profile. (See the top photo above.) For repetitive shapes, consider pattern routing. With a sharp bit, a pattern-routed surface needs very little cleanup and smoothing.

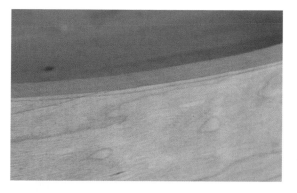

When shaping parts initially, cut a bit shy of the cut line—leaving it as a reference line for final smoothing. A pencil line shows through sanding dust better than a knifed line.

If you lack a lathe, you can hold spindle workpieces using bar clamps secured to your benchtop.

Holding Parts

Whenever possible, I smooth individual parts before gluing up a project. However, holding curved or round parts can be awkward. A shoulder or tail vise on a cabinet-maker's bench will secure many pieces, but you can also use pipe or bar clamps to hold turnings or odd-shaped parts like cabriole legs. (See the bottom photo above.) If you have a lathe, you can also mount legs and other long pieces between its centers. When smoothing edges, just clamp the workpiece so it overhangs your bench. Thin moldings can be temporarily spot-glued to a scrap panel using Super Glue adhesive, or you can slip them into an appropriately sized groove that you've cut in a scrap board.

Sanding Blocks and Pads

To sand curves and profiles, it's important to use a suitable backer for your sandpaper. If you try sanding a curved surface with a backing block, you'll almost certainly ruin the aesthetics of the shape. For example, sanding a concave surface using a random orbit sander with a hard backing pad will cause the edges of the pad to dig into the work surface. On the other hand, sanding a convex surface using a flat, hard backing pad may impart small flat spots to the workpiece surface. To avoid these problems, you can take a variety of approaches.

For sanding edge profiles such as a routed thumbnail or curved edge, you can use several types of backing blocks that match the profile shape. One approach is to make a custom block.

▶ See *"Making a Custom Sanding Block"* on p. 84.

Another is to use a commercially available contour sanding block that suits the shape.

▶ See *"Sanding Complicated Moldings"* on p. 83.

Adjustable contour blocks are also commercially available, as discussed in the sidebar below.

For sanding wider curved surfaces, the woodworking and automotive industries offer an array of flexible blocks that will conform to the shape of the workpiece. (See the photo below.) For general curved work, including turnings, you can use a variety of cushioned abrasives, such as commercially available foam sanding pads, synthetic steel wool, and sheet sandpaper backed up with a cushioned pad. These all have enough flex to follow odd workpiece contours. Foam hand-sanding pads designed to be used with flat sanding disks are also extremely useful. (See the left photo on the facing page.)

▶ AN ADJUSTABLE SANDING BLOCK

The Vario-Pro sanding block from Lignomat contains sliding plates that will adjust to any profile for sanding, working sort of like a contour gauge. To set up the shape, you

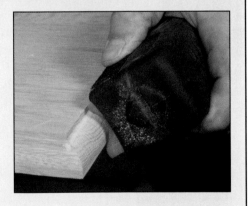

loosen a setscrew, press the block against the profile you're sanding, then lock the setscrew. The Vario-Pro won't sand a complicated profile without rounding over the details, but it's great for basic convex and concave curves.

Curved surfaces like this apron can be smoothed using PSA-backed sandpaper applied to a flexible pad available from automobile refinishing suppliers.

A grip-backed hand-sanding pad outfitted with a ½-in.-thick cushioned interface pad is perfect for sanding curved or complex parts, like this cabriole leg.

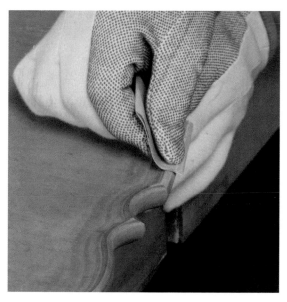

Cotton garden gloves with rubberized fingers protect your hands from abrasion and help absorb sweat.

This sandpaper gets its flexibility from a specialized glue bond, making it extremely easy to use for sanding details.

When dealing with complicated surfaces like carvings or complex moldings, sheet sandpaper folded into a suitable size and backed up with just your fingers can be the ultimate weapon.

Fair First

Leveling irregularities on a curved surface is called "fairing." Any high or low spots on curved edges should be faired before sanding. You can do this easily with a file or scraper. While performing the initial shaping with cutting tools, it's wise to leave a bit of your penciled cut line as a reference for final fairing. After fairing the surface, you can sand by hand or machine. Both fairing and smoothing can be done at the same time with a spindle sander. Another option is to fair and smooth using sandpaper backed up by a block shaped to a complementary curve.

Hand-Sanding

As fond as I am of using machines for smoothing, I find many complicated shapes are best done by hand. You'd be surprised at how much hand-sanding is performed in factories as well as small custom shops. One reason is that your hand will conform easily to just about any imaginable shape. The drawback is that sandpaper is rough on your hands, so wear protection. I find simple garden gloves effective. (See the center photo above.) I use gloves with rubberized palms for a better grip on the sandpaper and the workpiece. A-weight sandpaper is usually best for hand-sanding. Some manufacturers offer sandpaper with an extremely flexible glue bond, which allows you to form the paper to suit the work at hand. (See the right photo above.)

PSA paper is very handy to use with contour sanders because sandpaper that is firmly anchored to a backing block will create a sharp, clean profile.

A belt sander clamped in a vise makes quick work of smoothing these small, decorative tenon wedges. Note the bench slave that supports the front of the sander.

C- and D-weight papers are more appropriate for use with rigid backing blocks. I particularly like self-sticking pressure-sensitive adhesive (PSA) paper, which is sold in 4½-in.-wide rolls. You just tear off the length you need and press it onto a rubber sanding block or any other block with a smooth surface.

Power Sanding

When it comes to power sanding, an oscillating spindle sander is probably the most efficient machine for smoothing curved edges. A drum sander chucked in a drill press will work in a pinch, although most drill-press bearings are not designed to withstand axial (sideways) loads. Concave curves can be also sanded on the wheel section of an edge sander or belt sander. Stationary disk sanders and edge sanders can be used to fair and smooth convex curves.

Portable sanders can be also be used in some cases. A random orbit sander fitted with a cushioned interface pad works extremely well on domed surfaces. A belt sander mounted in a shop-made jig or clamped upside-down in a vise can be used to sand small curves quickly and effectively. (See the bottom photo at left.) Detail sanders are designed to reach into tight spaces and such, but I find sanding by hand faster and easier. When sanding crown molding and other complex shapes, it's often best to attack the various sections in steps. If you try to sand complex shapes all at once, you can destroy the crispness of the form.

▶ FOLDING SHEET SANDPAPER

When sanding by hand with lightweight sandpaper, it's best to fold the sheet to create a "pad" that's beefier and easier to grip. To ensure that the grit doesn't wear prematurely by rubbing against itself, fold the sheet in half, cut it halfway up, then fold it into quarters as shown here. After the first two exposed faces wear, turn the sheet inside out to expose fresh grit. For a smaller pad, fold a quarter-sheet of paper into thirds.

1. Make a cut halfway up on the short side.

2. Fold bottom-right quarter up.

3. Fold top-right side under.

4. Fold bottom half up.

Smoothing an Edge Roundover

The edge created by a roundover router bit is one of the most common profiles you'll encounter in furniture. To sand this profile, begin by fairing what's left of the original square edge into the roundover portion. When sanding the end grain, which is dense and tough, start with sandpaper wrapped around a cork-faced sanding block **(A)**. Hold the part securely and sand from the flat section of the edge onto the roundover, rolling the block around the profile so it's parallel to the grain at the end of the stroke. Next, smooth the roundover using a contour sanding block **(B)**. To remove the cross-grain scratches this creates, follow up by sanding the roundover shoe-shine style, using a piece of sandpaper folded into thirds for strength **(C)**. When you're sanding the long grain edges, a rubber contour sander takes care of all the operations above at once because the side grain isn't as tough as end grain **(D)**.

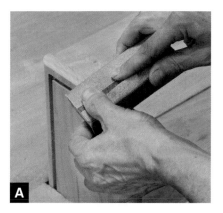

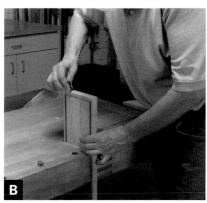

Fairing and Sanding a Curve by Hand

To remove the irregularities from a curve, begin by fairing it with a smoothing file. Hold the file with both hands at an angle to the edge, using the half-round side for concave curves **(A)** and the flat side for convex curves. Gauge the smoothness of the surface using your fingers and your eyes **(B)**. The best surface comes from using a custom sanding block made by tracing the profile of the curve onto a piece of scrap **(C)**. The sanding block need only be several inches long, but it should be slightly thicker than the edge to be sanded. Use double-sided tape or other adhesive to attach a piece of cork to the sanding block so the sandpaper will conform better to the profile **(D)**.

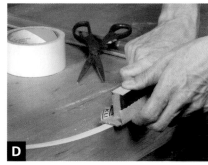

A

B

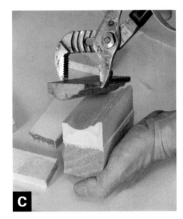

C

D

E

Making a Custom Sanding Block

Provided a molding isn't too complicated, you can save a lot of time by sanding its complete width all at once. To do this, you'll need a custom sanding block that is shaped to match the molding profile.

Begin with a 3-in.-to-4-in.-long section of the molding, applying a thin coat of furniture paste wax to it to act as a mold release. Using scraps of melamine, make a "dam" around the molding, butt-joining them at the corners with cyanoacrylate glue. Mix up some Bondo® or other polyester auto-body filler and push it down against the molding, leaving a small mound at the top **(A)**. Drive three screws into a piece of pine that's about ⅛-in. wider than the molding until the screw heads project about ¼ in. Then press the block into the auto-body filler **(B)**. This will push the body filler firmly onto the molding while forcing the excess filler out of the sides. After 5 to 10 minutes of monitoring the squeeze-out, you'll notice that it starts to turn rubbery. At that point (before the filler hardens), release the molding and the dam **(C)**.

Let the filler cure at least four hours. It may distort a bit as it cures, but you can fine-tune its shape by rubbing it along a sheet of A-weight, 220-grit sandpaper lying on the molding **(D)**. Next, spray the block with a thin coating of truck-bed liner **(E)**, a tough urethane that provides a slight cushion for the sandpaper while allowing easier removal of PSA sandpaper.

Sanding on the Lathe

I recommend sanding only on the lower quadrant, the 6 o'clock to 9 o'clock position of the work when viewed from the tailstock. Run the lathe slowly. Sand very carefully between the various elements to avoid destroying the crisp transitions that are the hallmark of good lathe-work.

I find the flexible hand pads that hold hook-and-loop paper first-rate for lathe sanding (**A**). For safety, don't use the hand strap, which might catch on the workpiece. You can easily conform the pad to match coves (**B**). Sand details and small grooves using the edges of a small sandpaper "pad" made by folding a quarter-sheet into thirds (**C**).

I usually sand lathe-work to 320 grit to minimize cross-grain scratches, then I stop the lathe and sand parallel to the grain using 220-grit paper (**D**). You can also turn the lathe back on and touch up just the transition edges with a turning tool.

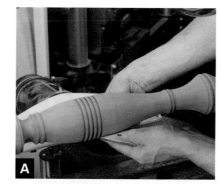

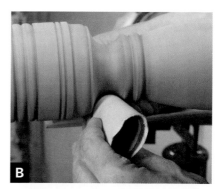

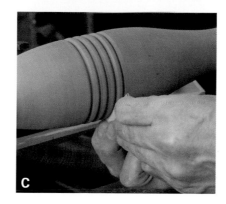

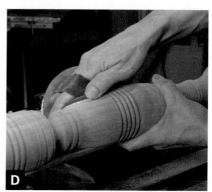

Sanding Complicated Parts After Glue-Up

My preference is to do as much surface preparation as possible before glue-up. However, sometimes you have to do it afterward in order to blend together various design elements, such as on the cabriole legs of this tea table.

I begin by using a smoothing file to blend the curves of the leg together (**A**). Next I use the concave edge of a curved scraper to remove the file marks and further refine the curves (**B**). A hand pad fitted with an additional interface cushion then smoothes the curves without flattening any areas (**C**). You can use a harder rubber profile pad to establish a crisp edge where needed, such as at the toe of this leg (**D**).

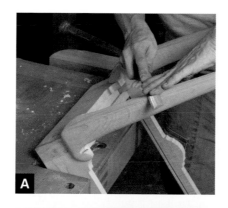

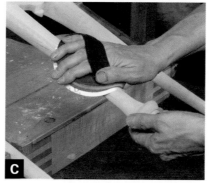

Fixing Defects

Preventing Problems

➤ Eliminating Glue Squeeze-Out (p. 95)

Repairing Damage

➤ Mending Broken Wood (p. 96)

➤ Steaming a Dent (p. 96)

Filling Gaps

➤ Filling Gaps with Putty (p. 97)

➤ Filling Gaps with Epoxy (p. 97)

Knots and Cracks

➤ Filling Cracks and Knots with Epoxy (p. 98)

➤ Filling Cracks and Splits with Cyanoacrylate Glue (p. 98)

Disguising Fillers

➤ Disguising Dark Fillers (p. 99)

➤ Disguising Light Fillers (p. 99)

I N SPITE OF every attempt to perfectly prepare a wood surface for finishing, you'll likely encounter last-minute defects. But don't start tearing your hair out at this point. Realize that fixing defects is not a detour; it's simply the final step in surface preparation. It's a natural part of the finishing process, and the more comfortable you are with handling defects and blemishes, the more enjoyable finishing will be as a whole.

Glue spots, sanding scratches, surface dings, and dents can be corrected much more easily before finishing. In this section, I'll show you how to spot these defects, how to correct them, and how to avoid them in the first place. I'll also suggest ways to treat natural defects like knots and cracks.

Avoiding or Minimizing Defects

By following a few general guidelines, you can minimize, and in some cases, eliminate defects and other blemishes on the wood surface.

- When you're done preparing surfaces, apply a finish as soon as possible. Unfinished parts risk getting dirty, dented, and scratched. They may also start to warp or change color while the rest of the parts are being made. It makes sense to build large flat tops, doors, and other panels last.

- Avoid glue spots by carefully assembling parts. Learn to apply just the right amount of glue to minimize or eliminate excess squeeze-out. Always perform a dry-

This door warped because it sat around unfinished in a humid shop most of the summer while the carcase was being made.

A glue-up table should be flat and easy to wipe clean. Melamine and plastic laminate are good surfaces for these purposes.

One way to clean up excess glue is to remove it immediately while it's still wet. This wetted fine-bristle toothbrush does a great job of reaching into corners.

assembly first to prevent surprises during the actual glue-up. Use a toothbrush or clean rag to immediately wipe away any glue drips or squeeze-out.

- Glue and clamp your project up on a glue-resistant surface like melamine or plastic laminate. Glue drips and smears are easy to detect on these surfaces and easy to wipe off. Wood also slides easily on them, reducing the chance of scratches. Use protective pads on clamp jaws to protect the workpieces.

- Use distilled water when cleaning up glue, as tap water contains dissolved iron salts that cause gray spots on tannin-rich woods like cherry and oak.

- If you break off a small piece of wood during cutting or shaping, glue it back on immediately.

Inspecting Surface Preparation

Always do a final inspection of your surface preparation before applying a stain or finish. Make sure that all square edges have been "eased" or "broken" to remove sharp, unfriendly corners that can wear quickly over time. Easing edges is also important because surface tension tends to draw wet finishes away from sharp corners, leaving them poorly protected. If an edge isn't properly covered with finish, it's easy to sand through to bare wood when scuff-sanding between coats. Ease your edges using the final grit of sandpaper from your finishing schedule. For a rounded edge, back up the sandpaper with your hand. Alternatively, you can back up the paper with a hard block, creating a small chamfer, which is one of those subtle details that distinguishes fine handcrafted furniture.

One artful way to ease an edge is to give it a small, crisp chamfer by sanding with 220-grit paper backed with a hard, flat block.

This unfinished panel reveals a small dent when wiped with alcohol. It's better to steam out dents before finishing rather than filling them with putty afterward.

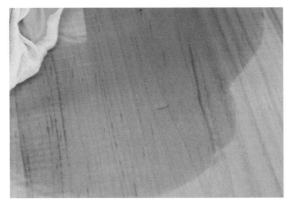

Simply hide defects whenever possible. The bark inclusion at the rear of the case side on this entertainment center will be hidden by the television.

Removing Imperfections

Sometimes it's possible to simply hide a defect in an unseen area. If this isn't an option, you can remove many blemishes by sanding, scraping, bleaching, or steaming. Here are some suggestions for handling various common imperfections:

Depressions can result from the incomplete leveling of a surface or from resanding an area to remove a deep residual sanding scratch. Although shallow depressions may not be very noticeable on dry wood, they'll usually be apparent after applying a finish. The solution requires releveling the entire area around the depression.

If you sand out just the low spot itself, you'll create a depression that will be noticeable after the finish is applied. If the low spot isn't too deep, you can "feather it out" into the adjacent area. (See the sidebar on the facing page.)

For final inspection, remove all sanding dust and debris using compressed air or a vacuum. Scrutinize the surface under raking light or wipe down the wood with mineral spirits, naphtha (which evaporates faster), alcohol, or acetone. Use either of the latter two if you're planning a waterborne finish. The solvent will wet the wood and accent any surface defects, glue spots, or sanding scratches. If you discover defects, repair them as described in this section, then carefully inspect the surface again. When the surface looks fine, you can proceed with staining or applying a clear finish once the wood feels dry, and there's no lingering solvent odor from the final wipe-down.

Residual sanding scratches can be removed by resanding the affected area with the finest grit capable of removing the scratch. Feather the resanded area back into the rest of the surface to avoid a depression. You can also use a scraper to remove the scratches, following up by sanding with the finest-grit paper you used the first time around.

Glue spots can be removed with a sharp chisel or scraper. Afterward, sand the area with the finest-grit paper you previously used on it.

Gray water spots caused by iron salts in tap water must be removed by treating the area with oxalic acid wood bleach.

▶ See *"Bleaches"* on p. 146.

Dents are best dealt with by steaming them out. Applying a combination of heat and steam swells the crushed wood fibers, brings the dent back to its former level or at least close enough to level it out by sanding.

▶ See *"Steaming a Dent"* on p. 96.

Patching with Wood

Whenever possible, it's best to patch wood with wood instead of putties or other fillers. Wood patches create a stronger, more attractive repair. A wood patch also provides more structural strength than most putties and will change color naturally over time with the rest of the surface.

Chipping is often caused by errant routing or other machining that breaks off sections of wood—particularly on corners and edges. If you can find the broken piece, the best

▶ FEATHER SANDING

Feather sanding is the technique of blending a slightly noticeable depression into the surrounding area so the resulting expanded depression isn't apparent. When feather sanding, use the finest grits of sandpaper possible to do the job. I usually start with 150- or 180-grit paper wrapped around a cork-faced backing block. Alternate your sanding strokes to fair the depression out in all directions, moving diagonally, cross-grain, and finally, parallel to the grain, as shown in the drawings below. Apply less sanding pressure as you move away from the heart of the depression.

Feather sanding is also used when smoothing hard fillers like epoxy or cyanoacrylate glue. Because these fillers are much harder than the surrounding wood, sanding only parallel to the grain will create depressions in the surface adjacent to the filler.

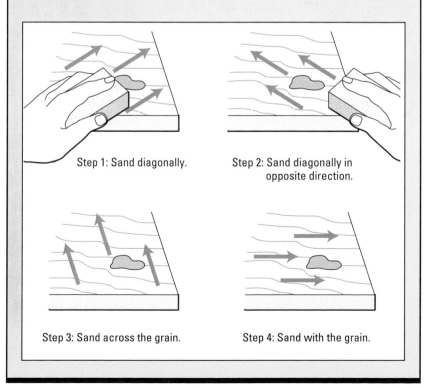

Step 1: Sand diagonally.

Step 2: Sand diagonally in opposite direction.

Step 3: Sand across the grain.

Step 4: Sand with the grain.

When patching with wood, you can use wedges to repair cracks (left), a "dutchman" patch to hide a knot (center), or a triangular patch to replace wood torn from a corner (right).

approach is to glue it back on immediately. Cyanoacrylate glue works best for this because it cures fast, allowing you to get right back to work. If you lose the broken piece, you can rebuild the area using a piece of wood that closely matches the grain, color, and texture of the adjacent area.

Splits and cracks that run parallel to the grain can be repaired by gluing slivers of wood into the affected areas. Large cracks and checks at the end of a board can be repaired this way, but the repaired area may not be structurally sound unless the patch is perfectly matched. As a result, you may want to avoid incorporating the repaired area into a load-bearing joint.

Knots or large damaged areas are best disguised with wood patches. The easiest approach is to drill a shallow hole of the appropriate size, then fill it with a plug cut with a plug cutter on the drill press. However, because of its shape, a round patch can be fairly evident.

For a more attractive repair, you can inlay an odd-shaped "dutchman" patch instead, using an inlay kit that's sold for use with a router. (See Resources on p. 287.) The heart of the kit consists of a router template guide that employs a removable spacer ring. To make the repair, you first rout a recess into the damaged area, guiding the router against a template with the spacer ring attached. Next, you make the patch using the same template but with the template guide ring removed. This "complementary routing" technique results in a perfectly matched patch and recess. If you take care to match the grain, color, and texture of the patch to the adjacent wood, the repair will be almost invisible.

You can also add an interesting decorative touch by using a patch that calls attention to a knot or crack. This type of design accent was popularized by furniture designers like George Nakashima, who often inlaid dovetail-shaped keys over cracks and splits.

Using Fillers

Sometimes filling a defect is your only option, particularly if you can't afford to remove any more wood by scraping or sanding. Splits, cracks, dents, gouges, knots, and joint gaps are all candidates for filler, whether it's a premixed commercial product or a filler you mix yourself. The fillers I'll discuss here are available in five different forms.

Wood fillers (clockwise from left): solvent-based and latex premixed putties; powdered putty; polyester resin, epoxy, and sanding dust; resin sticks; and wax crayons.

Premixed Putties

Premixed putties are among the easiest fillers to use. Also referred to as "wood filler," "wood dough," and "plastic wood," these products are widely available and sold under many different brand names. They're all easy to apply and they all sand well when dry, although some brands shrink more than others, and none has any structural strength. Most claim to be "stainable," but it's rare for the putty to take on the same color as the stained wood. However, you can add pigment to alter the color, testing the mix on scrap first.

These putties come in two basic types: solvent-based and latex (water-based). Solvent-based putty dries faster, which allows you to get back to work sooner. On the downside, it has a strong odor and tends to dry out quickly in its container, which can make it more difficult to apply. Latex filler has very little odor and doesn't dry out as quickly in its container.

Premixed putty can be used to fill dents and gouges less than $\frac{1}{4}$-in.-wide, as well as small joint gaps. It's also good for filling nail holes in trim work. I use both latex and solvent-based putty to repair work that will be stained, although I never assume that the color of the putty will match the stain color. If the color of the filler doesn't match the stained work, you can fine-tune it using touchup techniques.

▶ See *"Disguising Dark Fillers"* and *"Disguising Light Fillers"* on p. 99.

Powdered Putties

Powdered putties are very hard-drying, plasterlike compounds mixed with water before application. These putties can be very good fillers because they'll shrink very little when mixed with a minimal amount of water. The disadvantages are that they require mixing and have to be used immediately once mixed. They are also only available in an

To fill the gum deposit on this cherry panel, the author used a hot knife to lift a bit of material from a resin stick and apply it to the defect.

To smooth repairs made with resin sticks, rub the area with a piece of alcohol-wetted muslin wrapped around a cork block.

► COLORING FILLERS

Many fillers can be easily tinted to match the color of the wood being repaired. Any tinting medium that's compatible with the filler can be used. For example, you can use artist's oil colors in oil-based putties or acrylic artist's paint and water-soluble wood dyes in water-based putties. But be aware that the added solvent or water in these colorants can cause excessive shrinkage in the filler. Dry pigments can provide a better solution. Because they're inert and don't add other chemicals and solvents, dry pigments don't pose compatibility problems.

turn slightly yellow over time. In the case of cherry—which darkens quite a bit over time—go a few shades darker.

Resin sticks are typically used to repair damaged finishes or dents that occur during finishing. It's difficult to make an invisible repair, but if the dent is on a noncritical surface like a case side, it may not be noticeable. However, I don't recommend filling dents in tops and other prominent surfaces. Instead, scrape the finish off (which is easier than stripping), then sand or steam the dent out.

You can also use resin sticks on bare wood to fill defects in advance of finishing. Use a hot knife to lift a bit of resin from the stick and apply it to the workpiece. Afterward, level the resin using a cloth-covered block and alcohol, or just sand it level with sandpaper.

Eliminating Glue Squeeze-Out

When gluing up traditional mortise-and-tenon joints, you can eliminate a lot of glue cleanup by simply avoiding squeeze-out. Before assembling the joint, use a sharp chisel to pare away the top edge of the mortise all the way around **(A)**. Then use a block plane to chamfer the four leading edges of the tenon **(B)**. Apply glue carefully to the side walls of the mortise and to the leading edge of the tenon, keeping the glue about ¼ in. away from the tenon shoulder **(C)**. After clamping the joint, you'll be pleasantly surprised that there's no glue squeeze-out **(D)**. Keep in mind that the lack of squeeze-out does not indicate a starved joint; you've simply provided a "well" for the excess glue at the top of the mortise to prevent it from being forced outward under clamp pressure.

[**VARIATION**] **If you're using water-based polyvinyl acetate (PVA) glue or hide glue, and the work will be stained with a water-based stain, you can wipe off excess glue using a rag wetted with the stain.**

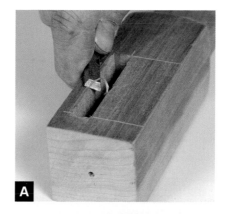

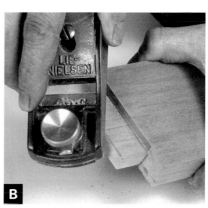

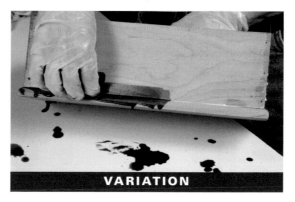

VARIATION

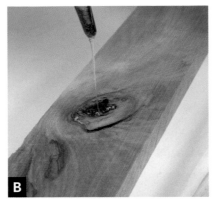

A

B

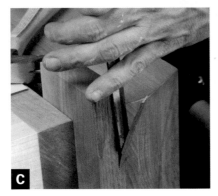

C

D

Filling Cracks and Knots with Epoxy

Epoxy serves as a great filler for large cracks and knots such as those on this walnut board. The epoxy will flow and settle better if you heat the knot first, using a heat gun on a low setting **(A)**. To apply the epoxy, simply dribble it into the knothole with a stick of wood or a small artist's palette knife **(B)**.

If you like, you can reinforce the board by driving slivers of wood into the splits after taping one side of the board and filling the holes with epoxy. It's best to rive the slivers from a scrap board using a chisel **(C)**. Because riven wood is split along the grain, it will conform to the shape of the crack better without breaking. Tap the slivers in lightly with a hammer **(D)**. After the epoxy has cured, saw off the ends of the slivers and sand the filled area.

A

B

C

D

Filling Cracks and Splits with Cyanoacrylate Glue

Cyanoacrylate glue is available in various viscosities, ranging from watery to molasseslike. Use the thin-viscosity glue to fill small stress cracks like the one on this white oak top **(A)**. Afterward, simply sand the area with 150-grit sandpaper, which compresses sanding dust into the glue, making the crack virtually disappear **(B)**.

For larger cracks, like the one on the end of this white oak board, use the thicker-viscosity glue **(C)**. After applying the glue to the crack, sand the area to mix sanding dust into the glue, creating a paste that fills the crack **(D)**. A quick spritz with CA glue activator hardens the paste immediately. A second application may be necessary for large splits.

Disguising Dark Fillers

Begin by sealing the entire wood surface with shellac. This darkens it to its finished state, providing a color reference for mixing the pigment. Next, mix pigment into a small amount of clear medium. (I use dewaxed shellac because it is fast-drying and compatible with any finish.) Using a no. 4 artist's brush, begin by blocking out the dark filler with a pigment mix that matches the darkest shade of the wood **(A)**. After that dries, fill in with shades of a lighter pigment mix **(B)**. Leave some of the darker pigment to create the impression of grain and detail **(C)**.

A common mistake is to make the touchup look perfect from a close perspective. Instead, try a procedure I call the "television" technique. Using the pointy tip of your brush, dab different-colored dots on the repair. This works much like a television screen, which produces all colors using three tiny round colored pixels. When viewed at a distance, the points blend together to make the repair appear more natural.

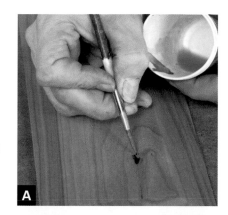

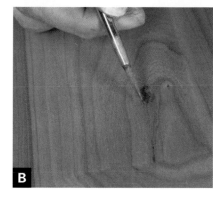

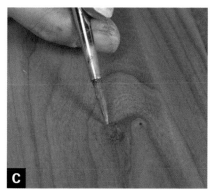

Disguising Light Fillers

Putty and other fillers often stand out because they dry lighter than the surrounding wood and interrupt the grain. One simple fix is to first darken the puttied area by applying a mix of pigment and shellac with a no. 4 artist's brush **(A)**. Next, paint some fine grain lines using a no. 1 artist's brush to simulate wood grain **(B)**. If the grain lines are too wide, use your no. 4 brush and original color to finesse the width of the lines **(C)**.

Stain Basics and Application

Hand-Applying Stains

➤ Applying Oil-Based Pigment Stains (p. 114)

➤ Applying Water-Based Stains and Dyes (p. 115)

➤ Applying Non-Grain-Raising Stains (p. 116)

➤ Staining Frame-and-Panel Doors (p. 116)

Spraying Stains

➤ Spraying Water-Based Stains (p. 117)

➤ Spraying Solvent-Based Stains (p. 118)

Dye Concentrates

➤ Mixing, Measuring, and Duplicating Dyes (p. 119)

Specialty Colors

➤ Making a Gilsonite/Asphaltum Stain (p. 120)

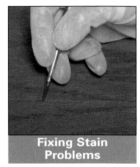

Fixing Stain Problems

➤ Fixing Glue Spots (p. 121)

➤ Dealing with Scratches and Sand-Throughs (p. 121)

S TAINING WOOD means coloring it without obscuring grain and figure. The visual effect is produced mostly by the colorant used. Most stains fall into one of two distinct classes: pigment-based or dye-based, although it's not unusual for a stain to contain both components. In this section, we'll look at pigment and dye stains. Specialty stains like chemicals will be covered in Section 9.

Pigment-Based Stains

Pigment-based stains are composed of three ingredients: pigment, binder, and thinner. The pigment consists of small colored inert particles that do not dissolve in any liquid. The combination of binder and thinner is referred to as the vehicle.

Pigments are broadly classified as either natural or man-made. Further classification divides pigments into inorganic and organic colors. The natural inorganic pigments widely used in wood stains are called earth colors

A typical oil-based wiping stain (right rear) consists of linseed oil (left rear) or alkyd binder, mineral spirits, and earth pigments (front).

because they're actually dug out of the earth's crust, then washed and dried. Unfortunately, the earth does not provide much in the way of white, black, or pure primary colors like red and yellow, so these must be made from either natural products or synthetic chemicals. Following are the basic industrial classifications for pigments.

Earth pigments are represented by the umbers, ochres, siennas, and Van Dyke brown. Included in this group are some naturally green and slate-tone earth colors. Most wood-tone stains are made with earth pigments.

White pigments were almost all lead-based up until the 1970s, when lead was banned from consumer paint. White pigment today is almost always titanium dioxide, a man-made pigment.

Black pigment is produced by a variety of processes. The predominant black pigment is carbon black, which is made by collecting the soot from a closed furnace after burning natural gas. Lampblack pigment is made from burning oil.

Organic man-made pigments include the bright reds, yellows, and blues you see in paints. These are classified by their chemical structure, such as phthalocyanine blue, cadmium reds and yellows, and quinacridone reds. Colors like the azos and phthalocyanines have similar chemistry to dye colors.

Transparent/micronized pigments have been reduced to a size under the lower limits of visible light, making them more transparent than traditional pigment stains. These pigments are very lightfast and nearly as transparent as dyes, and are popular as replacements for the less lightfast dyes used on furniture. Transparent red and yellow oxide are the two most easily available.

Bronze and pearlescent pigments are metal powders or flakes of mica coated with various metal oxides. Bronzing pigment—typically made from aluminum, zinc, and copper—produces an opaque metal-like appearance. Pearlescent mica pigments can be added to a glaze or clear finish to create a subtle, iridescent, pearl-like appearance.

HOW DYE STAINS WOOD

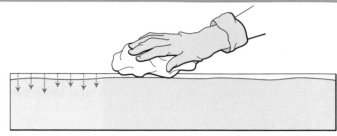

A

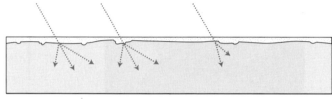

B

On smooth, close-grained woods like maple, dye stains color evenly, regardless of surface texture, because the small, molecular-sized dye particles are readily absorbed into the wood cells (A). The dye particles are so small that they don't bend or reflect light, so the dye appears transparent (B).

The right side of this ash panel was stained with alcohol-based dye, which creates a greater grain contrast than the water-based dye on the left side.

Dye stains can be mixed from powders or concentrated liquids. Modern dye stains are easy to use and produce consistently predictable colors.

alcohol-based and NGR dye stains do a better job of enhancing grain. It might sound like dyes are the miracle stain, but it's important to note that they are not as light-fast as pigment stains, particularly the natural earth pigments.

Up until the mid-19th century, all wood dyes were made of natural products. However, as soon as synthetic dyes became available, they were embraced by industry, which found them easier to use and consistently predictable in color.

Woodworking dyes can be classified either by solvent or by chemical structure, as follows.

Acid dyes dissolve primarily in water, though sometimes finishers add alcohol to a strong solution of the water-based mixture. Commonly available water-soluble powdered dyes are almost always acid dyes. They have good overall light fastness (for dyes) and are very economical.

➤ "ANILINE" DYES

When dyes were first synthesized back in the mid-1800s, the principal starting ingredient was aniline, a byproduct of coal tar—the sticky residue left after burning coal. These dyes became known as aniline dyes or coal-tar colors, to distinguish them from the natural dyes that were in use at the time. While the term "aniline dyes" technically refers to dyes made from aniline-based chemicals called "intermediates," it is often loosely used to refer to all synthetic dyes. However, because modern dyes used in woodworking contain no aniline in the final product, I prefer not to use the term, as it can lead one to think the dyes are hazardous, as aniline is quite toxic and a known carcinogen.

Basic dyes dissolve in water or alcohol and sometimes both. Basic dyes are extremely bright and vivid but not very lightfast. They've primarily been used to tint lacquers and shellacs, although they are being replaced by the more lightfast metallized solvent dyes discussed below.

Metallized acid dyes are similar to acid dyes, except that a metal such as chromium or cobalt is incorporated into the dye structure, making it more lightfast and bleed-resistant. These dyes are typically sold as concentrates.

Metallized solvent dyes are similar to metallized acid dyes, but they aren't soluble in water. Available in powdered form, they dissolve best in alcohols and ketones. They are widely used as a replacement for the basic dyes used to tint lacquers and other finishes. They're also used to make non-grain-raising (NGR) stains.

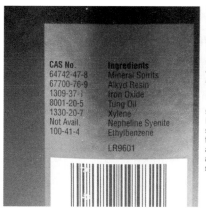

The ingredients on this label identify the thinners (mineral spirits, xylene, and ethylbenzene), the binder (alkyd resin, tung oil), and the pigment (iron oxide).

Stain Formulations

Pigment stains are available in premixed formulations that are classified by the binder/thinner vehicle. The most common consumer stains are oil-based or water-based products. They are typically available as either a pigment stain or as a combination of pigment and dye. The product label will often identify the contents of a stain formulation, but sometimes it doesn't. For basic identification of a liquid stain, you

CONCENTRATED PIGMENT COLORS

Oil Colors

Available from art stores, oil colors are made by grinding pigment into linseed oil.

Be aware that some oil paints may include raw linseed oil that may extend the drying time of oil varnishes to which they're added.

Japan Colors

These alkyd-based concentrates mix best with oil-based varnishes and products like linseed oil and tung oil. They dry much faster than the oil colors mentioned above and have some compatibility with solvent lacquer.

Acrylics

Water-based acrylic colors are available from art stores as acrylic artist's paint, or from specialty finish suppliers. Acrylics mix only with water-based finishing products.

Universal Tinting Colorants

Commonly referred to as UTCs, these colors were designed for compatibility with both oil-based and water-based (latex) paints and are the tints used by paint stores to mix paint colors.

Industrial Tinting Colorants

These colorants are specifically formulated by industry to tint products such as oil varnishes, lacquers, water-based products, and specialty urethanes and polyesters. They are usually repackaged by the finish supplier as products to be used with their proprietary finishes.

How Stains Handle

Two of the most important criteria in choosing a stain are how it handles and how it looks. I'll discuss handling characteristics first, then appearance.

The primary handling quality of a stain is its "open time," which is dictated by the type of binder and solvent used. Open time is the amount of time you have between applying the stain and wiping it off effectively. Oil-based stains have the longest amount of time before you remove the excess. The flip side of this is that you have to wait longer before applying a top coat. At the other end of the spectrum are the fast-drying lacquers and alcohol-based stains. Water-based products also dry quickly, but more so in hot, dry weather than under humid conditions. (See the sidebar on p. 111.)

The biggest advantage of oil-based and alkyd stains is that once they cure, any finish wiped over them will not redissolve the stain and remove some of the color. So for hand application of finishes with a rag or brush,

Oil-based stains have the longest open time, allowing plenty of time to wipe the stain off after application. Even after 10 minutes, this stain wiped cleanly.

oil and alkyd-based stains are very good products, which is why they dominate the consumer market.

Applying Stains by Hand

All stains can be applied by hand with rags, pads, or brushes. However, brushes only work well with slower-drying stains like the oil-based varieties. Rags and pads work better for medium and fast-drying stains because brushes tend to leave lap marks where the brushstrokes overlap each other.

Most consumer-grade stains are sold as "wiping stains," meaning the excess is meant to be wiped off after application. Other stains, such as fast-drying pigment stains and dyes without a binder, can be applied, then left to dry without wiping. Water-based dyes with no binder are the easiest to apply by hand with little wiping, because they have a wonderful ability to absorb evenly and spread over the surface, regardless of the amount applied. Alcohol-based and NGR dye stains can be very difficult to apply by

Don't judge the look of a stain until a coat or two of finish is applied. The left side of this stained board was given a top coat of finish, which brought the stain to life.

OPEN AND DRY TIME

Two very important characteristics of any stain are its open time and dry time. Open time is the period between application and a successful wipe-down. Dry time is the time necessary for a stain to dry before you can apply a top coat of finish.

Oil-based pigment or pigment/dye stains have the longest open time, followed by varnish-based gel stains. Lacquer-based stains and some fast-drying varnish stains have a shorter open time. Water-based products are next, followed by NGR stains, then 100 percent alcohol dye stains.

Oil-based stains require the longest dry times—typically six hours or more—while most water-based pigment stains dry a little faster. Water-based dye stains can be top-coated as soon as the wood feels dry, which can be within an hour under favorable conditions. The quickest-drying are the alcohol-based dye stains and some lacquer-based stains, which can dry in as little as 15 minutes.

To check whether a stain is dry, lightly wipe the surface with a clean, soft rag. If no color wipes off, you're ready to apply a top coat.

Fast-drying alcohol and NGR stains can be slowed down by adding as much as 10 percent retarder by volume.

To minimize raised grain caused by water-based stain, sponge the bare wood first, let it dry, then resand to remove the raised grain before staining.

hand because they dry so fast. Adding a retarder to these stains to slow the dry time is recommended.

Water-based stains will raise the grain of the wood after they dry. To minimize this, you can preraise the grain by sponging it with distilled water before staining, letting it dry, then sanding again. Sanding the bare wood to 320 grit also minimizes raised grain.

Spraying Stains

You can spray any stain to speed up the application or create a specific look. If you spray a pigment wiping stain, wipe off the excess for the cleanest effect. This also provides textural contrast between pores and flat grain. Pigment wiping stains can appear extremely muddy if not wiped off, and the excess may cause adhesion problems when applying a top coat of finish.

Fast-drying pigment stains and dye stains can safely be sprayed on and left unwiped. This technique saves time, makes the stain appear more uniform, and it's also used to control splotching, as you'll see in Section 10. As a general rule, wipe the stain after application if you want to accentuate the grain and figure. On the other hand, if you want the stain to color evenly, don't wipe it off. Dyes with no binder are the easiest to spray without wiping, because they absorb evenly.

> ⚠️ **WARNING When spraying stains, always wear respiratory protection and work in a well-ventilated area.**

The gel stain (center) or asphaltum stain (right) provide much better grain definition than the water-based dye applied to the left side.

Spraying a stain and leaving it unwiped (left) is the best approach to de-emphasizing grain contrast.

Selecting a Stain for Appearance

Just as important as the workability of a stain is its appearance on a given type of wood. In addition to choosing the appropriate color, you'll need to decide how prominent you want the grain to be, whether you desire or object to a yellow cast, and how important it is that the color remains stable or lightfast.

Grain Definition

To make the grain stand out on ring-porous woods like oak and ash, your best bet is to use pigment gel stains. NGR dyes, alcohol-based dyes, and pigment stains that contain Gilsonite also provide excellent grain enhancement. On the other hand, there are times when it's best to de-emphasize the grain, such as when you have to match a rough, textured wood like oak to a nontextured wood like pine or maple. In these cases, it's best to use a water-based dye with

no binder. Spraying the stain without wiping it off works well with fast-drying dye or pigment stains.

Yellowing

Yellowing will occur with any oil-based product but is usually only objectionable over white or pastel colors such as pickled finishes or whitewash stains. To minimize yellowing, use a stain made with an acrylic binder, and avoid using oil- or other solvent-based top coats, which are also prone to yellowing.

Lightfastness

Pigment stains provide the best color stability, particularly the earth colors, iron oxides, and Gilsonite. Indoors, strong sunlight from large windows can fade dye stains, so try to use metallized dye stains or pigment for these applications. An alternative is to set your undertone with a dye, and then simply wipe a pigment stain over it.

Applying Oil-Based Pigment Stains

To apply oil-based wiping stain, begin by stirring the contents thoroughly. Make sure you scrape all the pigment off the bottom of the can using the flat end of a stick and that you incorporate it into the liquid. Using a brush, rag, or pad, apply the stain to the wood in whichever direction you want **(A)**. Within five minutes, wipe away the excess stain with a clean absorbent cloth, turning the cloth frequently to expose clean sections as you work. Wipe off the stain in any direction you wish. After you've removed as much of the excess stain as you can, lightly wipe parallel to the grain to minimize any application marks. Because pigment stains contain binder, you should now have a good read on what the wood will look like with a clear finish. If the stained surface is then too dark, wipe it down with mineral spirits or naphtha. If you need to lighten it further or if the stain has gotten tacky, use a synthetic abrasive pad soaked with the appropriate solvent for the stain **(B)**. If the stain is the wrong color or not dark enough, simply apply a different stain **(C)**.

Applying Water-Based Stains and Dyes

Before staining wood like this coarse-grained oak, prepare the surface by sanding it through 220 grit. Then raise the grain by wetting it with distilled water **(A)**. After the water dries, resand the surface with 320-grit paper.

When staining casework like this nightstand, begin with the interior. This familiarizes you with the working quality of the stain and allows you to adjust the color if necessary before staining the more critical outside. Use a foam brush to work the stain into corners, but use a rag wherever possible, as it's faster and you'll avoid lap marks **(B)**. Work from the bottom up to avoid dripping the stain onto bare wood, and do the top last **(C)**.

If you need to darken the color slightly, apply a second coat of the stain. To darken or change the color dramatically, apply a stronger dye concentration or different color. It will be easier to judge the effect if you do this after the first coat has dried **(D)**.

[**VARIATION**] **When applying dyes to a complicated piece, a plant mister works particularly well.**

A

B

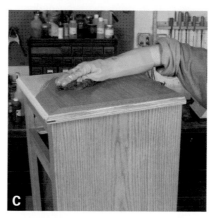
C

D

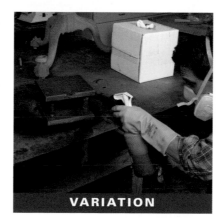
VARIATION

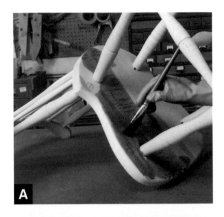

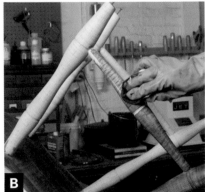

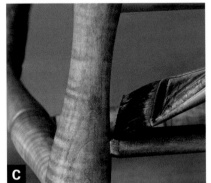

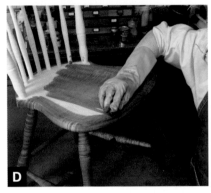

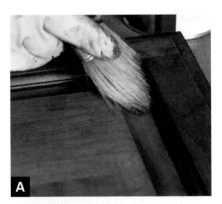

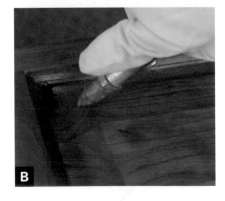

Applying Non-Grain-Raising (NGR) Stains

Although NGR stains were originally developed for spray finishing, they can also be applied by hand using the right technique. When applying the stain by hand on a complicated item, it's best to add retarder. Start by adding 2 oz. retarder per quart of finish, and begin on a secondary surface like the bottom of this chair **(A)**. Using a synthetic bristle brush, apply the dye quickly, then blend the brushstrokes together using a rag, which prevents lap marks from the brushstrokes. After staining the underside, do the legs and stretchers. For round parts like these stretchers, use a small dye-dampened rag **(B)**. You can use the tip of the brush to touch up spots or to work stain into crevices **(C)**. After staining the edges and top of the seat, finish up by staining the back spindles and crest **(D)**.

Staining Frame-and-Panel Doors

When staining frame-and-panel door assemblies, many finishers stain the entire panel before assembly. However, this requires that you stop midstream to do this prefinish work.

Alternatively, you can cut a slight back-bevel on the edges of the molded rails and stiles where they meet the raised panel, creating access for brush bristles when you're staining **(A)**. Liquid stain can also be driven under the rails and stiles using compressed air **(B)**. To further minimize the chance of exposing bare wood at the edges of the panels, it's a good idea to keep a panel centered in its frame by inserting rubber spacers in the frame grooves or by pinning the panel from behind to the center of the top and bottom rails.

Spraying Water-Based Stains

The easiest way to spray a water-based dye is with a small gravity-feed touchup gun **(A)**. These guns are inexpensive and can be easily powered by a small compressor. As when staining any project, first dismantle it as much as possible and tape off any drawer boxes **(B)**. Work from the inside out, spraying the dye generously and keeping the wood wet **(C)**. Blot up excess stain with a clean cloth **(D)**.

[VARIATION] **A good way to create depth and darken the figure in curly wood is to first dye it with a dilute brown dye, as shown in the photos above. Next, smooth the raised grain using sandpaper or maroon abrasive pads, removing some of the darker dye from the surface but leaving the curl darker. Finish by applying a caramel- or honey-colored dye to make the curl really pop.**

A

B

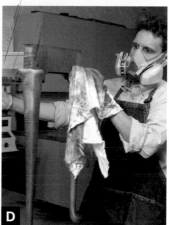

C

D

VARIATION

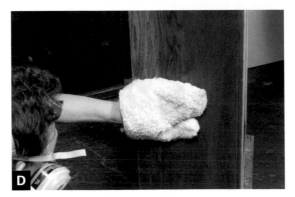

Spraying Solvent-Based Stains

Alcohol-based or solvent-based NGR stains are a good choice when you want to spray without raising the grain. For a bookcase like the one pictured, begin by removing the back to minimize spray bounce-back. Working from behind the case, spray the underside of the top first, then move down the right and left sides **(A)**. Spray the bottom afterward **(B)**. Since the vortex created by the spray gun may not allow the stain into corners, you can wipe the stain into them **(C)**. Next, spray the outside. If you want to wipe the stain to even it out, wear a painter's mitt on your free hand, immediately wiping after you spray **(D)**. Spray the outside frame and top last.

Mixing, Measuring, and Duplicating Dyes

To develop custom colors from dyes, I've developed a system based on calculated combinations of "master mixes," which I use to make custom colors.

When making your master mixes from powdered dyes, it's best to measure the powders by weight **(A)**. The directions for this particular dye suggest mixing 1 oz. powder to 2 qt. water. However, I'll mix up only half that amount, leaving myself ½ oz. of dye for making adjustments if necessary to create the color I'm after. Wearing a dust mask, measure the dye and stir it into hot tap water **(B)**. Once it has cooled to room temperature, transfer it into a labeled jar.

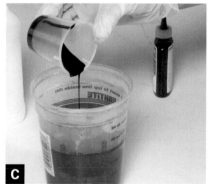

When making your master mixes from liquid dyes, measure them out by volume instead of weight **(C)**. Liquid dyes are more convenient if you don't own an accurate scale.

Once you make your master mixes, use them to create a stain board of the different colors **(D)**. This allows you to determine which stain might best match your intended color or which stain might serve as the base color to be adjusted with other stains. I also stain strips of copy paper with each mixture, noting on the paper the dilution ratio. Once you've selected the master mix, apply it to a scrap piece from the project and assess the color. If it's too dark, mix one part of the master with one part solvent and try that on the scrap. If it's still too dark, mix one part master with two parts solvent. If necessary, continue that approach until you reach the shade you want **(E)**. If you need to change the hue, it's best to add red, yellow, blue, or green.

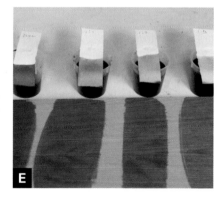

➤ See *"Basic Color Theory"* on p. 162.

Making a Gilsonite/Asphaltum Stain

If you hang around professional finishers enough, you'll invariably hear about the virtues of Gilsonite™ or asphaltum as a stain. Pure Gilsonite powder doesn't dissolve easily in mineral spirits, so use xylene or lacquer thinner as a solvent. Start by adding 1 tablespoon of powder to 3 oz. of solvent, then dilute that mix as necessary to suit your project **(A)**. Add 1 part boiled linseed oil to 9 parts solution to act as a binder.

Asphaltum is most commonly available in the form of nonfibered roofing tar **(B)**. To make a fairly dark stain, use 1 tablespoon tar to 3 oz. Danish oil or boiled linseed oil, which acts as a binder **(C)**. This mix makes a wonderful walnut- or oak-colored stain.

Fixing Glue Spots

When you detect errant glue spots during staining, it's best to correct the problem immediately. It's not unusual, for example, to encounter glue squeeze-out at a joint **(A)**. In a case like this, the glue can be immediately removed by wet-sanding the area with the same grit of sandpaper you used for your final bare wood sanding. Dunk a piece of wet/dry sandpaper into the stain and sand away the glue **(B)**. In certain situations you can use a sharp chisel to pare away the glue **(C)**. This will leave a bare spot that can be treated by blending the stain back in with an abrasive pad.

Sometimes glue will show through the veneer seams on plywood. In these cases, it's best to paint over the glue lines using a mixture of dry pigment and shellac, as discussed in Section 6. Often you can get away with simply brushing your stain over the affected area using a small brush **(D)**.

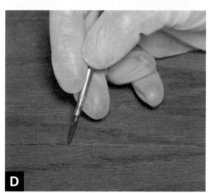
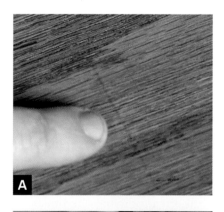

Dealing with Scratches and Sand-Throughs

Stains—especially pigment stains—will highlight errant cross-grain scratches **(A)**. To remove a scratch, use wet-dry sandpaper of the same grit that you used for your final bare wood sanding. Apply stain to the scratched area to serve as a sanding lubricant **(B)**.

When sanding a thin sealer coat, you can sometimes sand too far and break through the stain. If you applied a dye without a binder, just reapply more dye and it will blend right in. If you used a stain with an oil binder, it's far more difficult to make the stain blend in by simply rewiping the bare spot. Using your original stain, dab a fine bristle brush into a bit of the stain and lightly "dry-brush" it over the lighter area **(C)**. Dry-brushing feathers the stain to blend it in, but you can also use a soft cloth to help **(D)**.

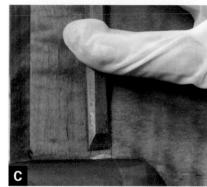
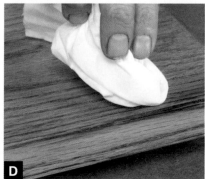

Glazes, Padding Stains, and Toners

Applying Glazes

➤ Subduing Bright Stains with Glaze (p. 133)

➤ Spraying a Glaze (p. 133)

➤ Striking Out (p. 134)

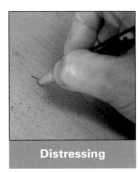

Distressing

➤ Physical Distressing (p. 135)

➤ Surface Distressing (p. 136)

Padding Stains

➤ Applying Padding Stain (p. 137)

Toners

➤ Toning for Consistency (p. 138)

➤ Shading (p. 138)

➤ Hiding Mistakes with Toner (p. 139)

➤ Spraying a Sunburst Pattern (p. 139)

E VEN AFTER WOOD has been initially stained and sealed, you can open up a whole new world of color and tonal possibilities by modifying the finish with glazes or toners.

Glazing is the process of sandwiching a layer of color between the initial sealer coat and the top coats of finish, whereas *toning* is the technique of mixing color directly into the finish itself for application. Glazing is often employed to highlight open grain and add texture, to selectively add color, and to

accent "distressed" elements to create an aged appearance. Both glazing and toning allow you to adjust the color and tone of a finish or to darken it. They can also be used to eliminate splotching and to make the overall appearance more uniform.

In this section, I'll discuss the nature and uses of glazes and toners and explain my methods for mixing and applying them.

Glazing Basics

A glaze is a thin coat of color applied between the initial sealer coat and the top coat of finish, as shown in the drawing at right. All glazes need to be top-coated after application, which not only protects the glaze but provides the optical mechanism by which glazes add richness and depth. Glazing is only done between coats of hard, film-forming finishes like lacquer, varnish, and shellac.

Glazes have a multitude of uses in finishing. They can be used to alter overall hue or value, control splotching, highlight pore structure, add richness to the wood, subdue stain brightness, and imitate age or grain.

Glazes are always pigment-based, as opposed to dye-based. In fact, they are very similar to pigment stains in that they contain pigment, binder, and thinner. However, glazes are modified to extend their dry time and viscosity for easier manipulation. The two major criteria for a glaze are that it cannot contain any solvents that may dissolve or soften the sealer and that it's able to be easily wiped around on the surface.

Glazes can be applied over a coat of sealer by spraying, brushing, or wiping with a rag. Then they are either wiped off clean—leaving a thin coat of glaze behind—or they are manipulated by hand to create certain effects before they set up and start to dry. The best thing about working with glazes is that you can easily wipe them away if you make a mistake or if you don't like the way a particular glaze looks. That's because glazes don't attack the sealer coat, so starting over is as easy as erasing a blackboard.

ANATOMY OF A GLAZE

Clear top coat

Glaze

Sealer

Wood

Glazes are similar in composition to pigment stains and will react to the texture of wood. However, unlike pigment stains, glazes are sandwiched between a sealer and a top coat of finish.

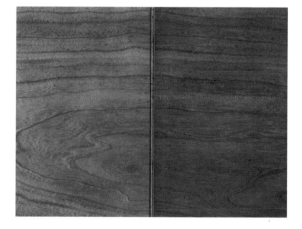

The reddish-brown glaze applied to the right side of this cherry panel subdues the brightness of the underlying golden dye stain seen at left and shifts the color to a richer golden-cherry color.

One of the more common uses of a glaze is to subdue the brightness of a stain. At the same time, you can alter the overall hue, making it redder or greener, for example. You can also alter its "value" to make the color darker. Because the surface has been previously sealed, splotching will be controlled as well.

Another useful application for glazing is to highlight the wood's pore structure or to bring attention to features such as carvings.

CREATING TEXTURAL MARKS

BRUSH PATTERNS   BRUSH TECHNIQUE

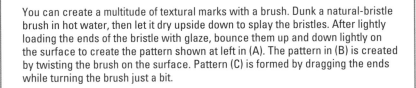

(A)

(B)

(C)

You can create a multitude of textural marks with a brush. Dunk a natural-bristle brush in hot water, then let it dry upside down to splay the bristles. After lightly loading the ends of the bristle with glaze, bounce them up and down lightly on the surface to create the pattern shown at left in (A). The pattern in (B) is created by twisting the brush on the surface. Pattern (C) is formed by dragging the ends while turning the brush just a bit.

A dark brown glaze applied over dyed and sealed mahogany highlights the grain and defines this carving by making it more three-dimensional. It also adds an antique look.

Glaze applied to this pine door highlights the physical distressing marks. You obtain an antique effect by deliberately leaving excess glaze in corners and moldings.

This technique can imitate aging at the same time. Glazing is often employed to darken "distressing" marks made in order to "antique" a piece of furniture. It can also be used to create textural marks on the surface of wood, as shown in the drawing at left or to create "faux grain."

Types of Glazes

Glazes are available in various forms. You can buy premixed, colored glazes that are ready to go, or you can get a colorless, translucent glazing base (sometimes called neutral) that you mix with colorants yourself. The latter approach is more economical because it allows you to create an endless variety of colors from one glazing base.

Precolored glazes and colorless glaze bases are sold in oil-based or water-based versions. Oil-based products typically contain linseed oil or long-oil alkyds as their binder, while water-based glazes use acrylic as the binder. Oil-based glazes are much easier to use than water-based glazes for certain applications because oil has the natural slip and "oiliness" required for easy manipulation. The open time of an oil-based glaze can also be easily extended by introducing additives.

The choice of glaze depends to some degree on the type of finish you intend to use for your top coats. Oil-based glazes are used in conjunction with solvent-based lacquers, varnish, and shellac. Water-based glazes can be used under any finish. Top-coating oil-based glazes with a water-based finish doesn't present compatibility problems, provided that a barrier coat of dewaxed shellac is applied over the glaze.

Most premixed glaze and glazing mediums are formulated to be thick in consistency, like a gel. They have a long open time as well as a clinging effect, referred to as "hang." These products are best used when creating decorative effects like faux-graining or antiquing, which involve leaving excess glaze in corners and in dents and dings created to "distress" a piece to imitate

GLAZING AND TONING DEMYSTIFIED

The terms "glazing" and "toning" are often confused. That's partly because both involve altering the color of a surface, and sometimes either approach can be used toward the same end.

The important distinction between the two is defined by the way they are applied. Just remember this: Glazes are colorants that are always applied between an initial sealer coat and the top coating, while toners are basically clear finishes with color mixed in.

The most commonly sold glazes are neutral bases that are colored by the finisher. This allows you to create an endless variety of colors with one glazing base.

old work. The thick consistency also helps when you're feathering, blending, or softening the glaze with a brush.

When coloring glazes, you'll need to use compatible colorants. To tint an oil-based glaze, you can use dry pigment powders, artist's oil colors, Japan color, asphaltum, oil paint, or UTCs. For water-based glaze, you can use artist's acrylic colors or UTCs. (For more on tinting, see Section 7.) You generally

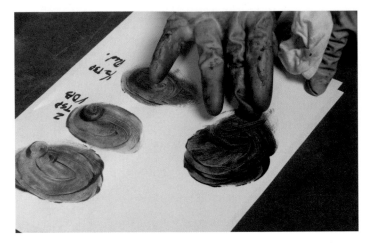

It's easy to gauge the color and intensity of a custom-made glaze mix by smearing some of the test mix on a sheet of white paper.

need very little colorant to tint a glaze. Add several tablespoons per cup to create dark colors; use less if you're after a light-colored glaze. To test the intensity of your mixture, smear some of the colored glaze onto a piece of glass or a sheet of white paper.

You can also use premixed commercial liquid stains for glazing, but only under certain circumstances. They're fine for spraying and for those times when you simply apply the stain as a glaze, then wipe off the excess in order to shift the color or to highlight the wood pores. However, the thin consistency makes these stains hard to handle on overhead or vertical surfaces. When you do use stain for glazing, do not use lacquer-based, alcohol-based, and NGR stains. They dry too fast and will usually dissolve or attack most sealers.

Gel stains work much better than liquid stains because of the gel's thick consistency. Even so, many gel stains dry too quickly to provide the time necessary for an easy wiping. To overcome this, you can add one tea-

spoon per cup of odorless mineral spirits to oil-based gel stains. To slow down the drying time of water-based gel stains, add a bit of propylene glycol, which is commonly sold to retard water-based finish products.

Applying Glazes

Glazes can be applied with brushes, rags, sponges, or spray equipment. The particular technique and tools you use will depend on the effect you're trying to achieve. I'll delve into the details of application in the photo-essays that complete this section. However, there are certain guidelines to follow regardless of the glazing you're using.

Whatever glazing technique you use, you must first prepare the wood surface by sealing it. You can use vinyl sealer, sanding sealer, or dewaxed shellac. You can also use a thinned version of your intended top coat—such as a water-based finish—as long as it's dry. Because glazes and sealers can affect the adhesion of top coats, it's wise to check with your finish supplier to ascertain which sealer-and-glaze combination will work best.

When applying the sealer, make sure to cover the wood surface consistently. Otherwise, unsealed or incompletely sealed areas may accept the glaze unevenly. Let the sealer dry thoroughly, then sand it smooth with 220-, 320- or 400-grit sandpaper. The glaze's ability to "take" to the sealed surface and spread easily is primarily determined by how many coats of sealer are applied and—to a lesser extent—what grit of sandpaper you use. A thin coat of sealer will only partially seal the wood, inviting more glaze penetration and a darker surface if desired. A thicker coat of sealer will result in a lighter surface.

➤ GLAZING VERSUS TONING

Your choice of glazing or toning a project will depend on the effect you're trying to accomplish and the tools available to you, as toning requires spray equipment. For example, glazing is the only real choice for highlighting pore structure or distressing. However, both glazing and toning can be employed to alter the overall hue of a finish or to blend light and dark areas. Here's a quick look at your choices of approach, based on solving a particular problem or creating a certain look.

Sandpaper Grit Comparison

OBJECTIVE	TECHNIQUE	COMMENTS
Increase richness and depth	Glazing or toning	Glazing is best.
Accent grain and distress marks	Glazing	
Faux graining	Glazing	
Imitate aging	Glazing	
Blend dissimilar characteristics	Glazing or toning	
Alter hue or color	Glazing or toning	For extreme changes, toning is best.
Subdue stain color	Glazing or toning	Glazing is best.
Hide mistakes	Toning	
Control splotching	Glazing or toning	Toning is most uniform.
Selective shading	Toning	

The intensity of a glaze is primarily controlled by how the wood surface is sealed. The left side of this cherry panel has one coat of sealer, and the right side has two.

After deciding what type of glazing technique you want to accomplish, apply your glaze as shown in the photo-essays. If you don't like the color or look of a glaze, wipe it off using the appropriate thinner before the glaze has cured. (Make sure the thinner will not dissolve the sealer coat.) When you're satisfied with the glazing, let it dry thoroughly before applying a finish. The necessary dry time before top-coating depends on the type of glaze, the type of top coat, and the method of applying the top coat. The general rule is that if you'll be applying a top

If you decide you don't like the color of a glaze, you can remove almost all of it from a well-sealed surface by wiping it away with the appropriate thinner.

Padding stains are easily made from pre-mixed dye stains. This NGR stain is mixed with an equal amount of water to make a padding stain for use on lacquer.

coat by hand, you should allow the glaze to dry long enough so that the friction from the top-coat applicator doesn't pull up the glaze.

There is one exception to that rule, however, which applies to using an oil glaze with a solvent-based spray lacquer top coat. In these circumstances, you can save time by spraying the lacquer as soon as the carrier from the glaze evaporates. This allows the solvents from the lacquer to "tie" the glaze to the previous coat of lacquer which is sometimes called "shooting through" the glaze.

Padding Stains

Padding stains can be used to add grain definition and depth to a partially finished surface. Padding stains are similar to glazes, except they contain a solvent that softens the sealer so the stain can bite into it. Padding stains are selectively wiped on to certain areas but not wiped off.

As far as I know, there are no premixed padding stains, so you have to prepare them yourself. They are always dye-based and mixed in a solvent that will soften but not aggressively attack the finish it's applied to.

Adding water to a solvent-based NGR dye or an alcohol-based dye will create a padding stain. I add water in a one-to-one ratio, which makes the padding stain easier to wipe and less aggressive. A water-based stain can be used on water-based finishes as long as it contains enough of the appropriate solvent to bite into the finish.

Toners

Toners are clear finishes that have been tinted with dye or pigment. They differ from glazes in that they are applied over a sealed finish and *not* wiped off, as glazes usually are. As opposed to glazes, which can be applied by hand, toners are always sprayed on. (Premixed toners are available in aerosol form if you lack spray equipment.) Top coats of clear finish are always applied over the toner to protect it from abrasion.

Many of the techniques you can perform with glazes can be done with toners, such as altering hue or value and adding richness and depth. (See the sidebar on p. 127.) They can be used to hide mistakes, to block out dark areas like mineral streaks, or to blend light areas into dark areas, such as when matching sapwood to heartwood. Toners allow you to neutralize strong areas of color like the green heartwood of poplar, or to apply color selectively by shading edges and other features. Because toner is applied with a spray gun, very subtle effects can be accomplished.

Toners tinted with dye transmit light and can be used to alter the hue or value of the underlying color without obscuring the grain and figure of the wood. Toners made with pigments can also be mixed to provide transparency, but because pigments have the capability of blocking light, they can be used in heavier concentrations to mask wood grain, cover mistakes, or make a dark area lighter.

When toners are applied over an entire surface, the process is generally referred to as *toning*, whereas toner applied selectively to certain areas is called *shading*. Toning allows you to shift color, prevent splotching, and consistently color combinations of woods like solid wood and plywood that would normally take stain differently. Shading can be used to create artistic effects, to mimic aged wood surfaces, and to highlight features such as moldings and carvings.

Making Toners

Premixed toners are available, but most finishers prefer to make their own by simply tinting their chosen finish with a compatible colorant.

Before mixing your toner, you need to decide how transparent you want it to be. Transparent toners can be made using either

To demonstrate the differences between shading and toning, the top half of this cherry door was shaded with a dye toner, while the bottom half was toned uniformly.

Toners are easily made by mixing thinned finish with a compatible pigment or dye colorant. A wooden stick gauges the intensity of the color.

dye stains or pigments. Dye stains added to finish will always produce a transparent toner. However, the transparency of a pigment-based toner depends on the amount of pigment added to the finish. For better transparency, add a minimal amount of pigment and avoid using very opaque pigments such as white, or the yellow or red iron oxides. The natural earth colors make good toners, as they are transparent by nature and wood-colored. White is used when you want to create a "pickled" effect.

A pigmented toner can be made by mixing concentrated pigment colorants into your finish medium. Strain the mixture through a medium mesh strainer.

A dye-based toner is made by mixing dye with a compatible finish. An alcohol-soluble dye was added to clear lacquer to make this amber toner.

Toners generally look best when they are applied in thin coats to prevent "building" the color too much. For this reason, commercial ready-mixed toners typically have less than 12 percent binder content, which will minimize the build of thickness and color. Some finishers prefer to tone with no

binder, using dissolved dyes instead of pigments and incorporating a thinner that softens or partially dissolves the finish it's being applied to.

To mix a shellac-based toner of the proper viscosity, add your pigment or dye to a 1-lb.-cut shellac mix. For solvent-based lacquer, start with one part lacquer to one part lacquer thinner before adding colorant. The ideal medium for water-based toners is a clear water-soluble stain base; however, that can be hard to find. Instead, you can simply add 10 percent water to your water-based finish to thin it appropriately. Many users of water-based top coats use dewaxed shellac-based toners, which are compatible with water-based finishes applied over them.

Tinting a toner is not a complicated process, but you have to pay careful attention to compatibility between the finish medium and its colorant. It's basically just a matter of adding to the finish a compatible stain or concentrated pigment. Concentrated colors in either powder or liquid form are best because they don't add a lot of solvent and other ingredients that might change the characteristics of the finish medium. The chart on the facing page shows the compatibility of many finish mediums and colorants. However, if you're unsure of a colorant's compatibility with a finish, check with the finish manufacturer, particularly when using two-component finishes.

Pigment toners are easily made by adding compatible concentrated pigment colorants to the finish medium. Dye-based toners are made by adding dye to the finish medium. Either dye powders or liquid dyes can be used, but powders should be dissolved before being added to the finish.

Toner and Colorant Compatibility

FINISH MEDIUM	COMPATIBLE PIGMENTS	COMMENTS
Oil-based varnish	Oil-based Japan colors; UTCs	
Solvent-based lacquer	Alkyd- or lacquer-based colorants; UTCs (only in small amounts)	
Catalyzed lacquers, 2K polyurethanes, 2-part polyesters, conversion varnish	Check with finish manufacturer	Colorant cannot contain any alcohol when mixing in 2K polyurethane.
Shellac	UTCs, some lacquer colorants*	*Typically acrylic base
Water-based finishes	Acrylic colorants, UTCs, water-based stains	After adding colorant, allow finish to sit 15-30 minutes to stabilize

FINISH MEDIUM	COMPATIBLE DYES	COMMENTS
Oil-based varnish	Oil-based dyes	
Solvent-based lacquer	Oil-based dyes, universal dye concentrates, NGR dye stains, alcohol dyes*	*Alcohol dyes require mixing with a mix of alcohol and acetone
Catalyzed lacquers, 2K polyurethanes, 2-part polyesters, conversion varnish	Check with finish manufacturer	Colorant cannot contain any alcohol when mixing in 2K polyurethane
Shellac	Alcohol-based dyes, universal dye concentrates, NGR dye stains	
Water-based finishes	Water-based dyes, universal dye concentrates	

NGR dyes and concentrated dye liquids can be added to most finishes, although it's wise to test for compatibility first by adding a bit of the dissolved dye to the finish. If it gels, turns cloudy, or separates, the two are incompatible.

[TIP] Concentrated colors in small amounts may be available at a friendly paint store for about a buck a squirt. If you're asking this favor of the store, be sure to bring your own small containers.

Applying Toners and Shaders

As discussed earlier, toners can be used for *toning* (consistent coverage of an entire surface) or *shading* (applying toner to selected areas only). Regardless of the technique, toners cannot be brushed or wiped on; they must be sprayed.

You can use any type of spray gun, but it should be capable of being adjusted for both a fine, tight spray pattern (for shading) and a wide, even pattern (for toning). Since toners are typically thin-bodied, use a combination of a small needle/nozzle and air cap to pro-

SPRAYING INTO CORNERS

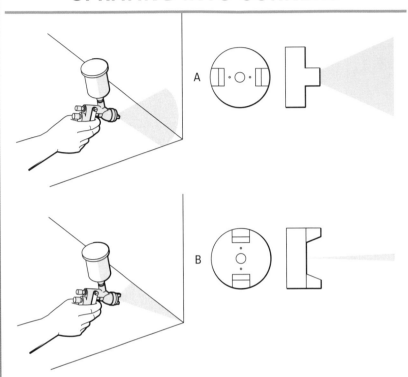

When spraying toner into a corner or other junction, orient the fan pattern to suit the direction of the junction, and spray at a low pressure.
(A) Incorrect: Fan pattern misalignment and high pressure prevent proper coverage.
(B) Correct: Align spray pattern to junction and spray at low pressure.

A good spray gun for toning should be adjustable to produce an elongated oval shape and a small, tight, round pattern, as seen in the photo. This gun has a fan-width control knob to produce both patterns.

vide consistent atomization across the width of the entire spray pattern. When spraying into corners, orient the fan pattern in the direction of the joint and use low spray pressure, as shown in the drawing at left.

For shading, I prefer to use a small gravity-feed touchup gun that allows precise application of the toner. These guns can be easily adjusted for a small, fine spray pattern.

To use a toner, select the proper size setup for the viscosity and turn the fan-width and fluid-delivery controls clockwise until they close. Open the fluid-delivery knob one or two turns and adjust the fan width for a 6-in.-wide fan pattern. Toners are easiest to apply if you "fog" them on in light, successive passes. Practice on a piece of white paper, cardboard, or a white wood like maple to see if the toner is the right color and the fan width correct.

To prepare for shading, pour some toner into the cup and turn your gun's fluid and fan-width controls clockwise to close them. While shooting against a piece of white cardboard or wood, adjust the fluid control knob until a fine spray pattern is visible. Then adjust the fan-width control to produce a pattern 1 in. to 2 in. wide.

To shade your workpiece, begin by slowly taking light passes until you achieve the intensity you're after. For effective shading, spray edges, interesting profiles, and recessed areas. You can feather in the shading by limiting the volume of finish sprayed and increasing the fan width and distance between the gun and the workpiece. This is particularly effective when you're blending in a repair or matching the color of sapwood to heartwood.

Subduing Bright Stains with Glaze

The most common use for glaze is to soften the brightness of a dye stain and enhance the grain. This cherry candle box was dyed with a golden-brown water-based dye stain, then sealed with one coat of a 1-lb.-cut dewaxed shellac. After the sealer dried for one hour, it was scuff-sanded with 320-grit sandpaper, then a maroon synthetic abrasive pad (**A**).

A glaze was prepared by tinting a neutral oil glaze base with Van Dyke brown and a bit of red, in the form of Japan colors. The glaze was applied with a brush, then the excess was wiped off (**B**). You can use a dry brush in corners and crevices if necessary to remove excess glaze (**C**).

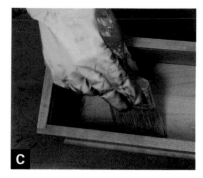

Spraying a Glaze

Any glaze can be sprayed, but you may need to thin a typical oil- or water-based glaze first. You can thin oil-based glazes with mineral spirits, but use naphtha instead if you want the glaze to dry faster. I find that water-based glazes often dry too quickly, so I usually add about 10 percent glaze retarder.

To apply the glaze, I often use a two-handed technique—applying the glaze, then wiping it off immediately (**A**). If the glaze starts to tack up before I'm done wiping, I simply moisten it with a mist of water for water-based glazes, or mineral spirits for oil-based glazes (**B**).

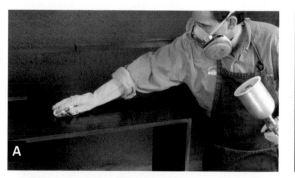

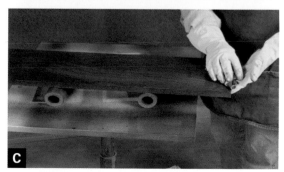

To spray two-sided parts like shelves, spray one side, wipe it, then turn it over, resting it on non-marring foam pipe insulation (**C**). This protects the wiped side from getting scratched. Then you can place the part on a nail or staple board to dry.

A

B

C

VARIATION

Striking Out

Striking out is a glazing technique in which you selectively remove glaze color from certain areas of a surface in order to create highlights that add dimension and overall depth to the appearance.

To perform the technique, stain the wood if you wish, seal it, then scuff-sand with 320-grit sandpaper or an abrasive pad. Apply a dark, contrasting glaze—spraying, wiping, or brushing it on. Next, wipe away the glaze. If you want to create a subtle contrast when you strike out, wipe away most of the glaze. If you're going after a starker contrast, wipe away less glaze for starters.

Now you're ready to do the striking out. Using a small piece of gray synthetic steel wool, remove glaze selectively, following the natural figure or grain **(A)**. After you've done this, blend the entire surface together using a soft brush to minimize the harsh edges created when you removed the glaze **(B)**.

After applying a clear top coat, you'll find that the resulting surface has an added dimension, as shown in the top half of this oak door **(C)**. Compare it to the bottom half, which was not struck out.

[**VARIATION**] Powder glazes are sprayed on like other liquid glazes, left to dry to a chalky appearance, then selectively sanded to reveal some of the surface below in order to simulate an old, worn finish.

Physical Distressing

One of the most effective ways to mimic age on a workpiece is to physically "distress" it, creating dents and scratches that imply years of use. The distressing is usually done after you've dyed and sealed the surface, and then the marks are accented with a glaze.

You can use various tools for distressing workpieces, but one of my favorites is an insidious-looking device that we call "The Tenderizer" in my shop **(A)**. This tool is made by driving different sizes of screws, nails, and staples into the end grain of a wooden mallet, then snipping off their ends. The art of using this tool is to strike the surface at random places and rotate the tool so you don't create a repeating pattern. Other tools you can use for physical distressing are keys **(B)** or small drill bits **(C)**.

In this case, asphaltum makes the best glaze for accentuating the marks and implying years of built-up grime and wax. To make the glaze, first mix up the standard asphaltum recipe for a stain.

▶ See *"Making a Gilsonite/Asphaltum Stain"* on p. 120.

Then add several tablespoons of chalk (known as whiting) per cup asphaltum **(D)**. Apply this glaze, wiping it cleanly over the marks but leaving excess in the crevices.

Surface Distressing

You can perform a less invasive distressing technique by applying marks to the surface rather than physically damaging the wood as previously described. This is usually done after the first top coat is applied so that any mistakes can be easily wiped away for another attempt. All surface distressing techniques should be protected with a clear-finish top coat.

Three techniques are commonly used to perform surface distressing: dry brushing, specking, and pencil distressing. For dry brushing, first make up some liquid colorant by mixing Japan color with mineral spirits. Apply some of this mix to a piece of scrap wood or cardboard, then dab the tip of a bristle brush into the color. Flicking the tip of the brush over a sharp edge will highlight the edge **(A)**. By holding the brush vertically and twisting it slightly, you'll get a different effect **(B)**. (See "Creating Textural Effects on p. 124.) "Pencil distressing" is done with china markers, making little arcs or lines on the surface **(C)**. "Specking" is the practice of spattering the surface with colored dots to resemble fly-specks. This is easily done by dunking a toothbrush into thin glaze, then flicking the bristles with your thumb to splatter a pattern of fine specks across the surface **(D)**. In fact, you can use just about any colorant you wish for this technique. Special spray guns are also available if you do a lot of specking finishes.

Applying Padding Stain

Padding stains are used after the first top coat of clear finish has been applied to lock in all underlying coloring methods. The padding stain in these photos is one part NGR stain with one part water added to slow the drying and to make the stain a bit less aggressive. This brown stain being applied to sealed, unstained maple provides a good visual contrast.

You can use padding stain to accomplish various aims. In the first photo, it enhances the figure of the wood. To create this effect, dip the corner of a rag into the stain, then follow the outlines of the grain (**A**). Padding stain can also create textural effects. Simply dampen the rag with the padding stain, crumple it up, then use it to blot random marks all over the surface (**B**). To soften the edges of the blots, blend them into the background using a gray synthetic pad (**C**).

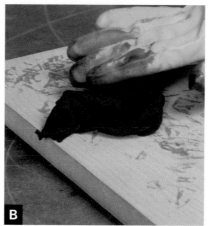

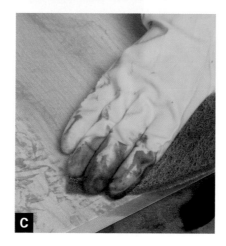

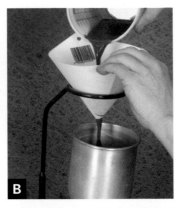
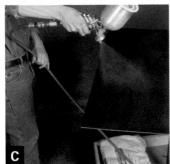
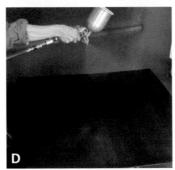

Toning for Consistency

It's obvious that the back of this cabinet was stained differently than the case **(A)**. To match the brown-colored back to the reddish color of the case, use a red toner made by mixing red dye into a water-based toner/stain **(B)**.

Whatever gun you use for toning, adjust it by first closing the fluid-delivery knob, then opening it one full turn. Adjust the fan width for a 6-in.-wide pattern **(C)**. I typically spray a toner in the direction of the grain. If you find you're getting an uneven pattern, you can pull the gun back farther and "fog" the toner on in light, successive passes **(C)**. It pays to practice on a piece of white paper, cardboard, or a white wood like maple to see if the toner is the right color and the fan width is correct.

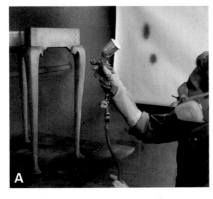
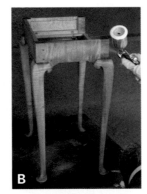
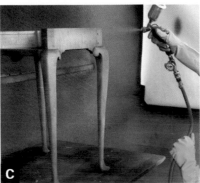
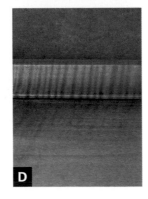

Shading

Adjust the gun's spray pattern while shooting against a sheet of white paper hung nearby. Close the fan width control to create a small, round pattern, as represented by the lower spray pattern on the paper in the photo **(A)**. On this maple table, first shade the pad feet with the table upside down. Then flip the table right side up to shade the edges and highlights **(B)**.

When blending, pull the gun back a bit to help feather the edges of the shading **(C)**.

If spraying results in areas that aren't colored, you can apply a glaze by hand after the toner has dried **(D)**. (NOTE: To show comparison, the scalloped edge in the left half of the photo was glazed, while the right half was not.)

Hiding Mistakes with Toner

A pigmented toner can be used to cover or block out mistakes, such as this dried glue spot that resisted stain, resulting in a light area (**A**). To cover a blemish like this, make a pigmented toner by mixing concentrated colors into clear finish. (I used water-based lacquer tinted with water-based colorants.) Mix the toner darker than the color of the finish, while staying with the same hue, whether it's red, brown, or yellow. Adjust the gun to spray a small, round pattern, then spray several layers of toner onto the area of the light spot, first from one direction (**B**), then the other (**C**). Blend the coloring into the adjacent areas by pulling the gun back a bit as you spray toward the outer edges of the affected area.

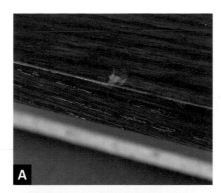

Spraying a Sunburst Pattern

A sunburst pattern represents the epitome of applying color with a spray gun. The most striking examples of this technique are often displayed on guitars. The process consists of both toning and shading. Starting with a guitar body that has been sealed and sanded to 600 grit, begin by covering the entire body with a yellow/amber toner (**A**). When that's dry, spray on a reddish-brown shader, aiming it inward from the edges. This creates a "two-tone" sunburst (**B**). To take it a step further, you can apply an additional dark brown toner to just the outer edges.

While a sunburst pattern may be too intense for most furniture, applying the same principles in finishing a curly maple drawer front can create a more subtle effect that is still quite striking (**C**).

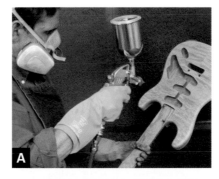

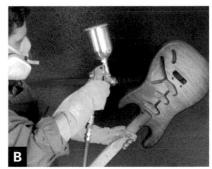

Natural Dyes, Chemical Stains, and Bleaches

Natural Dyes

➤ Making a Natural Walnut Dye (p. 148)

➤ Binding a Natural Dye with Mordants (p. 148)

Chemical Staining

➤ Staining with an Iron/Vinegar Solution (p. 149)

➤ Lye on Cherry (p. 149)

➤ Fuming with Ammonia (p. 150)

Bleaching

➤ Using Bleaches (p. 151)

Whitening and Ebonizing

➤ Pickling, Liming, and Whitewashing (p. 152)

➤ Ebonizing (p. 152)

THERE ARE MANY WAYS to color wood without using pigment stains, glazes, or toners. Prior to the use of synthetic dyes, finishers used to alter the color of wood with either chemical stains or natural dyes derived from plants. Another time-honored technique is to bleach wood in order to remove or lighten stains, or to whiten it by removing its natural color.

All of these approaches are still viable today. In this section, I'll explain how to treat wood with natural dyes, chemicals, and bleaches.

Natural Dyes

In the past, natural dyes were made from many different plants and trees. Today, the most important and easily obtainable natural dyes are made from walnut hulls, logwood, brazilwood, and catechu wood.

Although natural dyes aren't used extensively these days, they do have their appropriate applications. Furniture restorers sometimes use them for historically accurate coloring of reproduction pieces or repair work on antiques. Some finishers simply

Natural dyes extracted from walnut hulls, logwood, brazilwood, and cutch produce muted colors. The dyes are often applied over mordants, which help stabilize the colors.

SUNTANNING WOOD

Suntanning wood is a quick, easy way to accelerate the natural deepening of its color, which is caused by extended exposure to light and air. Suntanning works particularly well with cherry, quickly turning the pinkish color of the freshly cut wood to a nice brown. Woods like poplar and birch will react to the procedure too, although more slowly. To expedite the process, first apply a liberal coat of linseed oil or tung oil to your project, letting it soak in for several minutes before wiping off the excess. Place the project outside for a few hours, turning it occasionally to expose it fully to the sun. You'll notice the color change within a single day, but you may want to repeat the treatment daily for a week or so to really deepen the color.

like working with them and appreciate the muted colors they produce, which are less vivid than those created with synthetic dyes.

A natural walnut dye is easy to concoct if you have access to black walnut trees. The dye is made by soaking the walnut hulls in water and sodium carbonate.

See *"Making a Natural Walnut Dye"* on p. 148

Alternatively, walnut-husk extract is available from specialty suppliers, who also offer logwood, brazilwood, and cutch dye extracts. (See Resources on p. 287.)

To make a natural dye using an extract, dissolve 1 weighed oz. of the extract into 1 qt. of hot water. Let the mixture sit overnight, then strain it into another container through a fine-mesh strainer before using the dye. Always store the mixture in a

plastic container or a glass jar, as metal containers and caps can rust and corrode.

On the subject of natural colors, it's worth noting that there is a very natural, very easy way to color woods like cherry, and that is to "suntan" them, as explained in the sidebar above.

Binding Natural Dyes with Mordants
Unfortunately, natural dyes aren't particularly lightfast. To help overcome this, finishers often use them in conjunction with *mordants*, which are chemicals that help bind the dye to the wood, making the color more lightfast. Mordants include water-soluble metal salts like potassium dichromate, tin chloride, alum, ferrous sulfate, and copper sulfate. Some mordants, such as potassium dichromate, produce a distinct color of their own, as I'll discuss in a bit, under "Metal

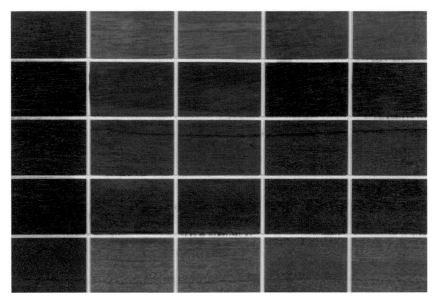

Natural dye/mordant combinations produce an array of colors. The top row shows mordants with no dye (from left, potassium dichromate, tin chloride, alum, iron sulfate, and copper sulfate). The four rows below show these mordants combined with logwood, brazilwood, walnut hull, and cutch dyes.

Working with chemical stains requires safety gear. Wear gloves, goggles, and a respirator specifically rated for the chemical used.

Salts." These particular metal salts can result in special colors when combined with dyes. Many mordants are available from specialty suppliers.

For the mordant/dye approach, the mordant is typically applied before you apply the natural dye. To mix a mordant for application, dissolve 1 oz. of the dry chemical powder into 1 qt. of warm water, stir the mixture, then let it cool to room temperature. For tin chloride, use $1/2$ oz. powder per qt. of water.

I want to point out that you don't have to use a mordant to bind a dye. In fact, you may want to avoid mordants, as some are toxic. Without a mordant, the dye will be less lightfast, but you can protect the color by keeping your project out of harsh light, such as from sunny windows.

[TIP] It can't be stressed strongly enough that any coloring treatment should be tested on scrap before you apply it to your finished project.

Chemical Stains

Chemical staining is an age-old technique that involves the use of *metal salts* or *alkalis*. These chemicals, which I'll discuss individually in a bit, react with the natural chemicals in wood to form colored compounds. With few exceptions, they are purchased as powders that the user dissolves in warm water for application. Almost all are applied to the workpiece just as you would apply a typical water stain.

I want to emphasize up front that many chemical stains are hazardous and definitely require the use of proper safety gear. However, in spite of these dangers, there are two worthwhile reasons for using chemical stains. The first is that the chemical reaction produces a colorant within the wood fibers, rather than simply on top of them. This makes chemical stains lightfast, transparent, and resistant to bleeding or lifting when a top coat of finish is applied over them with a brush or pad. The second reason is that you can obtain unusual effects that are difficult to create with dyes or pigment stains. For example, the intensity of color on a piece of wood can vary depending on the concentration of chemicals, such as tannins in the wood. Or the chemical stain might produce an attractive, offbeat effect.

Not just any project should be treated with these stains. Chemicals can be highly unpredictable, reacting differently with different woods, so it's best to build a project using sapwood-free boards from the same tree. When you need great control over color, as when matching an existing finish, for example, it's usually better to use dyes or pigment stains.

Metal Salts

Metal salts are typically purchased in raw form as dry chemicals that the user mixes with water for application. They're available from chemical supply houses or mail-order sources. Quite a few metal salts can be used as chemical stains, but I will focus on the ones below, as they produce consistent results and are fairly easy to obtain.

Potassium permanganate produces a yellowish-brown coloring that does not depend on high tannin content in the wood to create the color. The chemical tends to treat the wood surface consistently, even on areas of sapwood. It's very predictable and easy to use on any wood. While potassium permanganate is not technically a poison, it is hazardous.

Potassium dichromate is an orange-colored solution that creates deep, rich, red-brown tones on high-tannin woods like cherry, mahogany, and walnut. However, it won't color sapwood. Potassium dichromate has been used extensively in the past but is an

Water-based dye stain colors the left side of this cherry board fairly consistently, while the lye applied to the right side responds differently to the varying amounts of tannins in the board.

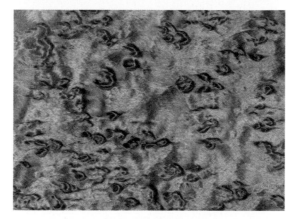

Chemical stains can produce offbeat, unusual colors impossible to attain with other stains. This bird's-eye maple was treated with ferrous sulfate, then lye. Note the dark "eyes."

Metal salt stains can produce very unique colors. Clockwise from top right, iron/vinegar stain on walnut, ferrous sulfate on ash, potassium permanganate on white oak, potassium dichromate on cherry.

Natural Dyes, Chemical Stains, and Bleaches | 143

Iron sulfate stain reacts to varying amounts of tannins in different woods. Clockwise from top left, it turns walnut almost black, while pine turns a brown color. Bird's-eye maple and ash turn various shades of gray.

> ## THE TERMINOLOGY OF MIXING

Chemical stains may be mixed by weight or by volume. When mixing from powders, measuring by weight is much more accurate. Simply weigh the manufacturer's recommended amount of powder and add it to the recommended amount of water or solvent.

When you mix liquids with liquids, the ingredients are measured out by volume and stated as a percentage. A 5 percent solution means that the ingredient in question represents 5 percent of the whole, or 5 parts of ingredient to 95 parts of solvent.

extremely toxic substance and a known carcinogen. I suggest using an alternative if possible. Frequent use should certainly be avoided.

Ferrous sulfate reacts with tannin in the wood to create the kind of grayish-black stains found on boards that have been in contact with iron. This chemical is useful in producing attractive grays on most species—a color difficult to obtain with dyes and pigments. Ferrous sulfate should be treated as a hazardous chemical.

Iron buff is the term for an old textile stain that produces a dull brown similar to the color of undyed ("buff") leather. The stain was originally made by soaking scrap iron in vinegar (acetic acid) for up to a week. When the resulting chemical (called iron acetate) is applied to tannin-rich wood, it forms iron tannate, an extremely lightfast black stain. Iron buff is one of the safer chemicals to use and handle.

Alkali Stains

Alkali stains work by oxidizing the tannin present in wood, converting it to colored byproducts. Following is a list of the most common alkali chemicals used for staining, along with suggested mixing percentages.

Sodium hydroxide, commonly called lye, has been used by finishers for ages to simulate the color of aged cherry. To emphasize reddish tones, use a 5 percent solution. For brownish tones, try a 2 percent or weaker solution. Sodium hydroxide (commonly available as Lewis Red Devil Lye™) can be found at most hardware stores. Wear protection when handling lye, as it is extremely caustic. Because of this, it needs to be neutralized with vinegar after application, as explained later.

Sodium carbonate is good for duplicating the yellowish color of photooxidation caused by exposure to light and air. It's commonly available as Arm & Hammer™ washing soda and is safe to use without a respirator. To make the stain, add 1 weighed oz.

Alkali stains react to tannins in the wood. Clockwise from top right, sodium carbonate on maple, lye on cherry, and ammonia on white oak. Note the unaffected sapwood on the edge of the oak.

(approximately 3 teaspoons) of the powder to 1 qt. of water. Very nice effects can be obtained by applying it after metal salts—for example, following a sodium carbonate treatment with a ferrous sulfate stain.

Ammonia is technically an alkali gas carried in a solution of water, creating a mix called ammonium hydroxide. Wood is typically treated with ammonia by exposing the wood to the fumes.

▶ See *"Fuming with Ammonia"* on p. 150.

This "fuming" results in a more consistent color than can be achieved with liquid stains.

Industrial-strength ammonia is typically used for fuming. This formulation is a 28 percent solution, which is hazardous and very irritating to the eyes and respiratory system. If you like, you can use a weaker

▶ WORKING SAFELY WITH CHEMICAL STAINS

Caution: When you're working with chemical stains and bleaches, it's critical to wear protective gloves and goggles and a respirator that is properly rated for the particular chemicals you're using. Work in a well-ventilated area and make sure you also wear your respirator when you sand the raised grain after the surface has dried.

Part of the fun of working with chemical stains is combining their effects with other effects achieved by dyes and pigment stains. However, you should never mix a chemical stain with another stain product in order to apply the combination at one time. Always apply each one separately and only after the previous stain has dried completely.

9 percent to 10 percent solution sold as strong, or "janitor grade" ammonia, at hardware and janitorial supply stores, but the process will take a little longer.

Preparing and Applying Chemical Stains
With the exception of ammonia, all these chemical stains are applied like a typical water stain. That is, you flood the surface liberally and consistently with the liquid, then blot up or wipe away the excess.

To prepare a stain from a powdered chemical, begin by slowly stirring 1 weighed oz. of powder into 1 qt. of warm water. If you don't have a scale, use 2 or 3 tablespoons per qt. of water. This makes a 3 percent solution, which is a good starting point.

Take care not to drip chemical stains onto your work-pieces. Otherwise, the "double-stained" drips will show up as darker spots when the primary coat of stain is applied over them, as on this drawer front.

Test this mixture on a piece of scrap, then dilute it or add more powder if necessary to obtain the color you want. (When using chemical stains, always test for color using scrap from your actual project, rather than just scrap of the same type of wood.) After the solution has cooled to room temperature, strain the mixture to remove any residue.

Apply the liquid solution using a foam brush, a synthetic-bristle brush, or a rag. Never spray a chemical stain. Work from the bottom up on your project to avoid dripping the mixture on bare wood. When you're done, wait at least four hours for the complete color to develop.

After the wood has dried completely, wipe it down with plenty of clean water to remove any residual chemical on the surface. In the case of sodium hydroxide (lye), it's advisable to neutralize the harsh, caustic nature of the chemical by applying a weak acid like vinegar. Sponge the surface with a solution of 3 tablespoons of vinegar per qt. of water. The other chemicals do not need to be neutralized.

Bleaches

Working with bleaches involves removing color rather than adding it. Bleaches have a variety of uses for the finisher, including lightening a wood's natural color or removing certain applied stains.

Bleaches do not really "remove" a stain; they simply render it colorless by changing its chemical composition. Not all stains can be bleached. As a general rule, inorganic colors such as the carbon black and iron oxide pigments used in wood stains will not react to bleach. These colors can only be completely removed by scraping or sanding the color from the surface of the wood. On the other hand, organic-based stains have less stable bonds and will usually react to bleach. Organic colors include dyes, the black stain created from iron, and the compounds that make up the natural color of wood.

There are three general classifications of chemical bleaches used on wood: oxygen bleach, chlorine bleach, and oxalic acid. Although all are sold as "wood bleach," each has specific uses. To determine the appropriate bleach for your purposes, you may need

The three types of bleaches commonly used on wood are (from left) oxalic acid, chlorine (calcium hypochlorite, laundry chlorine bleach), and two-part wood bleach.

to read the label carefully. In the next section, I've described the various types in an effort to help you identify them.

▶ See *"Using Bleaches"* on p. 151.

Oxygen Bleach

This bleach is sold as a two-part (A/B) liquid bleach. The two components are sodium hydroxide (A) and 30 percent hydrogen peroxide (B). The mixing of sodium hydroxide and hydrogen peroxide creates a third chemical called sodium hydroperoxide, which is the active bleaching agent. There are two ways to apply this bleach. The first is to mix the components together immediately before application; the second is to flood part A onto the wood, followed by part B.

Oxygen bleach is about the only product that will lighten or remove the natural color of wood. Up until the 1980s, it was used extensively by furniture companies as a pre-finish treatment to create color conformity on furniture made of dissimilar woods. It's not done as much today because of the extra steps involved and the severe grain raising caused by the process.

Chlorine Bleaches

Chlorine is a strong oxidizer that will remove or lighten most dye stains, as well as mildew and some food stains. A weak chlorine-based bleach such as Clorox™ (sodium hypochlorite) will work, but it generally requires multiple applications to be effective. A much stronger solution can be made from swimming pool bleach (calcium hypochlorite), which will work much faster. As when working with other chemicals, wear gloves and safety goggles.

Oxalic Acid

Oxalic acid is unique in that it will remove iron stain without affecting the natural color of the wood. This natural black stain is created when iron and moisture contact certain tannin-rich woods like oak, cherry, and mahogany. Drinking glasses and vases left on these woods can leave black rings due to the traces of iron in tap water. Iron is also the cause of the black stain often seen around the heads of installed nails and screws. For these reasons, you should also avoid using tap water to wipe down tannin-rich woods during the finishing process, as it can create small gray spots on the surface. Oxalic acid is a poison, so wear a respirator when mixing the product and sanding the wood afterward. Gloves and safety goggles should also be worn when applying it.

Making a Natural Walnut Dye

A stain made from walnut husks produces a nice brown **(A)**, but the color isn't very lightfast. Adding an alum mordant will help prevent fading and won't change the color of the dye, as some other mordants might.

Gather the fallen green nuts in early fall. Cut off the husks with a knife **(B)**, then let them dry out. To 1 qt. of hot water, add 1 oz. of sodium carbonate (washing soda) and 1 cup of the husks **(C)**. Let the mixture sit overnight, then strain and bottle it. Prepare commercially prepackaged husks in the same manner.

Drying husks contain worms and attract bugs, so to avoid these problems, immediately place the fresh green husks in an enamel pot, covering them with water, adding 1 oz. of sodium carbonate for every qt. of water **(D)**. Simmer for one or two days on low heat, then strain and bottle the liquid.

Binding a Natural Dye with Mordants

To use a natural dye/mordant combination, test for the color you want using a piece of scrap from your project wood. Here, I'm using cutch as the dye and potassium dichromate as the mordant.

Apply the mordant first, making sure to wear a respirator, goggles, and gloves to protect yourself from the chemical **(A)**. After the mordant dries, apply the dye with a brush or sponge. When the dye has dried, wash the surface with distilled water to remove any residual chemicals **(B)**. Finally, scuff-sand the washed surface after it has dried to remove the raised grain before applying a top coat of finish.

Staining with an Iron/Vinegar Solution

A solution made from iron and vinegar creates "iron buff," a nontoxic stain that is very easy to apply and that creates colors ranging from gray to jet black. To make the stain, first shred a pad of fine steel wool into a plastic or glass container. (If you're using steel wool from a roll, shred about ½ oz. worth.) Pour 1 pt. of white vinegar into the container **(A)** and cover it with a lid, punching holes in the lid to allow the hydrogen gas produced to escape **(B)**. After a day of sitting, the stain will be strong enough to produce a gray color. If you're after a black stain, let it sit for two or three days. When you're ready, double-strain the solution, first through a medium-mesh strainer to remove the partially dissolved steel wool pad, then again through a coffee filter to remove the fine bits of steel **(C)**.

Lye on Cherry

Lye can be used to mimic the appearance of aged cherry. For this table, a 1.5 percent solution, which is a weighed ½ oz. (or ¾ teaspoon) of lye dissolved in 1 qt. of warm water, was used.

When applying any chemical stain, it's very important to apply it from the bottom upward to avoid dripping the stain on bare wood **(A)**. After the stain dries, wash it with distilled water. When that dries, scrub the surface with a gray synthetic abrasive pad to level the raised grain **(B)**. Be sure to wear your goggles when scrubbing the wood, as drops of finish can flick off the surface. When that's done, apply a neutralizing solution made by mixing 3 tablespoons of white vinegar into 1 qt. of water. This step changes the harsh red of the lye to a more golden brown **(C)**.

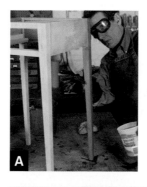

A

B

C

Fuming with Ammonia

Ammonia is a gas that causes strong color reactions in certain woods. It is often used to treat white oak, giving it a cool, almost greenish-brown color. You can offset this cool undertone by top-coating it with a strongly orange-colored finish like shellac **(A)**.

To get the gas into the wood, the ammonia and workpiece are first placed in a "fuming tent," which can be easily made from 1x2 furring strips and clear plastic sheeting **(B)**. Pour the ammonia solution into shallow dishes inside the tent along with your furniture. Include a few scraps from the actual workpiece wood that you can slip out from under the tent occasionally to monitor the color as it changes. Wiping your chosen finish top coat onto the scrap will indicate the color of the finished piece **(C)**. When you're satisfied with the color, remove the project from the tent. Let it sit for two days before finishing. The nice part about ammonia fuming is that it doesn't raise the grain of the wood.

Using Bleaches

Oxalic acid is the only way to remove black or gray stains caused by an iron/tannin reaction. To mix this bleach, dissolve 1 tablespoon of dry oxalic crystals into a pint of warm water. On bare or unfinished wood, apply the bleach with a rag or brush, and you'll see the bleaching effect almost immediately **(A)**. When the surface is dry, neutralize the bleach with plenty of distilled water, followed by a solution of 1 oz. of baking soda mixed with a quart of water.

To remove or lighten dye stains, make a bleach mix by adding 1 tablespoon of dry calcium hypochlorite powder to a pint of warm water. Let it sit for 10 minutes, stirring occasionally, and apply it with a rag or brush **(B)**. Multiple treatments are usually needed to affect modern dye stains, and complete removal isn't always possible. After the surface dries, rinse it with distilled water.

Two-part bleaches will remove the natural color in most woods. They're supplied in a kit with equal amounts of both parts, usually labeled A and B. You can use a brush to get the bleach into corners **(C)**. A rag or sponge works faster for the flat areas. If the first application doesn't lighten the wood satisfactorily, apply the bleach a second time.

Bleach raises the grain quite a bit, so you'll need to sand it after it's dry **(D)**. Just make sure you don't cut through the coloring at the edges. If you use multiple applications, most manufacturers recommend neutralizing the surface afterward with a mixture of one part vinegar to two parts water.

Pickling, Liming, and Whitewashing

Pickling, liming, and whitewashing all refer to the process of applying a white or off-white colored stain on wood. In pickling and liming, a white or off-white stain is applied, then wiped off, leaving most of the color in the pores of the wood **(A)**.

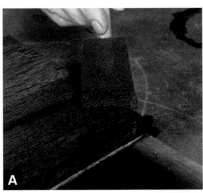

Whitewashing is the technique of applying a white stain so it appears more evenly distributed on the surface, rather than accenting the grain or wood pores. On ring-porous woods like oak, it's best to bleach the wood first with a two-part bleach before applying the white stain. This results in a more consistent, overall "bone" white-washed look, because the white color in the pores tends to match the color of the entire bleached workpiece **(B)**. On maple and other hard, dense woods with little grain definition, spraying the stain is the best application **(C)**.

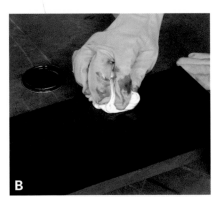

Ebonizing

"Ebonizing" wood simply means coloring it black without obscuring the grain. My favorite method is to begin by applying an "iron buff" stain, as described on p. 149.

➤ See *"Iron buff"* paragraph of *"Metal Salts"* segment on p. 144.

Cherry, walnut, and oak respond best to this particular treatment. After applying the iron buff stain to the wood **(A)**, let it dry, then lightly sand it with 240-grit sandpaper to remove the raised grain. Apply a second coat of the solution, then let it dry. Finish up by applying either an ebony pigment stain **(B)** or an alcohol dye. Although I prefer the look of the pigment stain, I use dye if the workpiece includes sapwood, like the walnut shown in the photo **(C)**.

Controlling Color

Controlling Stain

➤ Preloading Using Stain Controller (p. 166)

➤ Applying a Washcoat (p. 166)

➤ Applying Gel Stain over a Washcoat (p. 167)

Unifying Color

➤ Unifying the Color of a Board (p. 168)

➤ Matching Sapwood to Heartwood (p. 169)

➤ Matching Plywood and Solid Wood (p. 169)

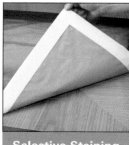

Selective Staining

➤ Selective Hand Application (p. 170)

➤ Selective Spraying (p. 170)

Color Matching

➤ An Exercise in Color Theory (p. 171)

➤ Tweaking Color by Layering (p. 172)

➤ Glorifying Cheap Woods (p. 173)

IN PREVIOUS SECTIONS, I've discussed techniques for coloring wood with dyes, pigment stains, and chemical stains. However, you're likely to encounter a variety of challenges due to the nature of wood itself, which doesn't always behave as we would like. For example, the end grain on almost all woods accepts stain differently from the face grain, and certain woods tend to splotch due to irregular stain absorption. In addition, plywood and solid wood on a project will accept the same stain differently.

Although glazing and toning can fix some of these problems (as discussed in Section 8), they are not always your best alternative. You may also need to match the color of your project to an existing piece of furniture. Or you may want to make an unattractive wood mimic a nicer species.

In this section, I'll discuss how to deal with these problems and how to perform a few specialized techniques, such as selectively staining a border or coloring the area around a strip of inlay.

The right side of this oak board was washcoated with 1-lb.-cut shellac before being stained with an oil-based stain.

To prevent heavy stain absorption on the end grain of this panel, the author seals it with a dilute coat of shellac, then sands it with 400-grit paper before staining. The panel was sealed before assembly to avoid getting the sealer on other parts.

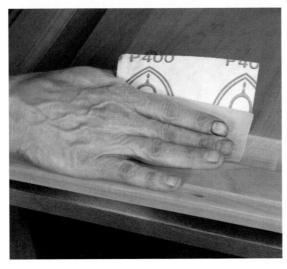

Controlling End Grain Absorption

The end grain of wood is more porous than face grain. Because of this, end grain absorbs more stain, typically resulting in a darker surface than that of the face grain. There are two techniques for controlling end grain absorption: One is to seal the end grain so it absorbs less color, and the other is to sand the end grain smoother than the face grain. Either works well with all wood species.

I find that the most effective approach is to combine the two techniques. I first apply a dilute coat of 1-lb. or 2-lb.-cut shellac to the end grain, taking care not to apply it too heavily. Otherwise the stain might not penetrate at all. After the shellac dries, I sand it using a grit that is two steps up from the finest previous grit used. For example, since I typically sand to 220 grit, I'll sand the shellac using 400-grit sandpaper.

You don't have to use shellac for the sealer. Instead you could use a thinned version of your finish, or lacquer-based sanding sealer, or vinyl sealer. A ratio of one part sealer to two parts thinner works well. Oil-based finishes don't seal very well, with the exception of gel varnish, which tends to stay near the surface rather than migrating deeply into the end grain. Some sealers may be ineffective when used with certain stains, so make sure you match the sealer to the stain. (See the chart on the facing page.)

Shaped workpieces such as turnings and carvings can be a trickier proposition. Because the transition from face grain to end grain can be very gradual, it's difficult or impossible to selectively seal just the end grain. For these pieces, I usually seal the entire surface.

Controlling Splotching

Splotching refers to a surface that exhibits random, unattractive patches of more darkly stained wood. It is caused by a variety of factors, including gnarly or swirled grain, density variations in the wood, or resin pockets at the surface. Softwoods like pine, hemlock, and fir are the most prone to splotching. However, hardwoods like birch, aspen, alder, cherry, and poplar suffer it as well, along with some species of soft maple.

Selecting a Washcoat

When choosing a washcoat, select one that won't be dissolved by the stain solvents. Here's a guide to basic compatibility.

	GLUE SIZE	SHELLAC	LACQUER-BASED[1]	WATER-BASED[2]
Oil-based stain	x	x	x	
Lacquer/fast-dry stain	x			
Water-based stain (pre-mixed)				x
Water-soluble dyes		x	x	x
Alcohol-soluble dyes		x		
NGR stain	x			

1. Sanding sealer or vinyl sealer, thinned 2:1 thinner/finish
2. Water-based thinned 2:1 water/finish or premixed stain controller

The splotchy hemlock spindle at left was not sealed before staining. The two others were first washcoated with glue size. The spindle at far right was stained twice with the same color of stain to get the dark color desired.

Splotching is a common staining problem with some woods. To prevent it on this cherry board, the bottom half of the board was washcoated with glue size prior to being stained with an alcohol dye.

To check for potential splotching problems before applying stain, wipe the wood with a non-grain-raising solvent like naphtha, mineral spirits, alcohol, or lacquer thinner. The figured cherry at left will splotch, but not the cherry plywood at right.

One approach to avoiding splotching is to avoid staining altogether. Instead you can simply use a strongly colored finish like the two shellacs or varnish shown here. From left, dark garnet shellac, orange shellac, tung oil/phenolic varnish, no finish.

Understand that the culprit here is not the stain. The fault lies in the way the wood's structure reacts to the stain. Although there are quite a few techniques for preventing splotching, there isn't any single solution that works with all woods. That's why it's important to be able to identify woods that will splotch and to practice the various solutions on scrap before staining your workpiece.

There are a handful of techniques for preventing splotching. You can use a gel stain or a water-based dye stain, both of which will minimize or eliminate splotching. You can preseal the surface to regulate stain absorption, or spray the stain to ensure a more consistent absorption. Another choice is to apply the color in the form of a toner, as discussed in Section 8. Of course you could also prevent the problem by avoiding stain altogether—simply applying a clear finish to your project. If you like, you can use a strongly colored finish as a "stain." Any one of the above methods will work on even the most splotch-prone woods, as I'll discuss below. You can also combine the techniques for the greatest flexibility in achieving the color you want.

Using Gel Stains

Because of their thick consistency, gel stains are remarkably good at not penetrating too deeply. They work well on most softwoods but can exhibit a lack of clarity. However, applying a gel stain over a washcoat, as discussed next, almost guarantees a splotch-free stained surface.

Preloading and Applying a Washcoat

The most effective form of splotch control involves sealing the wood with a clear, highly thinned finish before applying the stain. While the principle behind this technique is simple, it can seem confusing because of the number of different products used. When shopping for the various sealers, you'll encounter premixed products with names like Pre-Stain, Stain Controller, Wood Conditioner, Wood Stabilizer and even Glue Size. In addition,

Glue size is available in a concentrated liquid that is to be diluted with water. It makes fuzzy woods easier to sand, and it seals end grain to prevent excessive stain absorption.

APPLYING STAIN CONTROLLER

A

B

C

Stain controller is liberally applied with a brush or rag (A), then wiped off, leaving the controller puddled in the porous areas (B). Stain applied afterward stays on the surface on top of the filled pores (C).

you can make your own sealers by mixing various finishes with thinner.

But don't be confused. All these products basically serve the same purpose—to control the amount of stain that soaks into the wood. Their differences lie mainly in the type of resin and solvents they use and how they are applied. For the sake of clarity, I'll divide them into two basic classes: "preloading stain controllers" and "washcoat stain controllers." Each of these is distinguished by its method of application, which should be described on the containers of the various premixed products.

Preloading stain controllers are applied by flooding the surface with an oil-based product, then allowing it to sit for 10 to 15 minutes before applying the stain on top of the still-wet controller. You can use a premixed controller or make your own by mixing 1 part boiled linseed or tung oil with 9 parts mineral spirits. These products are typically sold for use with oil-based wiping stains.

I use preloading stain controllers for oil-based wiping stains. As a general rule, they are a good choice when you have a lot of area to stain or you simply wish to avoid the sanding involved after applying a washcoat, as described next.

Washcoat stain controllers are thinned finishes that are applied to the wood surface and then allowed to dry before being sanded. (Some oil-based commercial washcoats do not require sanding.) They all work by plug-

APPLYING A RESIN WASHCOAT

A

B

C

When applying a hard resin washcoat as a sealer, let it dry, then sand the surface (A). This leaves the hardened washcoat embedded in the porous areas (B). When stain is then applied, it tends to stay at the surface and appear more even (C).

best washcoats because they are compatible with all stains except those that are alcohol-based. For shellac, use a $^1/_2$-lb.- to 1-lb. cut.

► See "*Shellac*" on pp. 239-42.

You can make a lacquer washcoat by thinning lacquer-based sanding sealer or vinyl sealer with one to two parts lacquer thinner. Commercial water-based "prestains" are available for washcoating, but you can easily make your own by thinning water-based finish with two parts water.

Using Water-Based Dye
Splotching sometimes occurs because of a textural difference in the wood, such as sapwood that is more porous than the heartwood. In these cases, staining with a water-based dye can prevent splotching. However, water-based dyes are not always 100 percent effective, particularly when you use dark colors.

Spraying a dye without wiping it afterward almost always guarantees a splotch-free surface. Alternatively, you can wipe a water-based dye over a washcoat of shellac, but you'll have to apply the finish top coats by spraying, because a brush or rag will easily lift off the dye.

Spraying Stain
To avoid splotching, most professional finishers apply stain with a spray gun. To employ this technique, gradually work up to the color you want without wiping off the stain afterward. The problem with spraying is that it can be difficult to get the stain into corners and tight spots. To get into these areas, you can use either a small brush

ging up the porous, more absorbent areas with clear finish, while allowing the stain to penetrate the rest of the surface to some degree. The stain penetration is controlled by how much the washcoat was thinned and how much was sanded away afterward. This extra measure of control gives washcoats an edge over preloading stain controllers when you're applying dye stains, for example.

Whatever washcoat you choose, it's important that it won't redissolve the stains that contact it. Fast-drying products like dewaxed shellac and lacquer sealers make the

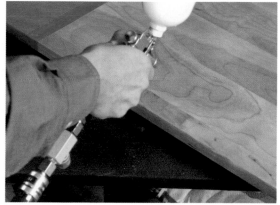

A small touchup
gun is perfect for
selectively staining
sapwood. Use alco-
hol or NGR dyes
to avoid raising
the grain.

For curved work like these cherry legs,
washcoating (left) or spraying the stain
(right) work well. Note that the washcoated
leg exhibits more grain definition and interest. If you make something too uniform, it
may start looking artificial.

or the sharp, pointy corner of a folded rag.
Another approach is to wipe an oil stain or
glaze onto these areas after sealing in the
underlying color.

Unifying Color

Part of the beauty of a nice piece of furniture
stems from the uniformity of its coloring. To
this end, it's wise to build a project with all
wood from the same tree and to construct
panels from matching boards. However, this
isn't always possible. Boards may not match

well and may include sapwood. Furthermore,
if your piece includes veneers, they will usually stain differently than solid wood. These
discrepancies can result in a project with
somewhat uneven coloring.

Dealing with sapwood is fairly easy.
Targeting just the sapwood, simply brush,
wipe, or spray on a stain that matches the
surrounding wood. I typically use alcohol-
based dye for this, applying it with a small
rag or a small touchup spray gun. The only
real challenge you'll face is when coloring
sapwood on cherry that won't receive a coat
of overall stain afterward. The difficulty lies
in the fact that cherry's colored heartwood
will darken dramatically over time, while
the stained sapwood won't. The way to
ensure a long-term match is to initially stain
the sapwood somewhat darker than the
fresh heartwood.

Unifying the color of an entire project
involves a two-step process. First, a light-
colored "uniforming" stain is applied as a
base color, then a second stain—referred to
in this process as the "overall" stain—is
applied over that. The result is that the
underlying uniforming stain pokes through
the overall stain, tricking the eye into per-
ceiving a unified overall color.

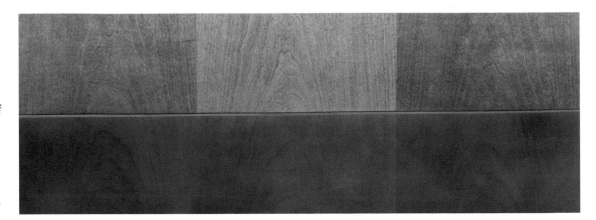

Stained plywood often exhibits a "barber-pole" effect caused by alternating grain direction, as seen at the top of this maple panel. The bottom half was first sealed, then sprayed with a lacquer-based toner.

When you apply an initial uniforming stain by hand, I suggest using a water-based dye, as it won't react strongly to textural differences in the wood. When spraying, you can use an NGR stain or an alcohol-based stain to take advantage of their fast drying properties. (Don't wipe off NGR or alcohol-based stains afterward.) I use a honey-colored uniforming stain if the overall color will be brown. I'll use a light reddish dye if the overall color will be red.

Whatever uniforming stain you use, apply it to the entire piece. After it dries thoroughly, apply a light coat of sealer; when it dries you can apply the overall stain. Later, you can further refine the color if desired by using toning and shading techniques. (See Section 8.)

Staining Plywood and Veneer

Plywood and veneers can include small stress cracks and splits created during manufacturing. These are impossible to remove, regardless of how well you prepared the surface. Another problem with plywood is the alternating light/dark pattern that appears as a result of book-matched veneers. Called the "barber-pole" effect, the pattern is caused by light reflecting differently on alternating grain.

Fortunately, all these problems are easy to handle by spraying on a stain without wiping it off afterward. Alternatively, you can spray the surface with toner. When dealing with stress cracks, you can mitigate the problem by using a water-based dye, because of water's unique tendency not to accentuate texture. However, spraying and not wiping the stain is the best solution.

Selective Staining

Sometimes you need to exclusively stain selected areas such as borders or inlays. Masking off the adjacent areas with tape is usually the best approach. However, the wood must be sealed and lightly sanded first, to provide a smooth surface for good tape adhesion. Any liquid or gel stain will penetrate underneath tape applied to bare wood.

Begin by applying a sealer coat to the entire surface, then masking off the area you want to protect from the stain. Use the correct tape for the masking job—one that will leave a fine, crisp line. The best tapes I've found are available from 3M in a variety of types to suit just about every purpose. The company's bright green tape is used for lacquer finishes because the adhesive isn't attacked by the lacquer solvents, but it can

The blue masking tape shown here can be left on for a week; the green tape resists curling or lifting from lacquer; the white "safe-release" tape is for masking sealed or delicate surfaces. The thin, flexible tape is for masking contours.

also be used with other finishes. Blue tape is for nonlacquer finishes and for circumstances when the tape needs to stay on longer without leaving a residue. Low-tack white tape is my preference and leaves no residue on a finish or wood. It's fine for most finishes, though heavy coats of lacquer may attack it. 3M's Scotch™ Fine-Line Tape 218 is good for all finishes and will stretch for curved shapes and is extremely thin, so you have a thinner ridge between the taped and untaped areas.

Another way to protect an area from stain is to mask off the adjacent areas, then spray several coats of finish onto the selected area. After removing the masking, you can stain the adjacent surface without the stain affecting the finished area.

➤ See "Selective Hand Application" on p. 170.

Color Matching

Matching an existing finish is one of the greatest challenges in finishing. Many variables affect the total makeup of a finished surface, including the texture and color of the wood, the color and vibrancy of the stain and top coat, and the sheen of the finish. You may be called upon to match a new project to an existing piece of furniture or to match a repaired section to the rest of the piece. There are two basic approaches to matching a stain. The first is to mix the appropriate colors together for a single application. The second is to layer the colors, tweaking each previous coat by covering it with a different color.

Mixing to Match

At its simplest, matching a stain involves finding the right single stain for the job. If you already own stain that may work, test some on a piece of your project scrap and compare it to the finish to be matched. Otherwise, compare store samples of actual stained wood against the project to be matched—perhaps a door or drawer front you've removed for that purpose. If you're lucky, you'll find a perfect match. It's more likely, however, that you'll find one that seems to be somewhere between two colors, and perhaps a bit lighter or darker.

➤ BASIC COLOR THEORY

When mixing and matching colors in finishing, it helps to understand the fundamental dimensions of colors and how the different colors relate to each other.

One of the standard systems to describe color was worked out in 1905 by an artist named Albert Munsell. Called the Munsell System, it organized the three fundamental dimensions that apply to colors as *hue*, *value*, and *chroma*. Hue refers to the degree of color—how red, blue, or yellow it is. Value defines how dark or light a color is. Chroma refers to a color's intensity or brightness.

The relationship of colors is typically portrayed on a six-segment color wheel representing the three *primary colors*—red, blue, and yellow, as well as the three *secondary colors*—orange, green, and violet. Red, blue, and yellow are called the primary colors because they cannot be mixed from other colors. Orange, green, and violet are the secondary colors because each results from the direct mixing of two of the primary colors. Two colors opposite each other on the wheel are called *complementary colors* because they cancel or neutralize each other when mixed, technically producing neutral gray, but also producing brown if mixed in the right proportions. Colors on the right side of the wheel are referred to as warm colors, and those on the left are called cool.

In wood finishing, our typical concerns involve altering natural wood tones, represented largely by various brown colors. To play with these colors, you'll also need white and black in addition to the primary colors. All colors except white are sold as dyes or pigment. White is only available as a pigment.

Here are a few basic rules for working with colors in wood finishing:

• Adding yellow brightens brown (increases chroma). Red warms brown and blue cools it.

• Adding black decreases the value and chroma of any color, darkening it. Adding white creates a lighter tint of any color.

• Adding black to white makes gray (in pigments only).

• Adding small amounts of any color to white creates a pastel.

• A complementary color will neutralize or weaken its opposite color. For example, add green to neutralize red. Mixing complementary pure colors produces grayish-brown.

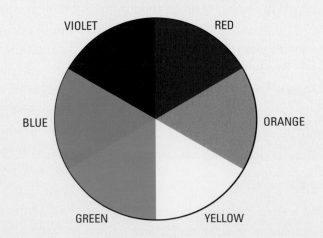

Experiment with the stain on appropriate scrap. If it's too dark, try diluting it a bit. If it's not quite the color you want, you can often "push" it toward a slightly different hue by wiping it with a different-colored stain while both colors are still wet. Try to approximate the lightest color in the wood you're trying to match. When you've got an idea of the proper colors to use and whether they need dilution, mix up a small amount of liquid to test, noting the approximate proportions of the mixture. Test it on your scrap again, and make any necessary adjustments to the mixture, again noting mixing proportions. As you mix and test, add other colors if necessary. To make the color distinctly redder, it's best to use a primary red colorant. To darken the color, add dark brown rather than black, which tends to have a cool, bluish hue.

Layering Color

Another approach—the one I typically use—is to apply colors in layers, building up to the desired final color. This method gives you the most control, particularly if you're trying to match a mystery finish.

The easiest layering technique is to apply a glaze over a dye, which allows you to "sneak up" on the final color. The first step in this process involves applying an "underlayment" of dye that approximates the hue of the final color but is a bit lighter. You then apply a sealer to this underlayment before applying a glaze that matches the desired final color. The beauty of this technique is that the sealer allows an errant glaze to be easily wiped away for a second (or third) try. The colors you achieve with this method can be spectacular and very rich

because the eye perceives both colors—the undertone and the top color. (For more on glazes, see Section 8.)

Experienced finishers are often able to intuit the result of applying a particular color over another. However, this can be a real challenge if you're not familiar with the process. Here's a trick to save you some trouble: Before applying your glaze to the workpiece, wipe it on a sheet of clear acrylic, then place that over the underlayment to get an idea of the final color. When using acrylic, first scuff the surface with gray synthetic steel wool to give the stain something to bite into.

[TIP] When it comes to color matching, there is simply no substitute for practice. And the practice will go more smoothly if you make some stain boards and understand some basic color theory to point you in the right direction.

Applying a glaze or stain over a sealed dye allows you to "sneak up" on the desired final color. The sealer over the underlying dye allows you to wipe away an errant glaze for another try.

A

B

C

D

Preloading Using Stain Controller

One of the easiest ways to control splotching is to "preload" the wood with a stain controller, which fills the porous areas of the wood prior to staining. Many manufacturers make a proprietary stain controller that's compatible with their stains. Apply the stain controller liberally, brushing it onto the entire surface **(A)**. The areas that soak up the controller almost immediately are the sections that would have been prone to splotching. After letting the controller soak in for 10 to 15 minutes, wipe off the excess **(B)**. Immediately apply your oil-based stain with a brush or rag **(C)**. After you wipe off the excess stain, the surface should exhibit a consistent overall color **(D)**.

A

B

C

Applying a Washcoat

Washcoating wood before staining is a great technique for preventing splotching. However, its success depends on picking the right product for the job. It's crucial that the dried washcoat won't be dissolved by the stain applied on top of it. If you're not sure, test compatibility on scrap first.

Apply the washcoat using a rag or foam brush **(A)**. Wipe off the excess immediately, then let the work dry overnight before smoothing the dried surfaces with 600-grit sandpaper **(B)**. After thoroughly removing the sanding dust, apply the stain **(C)**. For quick-drying stains like water-based products, I like to use a two-handed technique—applying the stain to just one section at a time, then wiping it off almost immediately with a rag.

Applying Gel Stain over a Washcoat

This is one of my favorite techniques for fool-proof staining of cherry—a notoriously splotch-prone wood. Make a ½-lb.-cut of shellac by mixing 1 weighed oz. of shellac flakes with 1 pt. of alcohol. If you're using premixed shellac from a can, dilute it according to the manufacturer's recommendations, or consult the chart on p. 242.

▶ See *"Shellac Conversion Ratios"* chart on p. 242.

I prefer to mix my own from flakes because it allows me to make lighter or darker-colored shellac, depending on the choice of flakes.

Using a rag, apply the shellac liberally to the surface of the wood **(A)**. After it dries thoroughly, sand the surface with 320-grit sandpaper **(B)**. Remove the dust and apply your gel stain. Although the stain used here is labeled "Country Maple," the color looks pretty good on this cherry top **(C)**. To darken it, apply a second coat of darker gel stain **(D)**.

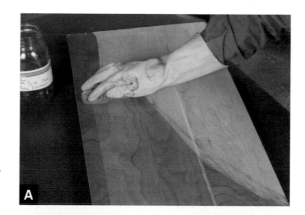

A

B

C

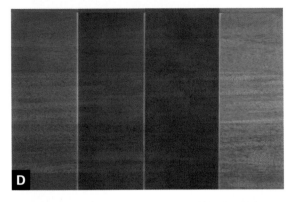

D

VARIATION

Unifying the Color of a Board

Sometimes a single board will exhibit several different colors, perhaps in the form of alternating light and dark bands, as seen on the mahogany board here. To equalize the differences, an amber/yellow dye stain was wiped on first **(A)**. The next step was to washcoat with a sealer, let that dry, then lightly sand the surface. Next, a gel stain was applied, brushed on thoroughly **(B)**. After the stain was wiped off, the surface displayed a much more consistent color **(C)**.

Sometimes, a board suffers from extreme color variation. In these cases, the best approach may be to apply a pigment-based toner, as shown in the photo **(D)**. The three sections from left to right show various shades of toner. The far right section was not toned. (For more on toning, see Section 8.)

[**VARIATION**]A different approach to unifying colors is to apply a two-part bleach to the entire surface before staining. It's particularly effective when two different species of wood are used, such as red and white oak in the same piece. This technique is fairly reliable, although it is more time-consuming and removes some of the natural depth and luster of the wood.

Matching Sapwood to Heartwood

Matching sapwood to heartwood involves selectively coloring the sapwood. In order to select the correct color of stain, first wipe the heartwood with mineral spirits to indicate the finished color of the wood.

I like to use alcohol dyes for sapwood touchups because they dry quickly. To avoid applying the stain too heavily, use the stain-dampened corner of a small cotton rag as an applicator. To dampen the rag properly, dip its corner into the mixed dye, then press it against the side of the container to squeeze out the excess. Lightly wipe the dye on the sapwood, using the tip of your finger **(A)**. When you're done, you can wipe the entire surface lightly with a solvent-dampened rag to even out the color if necessary **(B)**. For molded edges or other hard-to-reach areas, apply the dye using the sharp edge of an artist's brush **(C)**.

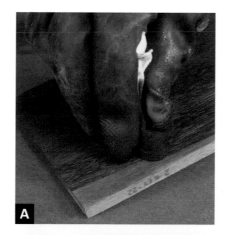

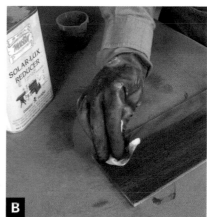

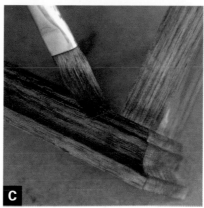

Matching Plywood and Solid Wood

Pigment stains will typically color plywood darker than solid wood **(A)**. Gel stains provide a good way to even out the colors because they can be applied in layers—selectively darkening the solid wood to match the plywood.

Apply the first coat of gel stain, then let it dry. Next, scuff it using 0000 steel wool or a gray synthetic pad **(B)**, then apply another coat of stain. In almost all cases this second coat equalizes the difference, though a third coat could be applied if necessary **(C)**.

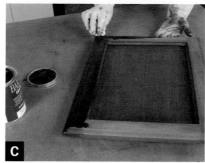

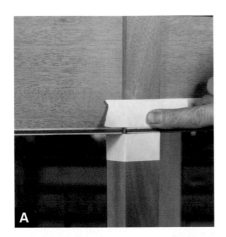

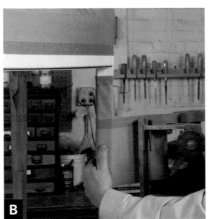

Selective Hand Application

When staining a piece, you sometimes want to leave selected areas uncolored, such as the inlay at the bottom of this table apron.

Begin by masking off the wood around the inlay with white, low-tack tape, burnishing down the tape with the tip of your finger **(A)**. Before spraying, protect any adjacent areas with tape and paper **(B)**. Now apply three or four light coats of a quick-drying lacquer or sealer that's compatible with your top coats but will resist the solvent in the stain you'll be using. I'm using here an aerosol version of the lacquer I'll be applying for the finish top coats **(C)**. Spraying is necessary in a case like this because wiping or brushing the finish on would drive it under the edges of the tape.

Remove the tape after 10 minutes and let the lacquer dry overnight before applying your stain. In this case, a water soluble dye was used, which is resisted by the lacquer on the inlay **(D)**.

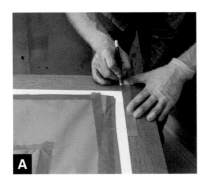

Selective Spraying

Masking your workpiece, then spraying color in the form of a toner, allows you to achieve the sharpest, cleanest edges. For this walnut and mahogany game table, the goal was a rich cordovan mahogany color surrounding unstained walnut veneer at the center. After sealing the whole table and letting it dry overnight, the walnut center section was taped off. To ensure crisp edges, trim the tape using an X-Acto knife and a ruler **(A)**. Next, spray the mahogany edges and legs with a commercial fast-drying lacquer stain **(B)**. After the stain dries, remove the tape to reveal a clean, crisp center panel **(C)**.

An Exercise in Color Theory

Practice is by far the best teacher when it comes to learning color theory, matching, and manipulation. Here is an exercise that should help you understand some of the basics.

Begin by mixing up the following five colors from dyes or thinned pigment concentrates:
- Rubine (a bluish-red)
- Lemon yellow
- Cyan (a turquoise-blue)
- Green
- Black

Working on a piece of white plywood like birch or maple, begin by staining the board yellow. Next, wipe rubine over it. You've just created orange—the secondary color made by combining red and yellow (**A**). Wiping cyan over the orange makes brown, which is a combination of the three primary colors yellow, red, and blue (**B**).

To "push" a basic brown color to alter its hue, it's best to use primary or secondary colors.

▶ See *"Basic Color Theory"* sidebar on p. 162.

To make the brown more red, wipe red over it. (**C**). If that turns the brown too red, you can neutralize the red somewhat by adding green, which is red's complementary color (**D**).

To darken a color, use black or dark brown (**E**). Be careful in your selection of a black, as many blacks have a bluish undertone that will "cool" a color.

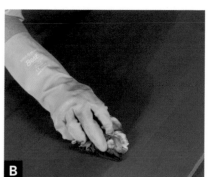

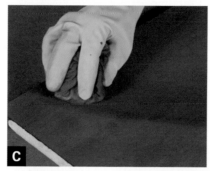

Tweaking Color by Layering

A quick, easy way to match an existing color is to tweak the color of the primary stain by applying modifying colors over it.

Here's where a stain board of sample colors really comes in handy.

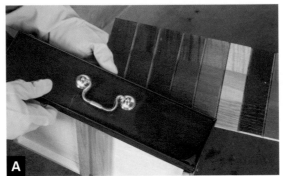

> See *"Making a Stain Board"* on p. 164.

Compare the match-piece (in this case a drawer front) against the colors on your stain board (**A**). If the match-piece has a satin or flat finish, squirt it with mineral spirits to mimic the gloss finish on your stain-board samples and to render a more accurate color.

Select the stain-board color that most closely matches the lightest tones on your match-piece. Then dye your workpiece using that stain (**B**). After the stain dries, apply a coat of sealer to "lock in" the dye. Let the sealer dry thoroughly, then smooth it with a light sanding.

Now you can "sneak up" on the final color by applying different colored glazes or stains over the dye. I used gel stains here, applying one, then comparing the color to the match-piece (**C**). The first color wasn't dark enough, so I followed it with a darker mahogany gel stain (**D**). When the stain was wiped off, it matched the drawer front nicely.

Glorifying Cheap Woods

I'll use the underside of this tabletop to demonstrate how you can get striking, uniform finishes using production finishing techniques. These techniques can be used to make inexpensive woods like pine, birch, and poplar look like more expensive woods.

Apply a sap stain first **(A)**. It doesn't have to be perfectly applied; your aim is simply to darken it enough to match the color of the heartwood. Next, apply a uniforming stain (in this case, a honey amber color) that will impart an overall golden undertone **(B)**. Seal the stain with a washcoat. Sand the dried washcoat, then apply an oil stain (in this case, a reddish-brown color) to provide some extra color and grain definition **(C)**. Apply a sanding sealer, then sand it smooth.

Now you're ready to spray toner to achieve your final color. I find that the most interesting finishes are created by applying two different-colored toners in succession. (You can see the two colors I used on the white practice paper in the background.) In this case, I started by applying an overall reddish-brown color. I followed that up with a dark brown, which I used to shade and highlight certain areas **(D)**.

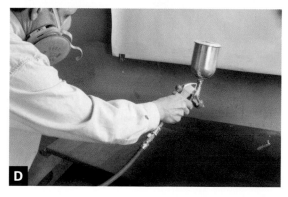

Filling Pores, page 176

Sealers, page 189

PART FOUR

Fillers and Sealers

WHEN FINISHING HARDWOODS, you have the option of applying grain filler—a technique that will result in a smoother finish. Using grain filler also provides another means of adding color. What you do with the grain can make the difference between a mediocre finish and a stunning one. Sealers perform an important part of the finishing process. Applied before the top coats, sealers can prevent many finishing problems, particularly when you're working with certain woods. In this part, we'll look at how and when to use certain types of sealers, and when they're not necessary.

Filling Pores

Finish as a Filler

➤ Sprayed Polyester (p. 185)
➤ Clear Varnish (p. 185)

Oil-Based Fillers

➤ Filling and Staining Simultaneously (p. 186)
➤ Filling after Staining (p. 186)

Water-Based Fillers

➤ Water-Based Pigmented Filler (p. 187)
➤ Plaster of Paris Filler (p. 187)

Partially Filling Pores

➤ Oil Slurry Filler (p. 188)
➤ Slush Fill (p. 188)

WHEN FINISHING HARDWOODS, you have the option of leaving the pores open or filling them. Although it's an optional step, filling the pores can create an elegant, glass-smooth surface in the final finish. In this section, I'll discuss the aesthetics of pore-filling and the various techniques involved in achieving the look you want.

To Fill or Not to Fill

Pores are the result of vessels that conduct sap in a living hardwood tree. (Softwoods are "nonporous.") When a board is milled from a hardwood tree, these vessels are cut open at various angles, exposing the channels we call pores. Finishers generally differentiate between hardwoods by calling them "open-pored" or "closed-pored" woods. Open-pored woods such as oak and ash exhibit large-diameter pores that result in a rough texture on the surface of the board. Closed-pored woods such as maple and cherry have a smoother texture, although pores are distinguishable if you look closely. The distribution of the pores also has an effect on the appearance of the wood.

PORE DISTRIBUTION

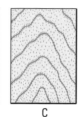

A   B   C

The size, number, and distribution of pores are what give the different hardwoods their character. When the large pores are concentrated mainly in the early-wood, the wood is called "ring-porous." These species include oak, ash, elm, chestnut, and teak (A). Woods like mahogany and birch have a pattern of more evenly distributed pores, and are referred to a "diffuse-porous" woods (B). "Semi-ring porous" species such as walnut and butternut display large pores in the earlywood and smaller pores in the latewood (C).

You certainly don't have to fill wood pores for finishing. An open-pored finish has a natural, unsophisticated look that is perfectly fine if you want to retain the sharp, crisp delineation of the pore outlines. (See the sidebar at right.) However, a filled-pore surface adds a refined, elegant look to a piece of furniture. Plus, if you want a mirrorlike buffed-gloss finish, you'll have to fill the pores; otherwise the tiny craters break up the surface, preventing the smooth, flat plane that defines a true gloss finish. You can also use thinned pore filler to partially fill the pores, creating an appearance somewhere between the other two.

There are two approaches to filling pores. One is to apply several coats of a suitable finish, then sand the surface flat. The other is to fill the pores with paste wood filler before finishing.

▶ OPEN-PORED FINISHES

You don't have to fill the wood pores for an attractive finish. In fact, many woodworkers prefer the "natural" look of an open-pored finish for some projects. In these cases, the choice of finish is critical to achieving a nice crisp look around the edges of the pores.

Open-pored finishes are best created by wiping on the finish, which pushes it into the pores. The best open-pored appearance is obtained by using thin finishes such as oil, an oil/varnish blend, or shellac. If you choose to spray instead, it's wise to work with low-solids finishes, like shellac and lacquer. High-solids finishes like conversion varnish or most water-based products tend to "bridge" the pores, creating the look of an incomplete fill. If you want to use these high-solids products, you can usually improve their appearance by thinning them, adding a retarder, or applying a lighter coat. When using water-based finishes, it can also help to apply a "slush fill" of thinned water-based filler to the pores beforehand.

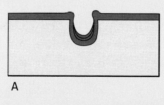

A

B

Applying an Open-Pored Finish
Thickly applied high-solids finishes and many water-based finishes pull up and "bridge" as they try to coat the walls of an open pore (A). This results in the soupy "plastic" look associated with these finishes.

It's much better to use low-solids finishes for an open-pored finish, because these thinned finishes hug the wall of the pore as they flow down, resulting in a crisper, more sharply defined pore (B). It also helps to wipe the finish on rather than brushing or spraying it.

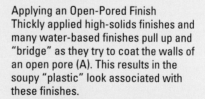

FILLING WITH FINISH

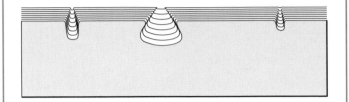

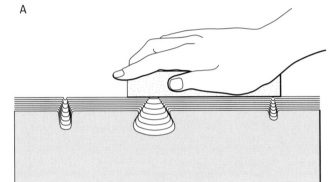

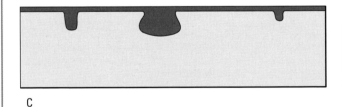

When you fill pores using a finish, you apply several thick coats and let them dry (A). Then you sand back the excess build until you can no longer see the outline of the pores (B). It's possible to use a scraper instead to cut back the finish but because an errant scrape may dig too deep, it's better to sand the finish if the work was stained first. Properly done, the pores are filled with finish and a smooth thin coat left on the surface (C).

Filling with Finish

Filling pores with finish involves applying enough coats of an appropriate finish to fill the pores. There's no need to sand between coats. After the finish dries, sand it level

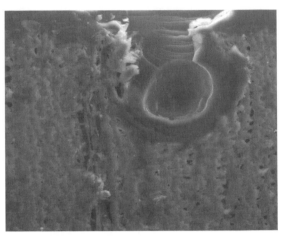

This cross section of mahogany taken at 150x magnification shows polyester filler-in a single pore. Note how the polyester flows down into the pore and fills it completely.

until the surface is uninterrupted by pore craters. Although you can use a scraper to cut back the finish, it's safer to sand a stained surface rather than risk cutting through to bare wood with an errant stroke of the scraper.

Only certain finishes work well for pore-filling. In years past, filling pores with low-build finishes like lacquer and shellac was very time-consuming. To make matters worse, these finishes invariably shrank down into the pores over time. Fortunately, modern high-solids finish resins allow faster fills with minimal shrinkage. The best products to use are tough thermosetting resins like polyester, urethane, and epoxy (see Section 13). Of the two, polyester and 2K urethane (see Section 14, p. 236) are typically used for spraying and are available from specialty suppliers. Polyester works best because it is nonshrinking and the hardest of all the finish resins. After sanding, it can be top-coated with other finishes. It is also heat-resistant, so it

The best finish for filling pores is polyester resin, which is the hardest and shrinks the least of all the finish resins. At right is the hardened residue removed from a mixing container.

This cross section of mahogany at 200x magnification shows how traditional paste filler bulks up the pore cavity but doesn't fill it completely. Three sealer-coats of lacquer were required to fill the remaining area before a clear lacquer could be built on top.

won't be softened by the heat generated from buffing out the final finish. That said, conversion varnishes, catalyzed lacquers, alkyds, urethanes, and thermosetting acrylics can also be used.

Filling with Paste Wood Filler

Instead of filling pores with finish, many shops use paste wood fillers. These products are widely available, easy to apply, and well suited to use by both professionals and novices. Paste wood fillers are available in various formulations, although all are used in a similar manner. They are applied to the surface of the wood and worked into the pores. Afterward, the excess is removed by wiping and/or sanding. Because paste wood filler doesn't always fill pores completely, it's often necessary to apply several coats of finish on top of the filler to completely fill the surface before applying top coats of finish.

The ideal paste wood filler would work easily into the pores and not dry too fast. You would be able to easily wipe the excess from the surface without removing the filler from the pores. The final product would

become as hard as a rock without shrinking. But that's asking a lot. At best, most paste wood fillers compromise some features in favor of others, as I'll discuss. The various formulations of paste wood filler can be divided into two basic categories: oil-based fillers and water-based fillers.

Oil-Based Paste Wood Fillers

Oil-based paste wood fillers are composed of binder, a bulking pigment, and solvent. The oil or alkyd binder determines the filler's handling characteristics and drying time. It's also what locks the filler into the wood pores. The translucent bulking pigment, which prevents shrinkage, consists of fine silica or a quartz-silica mineral. It constitutes about 65 percent of the filler's total weight. Solvent adjusts the viscosity of the filler and affects how soon the product can be wiped clean. Colored fillers additionally contain colored pigment.

I typically prefer oil-based fillers because they're easier to control than their water-based cousins, especially in subtle coloring situations like matching a finish. Oil-based fillers are commercially available in either "natural" or colored versions. "Natural" is actually an off-white, putty color to which you can add your own colorants.

Preparing Oil-Based Fillers

Not all paste wood fillers are ready to use straight from the container. Some may need to be thinned, and some may require additional color to suit your purposes.

For proper application, a paste wood filler should be the consistency of heavy cream. If necessary, thin a premixed filler with mineral spirits or naphtha. Naphtha will make the filler dry faster, which may be desirable for a small project. However, if you're likely to need more "open" time in which to apply and wipe off the filler, use mineral spirits. Always thoroughly stir filler immediately before use, as the bulking agent and pigment tend to settle to the bottom of the container.

If your workpiece is to be stained, you also have the option of adding oil-based stain to the filler in order to simultaneously

Applying filler over sealed wood creates a better aesthetic, because the filler colors the pores darker than the intermediate areas, providing contrast, as seen at right.

fill and stain your project. However, because liquid stain will thin the filler, it's best to use a concentrated colorant, which won't affect its consistency. You can use any colorant that's compatible with the filler—dry pigment powder, artist's oil colors, UTCs, or Japan colors. Simply stir the color into the filler. When using thick, pasty colorants like artist's colors, thin the color with a bit of mineral spirits or naphtha first.

Applying Oil-Based Fillers

You can apply the filler to bare wood or sealed wood. In many cases, it's fine to apply it to bare wood, rubbing it into the surface, then wiping away the excess as described below. However, sealing the wood before filling it can result in a surface with a more aesthetic contrast between the filled pores and the intermediate wood. Sealing before filling also provides more control over filler application, because filler will wipe more easily and evenly from a sealed surface. The amount of sealer you apply also helps control the amount of color imparted to the surface when you're using colored filler. For example, a thick sealer coat will completely seal off the wood surface, allowing filler into only the pores. On the other hand, a thin sealer coat will allow some of the color from the filler to stay on the surface.

You can use any sealer as long as it's compatible with both the filler and top coat. Dewaxed shellac is one of my favorites because it's widely available, compatible with all finishes, dries fast, and seals well in a thin film. It can also be used as a sealer and barrier coat when you're using oil filler with water-based top coats. Thinned lacquer works for lacquers. Specialty sealers like

You can apply oil-based pore filler directly to bare wood. The colored filler here darkens both the pores and the surrounding wood but leaves the pores darker.

The other option is to first apply a wash-coat to bare or stained wood, then apply the filler. This method offers more control over the final color of the surface.

vinyl work for conversion varnishes and lacquers. If you're in doubt, a thinned version of your finish will work.

When preparing the sealer, I like to aim for a solids content ranging from 7 to 10 percent. For shellac, this means mixing up a $^1/_2$-lb. to $^3/_4$-lb. cut. I'll typically cut sanding sealer or vinyl sealer 50-50 with thinner. Apply the sealer with a brush or spray gun. After it dries, lightly scuff-sand it smooth with 320-grit sandpaper.

Although you can spray filler, I find it easier to apply it with a brush, packing it into the pores using a coarse cloth like burlap. Alternatively, you can push it into and across the pores using a squeegee or rubber scraper. The idea is to drive the filler into the pores at the same time that you are removing the bulk of the excess.

Wait until the residual filler on the surface turns hazy, which indicates that the majority of the solvent has flashed off but the surface residue is still moist enough to wipe. Using a clean cloth or piece of burlap, lightly wipe the surface to remove all traces of residue while leaving the pores filled. Allow the filler to dry overnight, then per-

form a second application if necessary. After filling the surface as described, I sand it with 320-grit sandpaper before applying a finish.

[TIP] On some coarse woods like mahogany, you may get better results from filler by initially applying a "slush fill" of highly thinned filler for the first coat, then following up with an unthinned coat.

Most oil- or solvent-based finishes can be applied directly over oil-based paste wood filler without a problem. However, when using a water-based finish, it's wise to first apply a sealer coat of dewaxed shellac over the filled surface to prevent adhesion problems. If you're using lacquer as a top coat, avoid applying it too thickly, as its solvents can soften and wrinkle the dried filler. To counter this when applying lacquer with a brush, seal the surface first with shellac. If you're spraying the lacquer, simply apply the first several coats as light "mist" coats. When you use conversion varnishes, catalyzed lacquers, and other two-component finishes, you may apply a vinyl sealer coat over the filler to prevent any possible adverse reactions with the top coat.

Water-Based Fillers

Water-based fillers have the same basic constitution as oil-based fillers, except that the solvent and the oil-based binder in the latter have been replaced with water and a water-compatible resin. Water-based filler formulations allow the manufacture of totally transparent fillers, as well as "natural" off-white and pigmented fillers. Several formulations are available as a transparent gel that will dry water-clear.

Water-based fillers have both advantages and disadvantages when compared to oil-based fillers. On the plus side, you can use solvent-based stains like alcohol dyes and NGR stains over a dried water-based filler, whereas this isn't possible with oil-based fillers, because the stain doesn't bite into the oil-sealed surface. Water-based fillers are also much easier to sand and can be top-coated with any finish without risking adhesion problems.

On the downside, water-based fillers dry so fast that it's very difficult to apply the filler and wipe it off cleanly in time. These fillers also stick to sealer coats, so it's impossible to remove them from the surface of sealed wood without removing the sealer. And finally, because they are water-based, they may raise the grain of the wood in use.

Applying Water-Based Fillers

Because of its fast dry time and its habit of adhering to sealers, the best way to handle a water-based filler is to brush it directly onto bare wood, then quickly wipe off as much of the excess as possible with a rag or a squeegee, and let the filler dry thoroughly. Afterward, sand the excess filler level to the surface of the wood. The filler is dry enough to sand when it powders easily. Humidity extends the dry time, but at 50 percent to 60 percent relative humidity (RH), water-based filler should be dry enough to sand in two hours.

Most water-based fillers are ready to go from the can, but you can add small amounts of water, up to 10 percent, to adjust the viscosity if necessary. This speeds up the dry time. To slow the dry time down, add retarder, if available from the manufacturer, or propylene glycol. (Five percent is a good starting point.)

Some water-based fillers dry chalky. However, you can deepen the appearance by applying stain or a thin coat of oil. But don't apply oil over water-based clear acrylic fillers.

You then have the option of staining, as long as you do it within 12 hours after sanding and use a stain that is based on alcohol or glycol ether. This includes alcohol and NGR dyes, fast-drying pigment wiping stains, and many water-based stains, provided they contain solvents in addition to water. To see if the stain will take, wipe some on the dry, filled surface. If the filler changes color or deepens, it indicates that the stain has enough "bite."

Colored versus Natural Fillers

To achieve certain effects you need to use the proper filler—whether colored or "natural." And particular special effects require the right choice between water-based or oil-based fillers. Keep in mind that the finish you put over the filler affects the look. Following are some general guidelines.

Colored Oil-Based Fillers

To make the wood natural looking, apply natural filler to the bare wood. The wood color will deepen from the binder, much as it would if you applied an oil-based product. The binder may yellow over time, so it may not be advisable to use natural filler on very light woods like ash.

To stain the pores and the wood at the same time, apply filler mixed with stain to the bare wood. This takes some trial and error to get the color right, and you'll have to practice on samples. This technique usually accentuates the pore structure.

To de-emphasize the pores by making them the same color as the rest of the wood, seal the wood, then apply filler that matches the natural color of the wood in the intermediate areas between the pores.

Oil-based filler on mahogany: from left, "natural" filler; brown-colored filler applied to bare wood; mahogany-colored filler applied to a sealed surface; white filler applied over sealed black dye.

Filler Colorant Compatibility

COLORANT	COMPATIBLE FILLER
Dry pigment powders	Oil- or water-based filler
UTCs (Universal Tinting Colorants)	Oil- or water-based filler
Bronzing powders, pearlescents, and metal flake (aluminum)	Oil- or water-based filler
Oil-based dyes	Oil-based filler
Oil-based stains and paints	Oil-based filler
Artist's oil colors	Oil-based filler
Japan watercolors	Oil-based filler
Water-based stains and latex paint	Water-based filler
Water-based dyes	Water-based filler
Artist's acrylic colors	Water-based filler

To accentuate the pores by contrasting them with the color of the wood, first stain the wood to the color you want, or leave it unstained. Seal the wood, then apply a colored filler that creates either a lighter or darker contrast with the wood.

The photo above shows the effects of the above techniques.

► TWEAKING FILLER COLOR

You can adjust the color of paste filler by adding a colorant compatible with the filler, as shown in the chart on p. 183. The important thing to remember is that the color of the filler in the pores has an impact on the overall finish. Even a slight difference between the color of the pores and the color of the intermediate areas can have a dramatic effect.

The same color-theory rules that apply to stains apply to paste wood fillers. (See "Basic Color Theory," on p. 162.) However, following are a few guidelines specifically geared toward coloring fillers.
• To make any filler darker, add black, Van Dyke brown, raw umber, or burnt umber. Adding black usually cools the overall color, so you may have to add some red to counteract it.

Oil-based filler on mahogany: from left, natural filler, burnt sienna added, black added which cools the color, red added to warm the color.

• To lighten a wood-tone filler, use raw sienna or golden ochre. Using white will result in a pastel color.

• To "cool" down a wood tone color, add a small amount of raw umber. This pigment has a greenish undertone that will neutralize warm colors.

• To warm up a wood tone color, add a bit of orange or red.

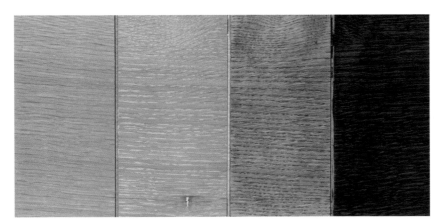

Water-based filler on white oak: from left, transparent filler; un-tinted neutral filler; dark brown filler; dark brown filler under alcohol dye stain.

Colored Water-Based Fillers

To blend in the pores with the surrounding wood, apply natural filler or filler colored to match the wood. Natural water-based fillers dry to a chalky, off-white color that may have to be tinted on light woods, as well as darker woods like mahogany and walnut.

To make the wood look completely natural, use transparent filler. To make the pores darker than the color of the wood, apply a dark brown filler and sand off the excess when dry.

To color both the pores and the intermediate areas, use a solvent-based dye (alcohol or NGR) to color the wood. The dye will deepen the color of the filler while staining the nonporous areas of the wood.

The photo at left shows the effects of the above techniques.

Sprayed Polyester

Over a stain or certain woods, it's advisable to first apply a catalyzed urethane barrier sealer called an isolante. Spray the barrier coat, let it dry about two hours, then apply your first polyester coat **(A)**. Spray in a cross-hatch fashion.

➤ See *"Spray Basics"* on p. 217.

Polyester is sprayed "wet-on-wet," meaning you apply each subsequent coat before the prior coat has cured. Touch the previous coat with your finger. If it's still liquid, wait. If it feels sticky and you can see a fingerprint, you're ready to shoot another coat **(B)**. After three applications, most surfaces should be filled enough to sand back the excess.

Wait 12 hours, then sand the polyester until the outlines of the pores are no longer visible **(C)**. Sand-throughs are common with this technique. Correct them by using a small touchup gun to replace color **(D)**.

Clear Varnish

If you want to apply finish by hand to fill the pores, the best low-tech method is to use a varnish with a solids content that exceeds 40 percent of the finish by weight or volume. Brush on three to five coats, waiting for it to dry between coats **(A)**. After the last coat has dried enough for the sandpaper to powder it, you can sand the surface level, using a flat block **(B)**. After several passes with the block, switch to a folded piece of sandpaper **(C)**. You're done when the outlines of the pores are no longer visible in backlighting.

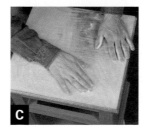

Filling and Staining Simultaneously

If you wish, you can simultaneously stain and fill the wood pores by applying colored filler to bare or washcoated wood. To get a redder tone, add a compatible premixed stain to the filler **(A)**.

Remove all dust from the pores of your project **(B)**. Then use a piece of cloth to "pad" the filler into the pores using a circular motion **(C)**. On small workpieces, it's possible to apply the filler all at once, but if the filler is drying too fast, you can always tape off more manageable sections **(D)**. As soon as the filler hazes, use a piece of burlap to clean the residual filler from the surface **(E)**.

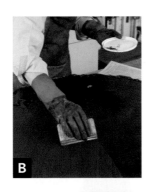

Filling after Staining

Stain the wood, then apply a sealer to lock in the stain and to prevent the filler from coloring the wood. Lightly sand the filled surface **(A)**, then remove the dust. Next, apply the filler evenly with a brush, then immediately take a rubber squeegee, credit card, or piece of cardboard and scrape the excess filler off, moving in the direction of the grain **(B)**. Scrape the filler off the edge and periodically clean the excess filler off the squeegee blade. After the filler hazes, wipe any remaining filler off the surface of the wood with a piece of burlap or cheesecloth. Wad the burlap and wipe the surface, moving across the grain this time **(C)**. For moldings and intricate areas, use a piece of soft wood to pick out the filler **(D)**. When you've removed all the excess filler, wipe the surface in a figure-eight pattern. Sand it lightly with 320-grit sandpaper.

Water-Based Pigmented Filler

Because of its fast dry time, it is best to apply water-based filler to bare wood and sand the excess. Using a brush, roller, or spray gun, apply the filler liberally to the surface of the wood **(A)**. Immediately squeegee the excess off, moving in whatever direction you want **(B)**. (It's not necessary to scrape in the direction of the grain.) Then wipe off as much of the filler as possible using a clean rag dampened with water. The filler is ready to sand in several hours, or when it powders easily when you sand it. If it gums up, let it dry longer. I sand flat parts using 220-grit sandpaper on a random orbit sander **(C)** and sand moldings by hand **(D)**. You're finished when you can see clean grain but also see filler in the pores.

[**VARIATION**] If you don't want the filler to color or change the natural appearance of the wood, use a transparent water-based filler.

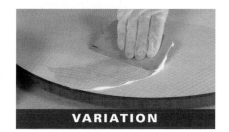

VARIATION

Plaster of Paris Filler

Plaster of paris is a great low-tech product you can use to fill pores. It's the traditional method used in Britain for French polishing. Make up the

See *"French Polishing"* on pp. 248-249.

filler by mixing water and plaster of paris until you have a fairly stiff consistency. Work it into the pores of the wood with a cotton cloth using a circular motion **(A)**. Once you've covered the entire surface, let the plaster sit until it feels dry, then wipe off some of the excess with a dampened cloth **(B)**. Let it dry overnight, then sand it with 220-grit sandpaper. You can then apply clear boiled linseed oil, or color the oil with dye to darken it, if desired. Note how the chalky surface turns translucent with the application of oil **(C)**.

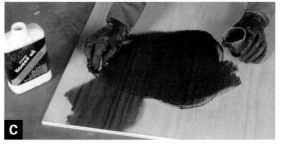

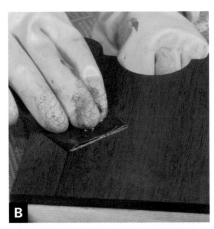

Oil Slurry Filler

An easy and classic way to create a partially filled surface is by wet sanding an oil-type finish into the pores. Begin by wiping a generous coat of boiled linseed oil, tung oil, Danish oil, or an oil/varnish mix into the wood **(A)**. Wipe it off after 15 minutes or so, and let it dry overnight.

The next day, apply another coat, this time wet sanding it in a circular motion with 600-grit wet/dry sandpaper **(B)**. The idea is to create a slurry of sawdust, dried finish from the previous day, and new finish, and work it into the pores. Wipe the excess off after it has set for 30 minutes but before it becomes too tacky to remove. If you want to add just a hint of color to the pores, you can sprinkle some rottenstone on the surface and wet sand it into the pores along with the oil **(C)**. You can add more coats if you like, or stop here for a natural look. If you wish, you can top-coat with a harder finish that has been thinned. For example, you can use a 1-lb.-cut of shellac, a thinned lacquer, or a varnish cut 50-50 with thinner.

Slush Fill

A single application of thinned filler will create a partially filled appearance. If you use a dark filler and don't want to color the intermediate wood surface, seal the wood first, then sand it with 320-grit sandpaper. Thin the filler to the consistency of cream using mineral spirits or naphtha **(A)**. (This is typically a one-to-one ratio of filler to solvent.) Work the filler into the wood pores using a brush **(B)**. Then pad the filler into the pores using a rag and working in a circular motion **(C)**. The filler will haze in 15 to 30 minutes, depending on the thinner used. At that point, clean the excess off the surface with a clean wadded rag **(D)**.

Sealers

Sealer Basics

➤ Brushing Sealers
  (p. 194)

➤ Spraying Sanding
  Sealer (p. 195)

➤ Scuff-Sanding
  Complex Surfaces
  (p. 195)

Specialty Sealers

➤ Mixing and Using
  One-Pound-Cut
  Shellac (p. 196)

➤ Fixing Fisheye
  (p. 197)

SEALERS PERFORM a number of tasks in finishing, including splotch control, as discussed in Section 10. However, one of the primary purposes of a sealer is to prepare the surface of the wood for subsequent coats of finish. In the process, it may also perform a variety of other functions, such as promoting adhesion, accelerating dry time, minimizing grain raising, and preventing contamination or migration from underlying substances.

In this section, I'll discuss the various purposes for sealers and help you decide which ones to use and when.

Simplifying Sanding

The initial base coat of any finish is the one that penetrates into the wood. After it hardens, it normally leaves behind a slightly rough or irregular surface, caused by the finish encapsulating any raised grain. This hardened raised grain can now be effectively sanded flat, creating a smooth surface that promotes good "layout" when the next coat of finish is applied. (Because subsequent coats don't penetrate the wood, they don't require nearly the sanding effort that the first coat involves.)

Many water-based finishes and oil-based polyurethanes sand out perfectly well, so you don't need a special sealer for them. For the first coat, simply thin the finish itself for better penetration and quicker drying.

189

In this greatly enlarged photomicrograph, you can see how a single coat of sealer encapsulates the raised-grain "whisker" at center, hardening it for easy shearing by sandpaper.

This finish separation shows the result of poor adhesion caused by applying a water-based finish over an oil-based glaze. Dewaxed shellac would have "tied" the two dissimilar materials together.

► SEALING WITH FINISH

There's a common misconception that wood must be "primed" with a special sealer before you apply a finish. The truth is that the first coat of any finish will serve as a "sealer." However, it's important that this first coat can be sanded easily to provide a smooth surface for subsequent finish coats. Because some finishes don't sand easily, they don't serve as a great seal coat. This is why manufacturers have developed special sealers that expedite the sanding process.

However, most varnishes and lacquers tend to gum up when you sand them. In these cases, using the appropriate sanding sealer for the first coat will speed up the job. Your finish manufacturer or dealer can recommend a sealer compatible with your finish.

Preventing Adhesion Problems

Adhesion problems can arise from chemical incompatibility between a finish and resins in the wood or between different finishing products. For example, the chemicals in aromatic red cedar will soften lacquers and varnishes. In other cases, oil-based paste wood fillers and glazes used between coats of water-based finish may not adhere properly. Mechanical adhesion can also be a problem with modern, high-solids conversion finishes that aren't thin enough to grab onto a well-sanded wood surface. In these cases, sealers are routinely used to promote adhesion.

Promoting Dry Time and Preventing Grain Raising

Fast-dry sealers can take the place of an initial coat of thinned polyurethane or varnish that would normally take a long time to dry hard enough for proper sanding. These fast-dry sealers allow for same-day application of the sealer and at least one top coat.

Grain raising can be a problem when using water-based finishes, which also don't penetrate wood very well. To solve these problems, many manufacturers offer a neutral-pH sealer that minimizes grain raising and increases penetration.

Preventing Stain Migration and Contamination

Stain migration occurs when the stain and finish share a similar thinner. In these circumstances, a sealer can prevent the stain color from migrating into the finish coats. This typically happens when water-based finishes are applied over water-soluble dye stains.

Contamination from wax, silicone, and spilled machine lubricant can result in "fisheye" on a finished surface. This is often encountered when you're refinishing furniture.

▶ See "Fixing Fisheye" on p. 197.

A barrier coat of sealer applied before the finish coats will usually prevent this.

Types of Sealers

Various types of sealers are available to suit your particular chosen finish and sealing requirements. If you're unsure of a sealer's compatibility with your finish, check with the finish manufacturer.

Sanding Sealer

A sanding sealer is simply a thinned version of a lacquer- or varnish-based finish that has been modified with zinc stearate or a resin (usually vinyl). These additives make the finish easier to sand and give it better "hold-out," which is the ability to make subsequent coats lay out smooth.

The downside of sanding sealers made with zinc stearate is that they decrease adhesion and are softer and less durable than the unmodified finish. Because of this, they should be used with discretion in situations where moisture resistance is an issue, as on

Fisheye shows up as craters randomly spaced throughout the finish. If the finish has dried, they're removed by sanding.

Sealers, from left, include oil-based fast-dry sanding sealers, shellac sealer in clear and pigmented forms, primer for paint, lacquer-based vinyl and stearated sanding sealer, glue size, and water-based sealer.

Though both are "fast-dry" varnish sealers, the one on the left includes zinc stearate (seen on the stick), making it unsuitable for use with polyurethane. The one at right has no zinc stearate and is suitable for polyurethane.

The zinc stearate additive in this lacquer-based sanding sealer makes it much easier to sand and provides a better base for subsequent lacquer coats.

kitchen and bath cabinets. And they should never be used to "build" a base. Ideally, they should be applied thinly, then sanded to leave only a thin layer behind.

Vinyl Sealer

Vinyl sealer is used in cases where finishes will react adversely to the zinc stearate in the sanding sealers discussed above. Polyurethane varnish, for example, will not bond to stearated sealer, nor will high-performance lacquers and varnishes.

Vinyl sealers provide excellent holdout and are very moisture-resistant. They also have excellent adhesion qualities to help "tie," or adhere, different finishing products together. In fact, professionals routinely use vinyl sealers when using oil-based glazes or paste wood fillers with solvent-based lacquers and conversion varnishes. Vinyl sealers will also stop the natural oils in woods like teak and rosewood from preventing oil-based finishes from curing.

Vinyl sealers are available only in commercial, fast-drying spray formulations, although it is possible to apply them by brush or rag if you work quickly. Vinyl sealers should not be confused with the

vinyl/alkyd-based varnishes sometimes sold as "one-step sealer/finishes." Unfortunately vinyl doesn't sand well, so vinyl sealers usually include other resins like nitrocellulose to make them sand better.

Shellac

Shellac is a natural resin that is commonly available and easy to apply. Of all the sealers, shellac is perhaps the most universal in its ability to prevent finishing problems. For the best results, only dewaxed shellac should be used in conjunction with water-based finishes and polyurethanes.

Shellac sands fairly well and provides good holdout for subsequent coats of finish. It prevents grain raising from water-based finishes and imbues their normally "cool" color with a warm, amber hue. And dewaxed shellac will keep water-based dye from migrating into a water-based finish coat.

Dewaxed shellac was applied to the left side of this dyed curly maple, after which a water-based lacquer was applied. The shellac prevented the water-based lacquer from pulling the dye up, resulting in a sharper, cleaner, and richer look than on the right side.

Natural oils in cocobolo impede curing of oil-based finishes. The left side was sealed with glue size before an oil varnish was applied. The unsized right side was still not dry after three weeks, as evidenced by the tissue paper stuck to the surface.

Shellac minimizes grain-raising, provides good holdout, and sharpens and warms up the grain of this walnut board. The pasty, plastic look at left is a common complaint about water-based finishes.

As a barrier coat, shellac can perform wonders. It will block off the natural oils in rosewoods and the chemicals in aromatic red cedar, which can stop the curing of oil-based top coats. Applying a coat of shellac over oil-based pore fillers or glazes will prevent potential adhesion problems with water-based top coats.

Of course shellac isn't perfect. It's a less durable finish than lacquer or varnish, and it is not very resistant to heat or alcohol. Because of this, it may not be appropriate in applications where durability and moisture resistance are important.

Glue Size

Glue size serves several purposes as a sealer. For one, it can be used to "lock down" wood grain—stiffening and strengthening the fibers to make them easier to sand. It can also be used to seal the extremely porous edges of medium density fiberboard (MDF). When you use oil-based finishes over rosewoods, glue size will block off the natural

oils in the wood, allowing proper curing of the finish.

In the past, finishers made their own glue size by thinning hide glue or polyvinyl acetate (PVA) glues with water. However, commercially prepared glue size is now sold based on a water-soluble resin called polyvinyl alcohol. My opinion is that it performs better than homemade versions. If you make your own size, try 10 parts water to 1 part PVA glue (the commonly available yellow or white wood glue).

Glue size is available as a concentrate that you mix with water to make a sealer for porous woods and MDF. A homemade version can be made by mixing 1 part PVA glue with 10 parts water.

Brushing Sealers

As the name implies, a "brushing sealer" is intended for hand application. This type of sanding sealer is a clear vinyl/alkyd and can be used with oil-based polyurethane or varnish. It should be used unthinned straight from the can. Using any kind of brush, apply the sealer to the wood with even strokes **(A)**. Let the sealer dry thoroughly before sanding. It's ready to dry when the sandpaper causes it to easily "powder up" like chalk.

I sand flat parts using 600-grit stearated sandpaper folded into thirds **(B)**. Using my hand as a backup pad, I scuff the surface lightly with the sandpaper, being careful not to round over any sharp edges. Wear a respirator as you would for any sanding application **(C)**. A hook-and-loop hand-sanding pad can be used with round disks. **(D)**. To avoid cutting through edges, use your index finger to back up the pad of sandpaper and keep it level **(E)**.

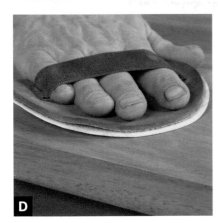

Spraying Sanding Sealer

If using a sanding sealer that includes zinc stearate, make sure you stir it well before application. Spray it on **(A)**, then let it dry at least one hour before sanding. To sand complicated forms like the piecrust tabletop shown here, I fold a quarter sheet of P-grade 600-grit sandpaper into thirds, and sand right up the raised molded edge **(B)**. To sand the molded profile itself, I use synthetic steel wool instead of sandpaper **(C)**. Wipe all the dust off completely, using naphtha or mineral spirits before applying more finish **(D)**.

Scuff-Sanding Complex Surfaces

To sand a complex surface like this frame-and-panel door, I use a cushioned interface pad mounted between a round hand-sanding pad and the sandpaper disk **(A)**. Use a piece of synthetic steel wool to smooth the molded edge **(B)** as well as the gentle cove of the raised panel **(C)**. If you happen to rub through the sealer and stain, touch up the affected area using your original stain. Alternatively, you can use shellac tinted with touchup powders **(D)**.

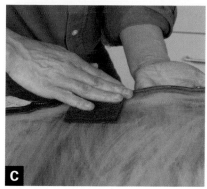

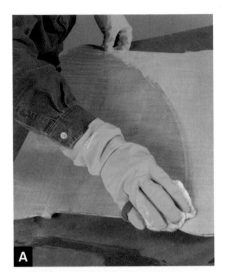

A

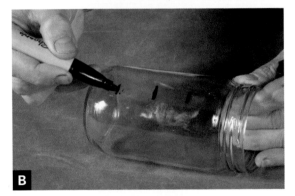

B

C

Making and Using One-Pound-Cut Shellac

Because it serves as such a good general-purpose sealer, 1-lb.-cut shellac is very popular in my shop. It solves a lot of finishing problems and is easily wiped on with an absorbent cloth **(A)**.

I go through so much of this stuff that I just mix it up quickly using the following method: Take any size clean glass jar and mark lines on it to divide into four equal parts **(B)**. Fill up the first quarter with dewaxed shellac flakes **(C)**. Then fill the rest of the jar with denatured alcohol and shake it every 10 minutes for about 2 hours.

Fixing Fisheye

If fisheye turns up when you're applying a finish, the best solution is to remove the finish before it sets up. This may work with slow-drying finishes like varnish or polyurethane, but other finishes may dry too fast for this approach, or you may risk removing an underlying stain in the process. And sometimes fisheye doesn't show up until after the finish has hardened. In these cases, you'll have to sand the fisheyes out after the finish has cured.

Using a piece of 400-grit sandpaper wrapped around a sanding block, sand the surface until the outlines of the fisheyes disappear **(A)**. Be careful not to sand through the finish to the stain or bare wood. If this is a danger, switch to an ultrafine synthetic steel wool pad that has a bit more deflection and cushion to it **(B)**. Afterward, remove the dust and selectively apply several coats of dewaxed shellac to the affected areas **(C)**. In minor cases, this will seal in the contamination that is causing the fisheye. However, if the problem is extensive, you may be better off adding a fisheye additive to your finish. Only several drops per cup are needed. If you don't have a small dropper, you can dispense drops off the end of a small wooden stir stick **(D)**.

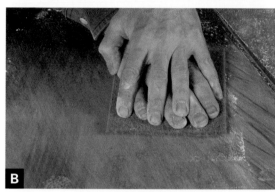

Choosing a Finish, page 200

Reactive Finishes, page 222

Evaporative Finishes, page 239

Water-Based Finishes, page 257

Rubbing Out Finishes, page 273

PART FIVE

Finishes

WOOD FINISHES SERVE two basic functions: protection and decoration. A finish protects wood by enveloping it in a continuous film to provide a barrier against damage and the fluctuations of humidity. A finish can also make wood deeper and richer looking by providing gloss, reflectance, and perhaps additional color.

As simple as it may seem, it can be difficult to choose an appropriate finish because products vary widely in durability, ease of application, and drying characteristics. In this part of the book, I'll discuss how to select the proper finish for a particular project and how to apply it. You'll learn which application techniques work best and how to rub out a finish to achieve spectacular results.

Choosing a Finish

Evaluating a Finish

Brushing Basics

Spraying

Special Situations

THERE IS SUCH A bewildering array of finishes available that it can be difficult to choose the right one for any particular project. Some finishes are attractive and easy to apply but perhaps don't offer the level of protection that a particular project warrants. Another finish might offer the durability you're looking for but may add an undesirable color. In some cases, you may not own the proper equipment needed for application.

In this section, I'll try to help you sort out these variables to arrive at a good choice. In the process, I'll delve into the composition of the basic types of finishes and how you can amend them to suit your application purposes. I'll also discuss common application techniques that apply to the various types of finishes.

Choosing a Finish

When it comes to choosing a finish, there are three primary considerations to take into account: durability, appearance, and method of application. Secondary considerations may include reparability, ease of rubbing out, or nontoxicity.

The first step is to determine how the piece will be used. Will it be subjected to a lot of moisture, solvents, or food? Is it likely to suffer abrasion and scrapes, or will it be primarily a display piece? This affects the level of durability you'll need from a finish.

Hard film-forming finishes like shellac bring out the brilliance and luster of the figured mahogany-and-satinwood top shown here. Underneath it is a quarter-sawn white oak top treated with a penetrating finish for a less sophisticated, natural look.

This dictionary stand received two sprayed coats of a flat lacquer, which provides the minimal protection it needs while maintaining a natural "in-the-wood" appearance.

The next important decision is how you want the finish to look. Do you want the "in-the-wood" appearance that a thin finish provides, or do you want a thicker finish that accentuates depth? And do you want the finish to add color to the wood, such as a yellow tone? Or do you want to minimize the chances of the wood changing color as it ages?

Do you have the right equipment to apply your chosen finish? And do you have a finish area that is clean, heated, and dry for properly doing the work? Is it equipped so you can safely spray flammable solvents?

The yellowing on the white stained sample at left comes from the alkyd base in the pickle stain and the nitrocellulose lacquer applied over it. The sample on right received a water-based acrylic stain topped with a nonyellowing CAB-acrylic lacquer.

EVAPORATIVE FINISHES

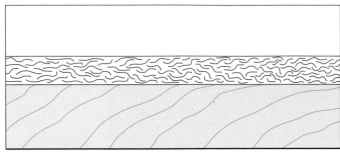

A

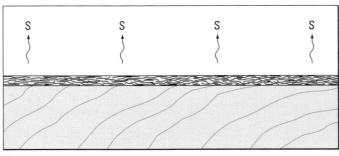

B

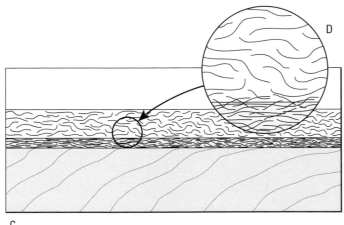

C

In wet form, evaporative finishes are composed of long, stringy strands of molecules separated by solvent (A). Think of cooked spaghetti (the polymer molecules) floating around in boiling water (the solvent). When the water is removed, the spaghetti packs down into a hardened mass. This is exactly what an evaporative finish does when the solvent evaporates (B). When you apply another coat of finish, the solvents in the new coat redissolve the packed-down strands (C), knitting the two coats together (D).

Determining the answers will help you target the best finish for the job. But before I discuss the appropriate finishes, it's important to understand the two basic categories of finishes: evaporative and reactive.

Evaporative and Reactive Finishes

All finishes fall into one of two types: *evaporative* and *reactive*. These classifications are based on how the liquid resin cures into a solid, protective finish and can tell you a great deal about what to expect from a particular finish.

Evaporative finishes are made by dissolving the finish resin in solvent. These finishes cure by evaporation of the solvents in the finish. Common evaporative finishes include shellac and nitrocellulose lacquer. Because the resin does not undergo any chemical change, these evaporative finishes are referred to as "nonconversion" finishes. They are also called "thermoplastic" finishes because they are softened by heat.

Reactive finishes cure as a result of the resin converting into a different chemical compound. A reactive cure is known as cross-linking or conversion curing, because the liquid resin reacts with something else to form a new chemical compound. Two examples of reactive finishes are oil-based varnish and catalyzed lacquer. Varnish cures automatically by exposure to the oxygen in the air, while catalyzed lacquer only cures when you add a catalyst. Once the resin molecules convert into the hardened finish, they are no longer soluble in their original solvent, nor are they easily softened by heat.

Durability

The durability of a finish refers to its resistance to scratches, marring, heat, and damage from liquids. Durability is a prime consideration when you're choosing a finish. If you're looking for greater durability, a reactive finish is a better choice than an evaporative finish.

Evaporative finishes are less durable overall than reactive finishes because their resins can be softened or remelted by heat or certain solvents. This feature is good if you want to repair the finish later or rub it out, but the downside is that the finish scratches easily. Of the evaporative finishes, nitrocellulose lacquers and the acrylics fare the best for overall durability.

Evaporative finishes will redissolve in their original solvent, making repairs at a later date easier. Lacquer thinner brushed onto this scratched lacquer finish instantly removes the white scratches on this guitar.

REACTIVE FINISHES

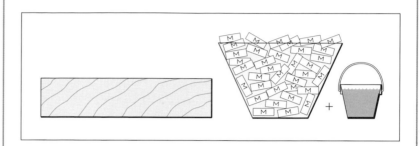

A

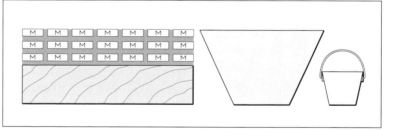

B

C

Reactive finishes consist of large molecules formed from smaller ones through the process of polymerization. Think of a bucket filled with individual bricks mixed with the mortar components of lime, clay, and sand (A). The bricks represent the one-part finish monomers. The mortar components represent the individual chemicals in the finish. Just as adding water to the mortar components creates a cement to hold the bricks together, adding catalyst to the finish chemicals creates a multipart polymer finish (B). The dried mortar is like the chemical cross-links formed. When a new row of bricks (another coat of finish) is applied, it doesn't re-dissolve the previous row, it simply sticks to it (C).

This stool requires scratch resistance, so it was finished with polyurethane. It's also wise to use a very hard wood, such as the elm shown here.

Except for the pure oils, reactive finishes are much more durable than evaporative finishes. Because the resin molecules are more tightly cross-linked, water cannot permeate the finish easily. They are also more solvent-resistant than evaporative finishes. Oil-based polyurethane is the most durable finish that you can apply by hand, while catalyzed lacquers, varnishes, urethanes, and polyester are the best for spray application. While there are exceptions, reactive finishes are generally harder to rub out and repair than evaporative ones.

Appearance

The three primary contributors to the appearance of a finish are its film-forming qualities, its color, and its depth of penetration into the wood. The main decision you'll need to make is whether you want the kind of natural, "in-the-wood" finish look provided by a penetrating, nonfilm-forming finish, or the hard, clear, protective "lens" of a film-forming finish.

For a natural finish, woodworkers have long used true oils like tung oil and linseed oil, wax, or oil-varnish blends (like Watco™). These nonglossy penetrating finishes harden within the wood, imparting a nice low luster to the surface. However, since they don't form a hard, solid film on the surface, they offer limited protection against abrasion and liquids.

If you want durability and the deep, lustrous look of a filled-pore finish, you'll need to use a hard, film-forming finish like shellac, lacquer, or varnish. These are the finishes used in conjunction with complex coloring options like toning and glazing. A point to consider is that as long as you don't build up the finish beyond several coats, shellac, lacquer, varnishes, and catalyzed finishes can all be used for natural-looking finishes and will provide better protection than pure oil.

The color of a finish is also a consideration. Some finishes significantly deepen or darken the wood surface, increasing both depth and luster. Oils and oil-based varnishes do this the most, followed by solvent-based lacquers and shellac. On the other hand, most water-based polyurethane or acrylic finishes, as well as some catalyzed finishes, have a minimal effect on the natural color of the wood because they're optically clear and tend to lay on the surface without penetrating deeply.

Dark finishes like orange shellac or tung oil/phenolic resin varnish may be too dark

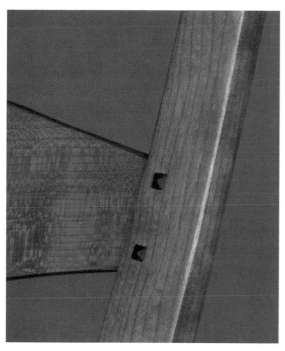

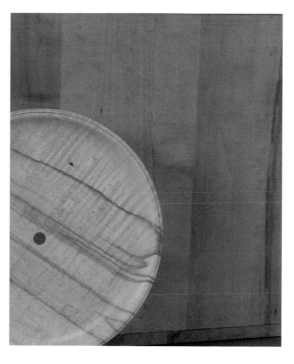

A nonyellowing acrylic water-based finish was applied to the plate on the left to prevent yellowing. A phenolic resin/tung oil wiping varnish was applied to the maple storage box behind it, imparting a yellow hue.

The wiping varnish on this cherry chair by Brian Boggs provides the luster and sheen necessary to bring out the delicate ray fleck of the cherry. It provides durability with a thin coat, displaying the chair's carefully handcrafted tenon pegs and carved facets.

for woods you want to keep as light as possible. Some finishes can impart a yellow hue when applied over white-painted finishes.

Application Safety and Environmental Concerns

Solvent-baZsed finishes like varnish and lacquer contain flammable and toxic solvents. Water-based finishes eliminate the danger of fire during application and mitigate the environmental and health impact. True oils are an alternative to solvent-based lacquers and varnish, as they are 100 percent solids with no solvents and come from renewable resources. Shellac is also a safe finish to apply because its solvent is ethyl alcohol, which is distilled from corn. It isn't particularly toxic nor are its fumes unpleasant.

Ingestion of finishes used for food preparation surfaces or for infant furniture used to be a serious concern before lead was banned

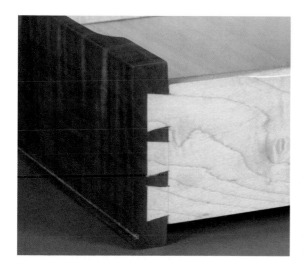

Boiled linseed oil was applied to this drawer to contrast the cherry and maple and to make the figure "pop." The oil was then topped with a nitrocellulose finish for more durability.

Beeswax, shellac, or mineral oil can all be used as food-grade, edible finishes. You can mix the beeswax shavings with the mineral oil by heating them both in a double boiler.

from paint in the 1970s. However, these days, consumer-brand clear finishes are non-toxic when *fully* cured. All the same, when a finish is to be used for toys or in other cases where it may be ingested, it's wise to consult the finish supplier or manufacturer. The only totally safe edible finishes I'm aware of are food-grade wax, pure natural oils, mineral oil, and shellac.

If your finishing environment is cold or dusty, fast-drying evaporative finishes and spray-applied reactive finishes like catalyzed lacquer are engineered to dry dust-free in minutes. Evaporative finishes like shellac and lacquer are the least temperamental in cold temperatures and can be easily modified by adding retarder in hot and humid conditions.

Resins, Solvents, and Additives

Most clear finishes consist of a resin, solvent, and additives. The resin provides the finish's protective and decorative qualities. Solvents adjust the viscosity so the resin can penetrate and adhere to the wood. Solvents also help control flow-out and leveling and make application with various tools possible. Additives adjust viscosity and determine the satin or matte appearance of a finish. Some additives promote curing or extend the life of the finish—both in the can and after it's applied.

Resins

Rather than choosing a finish based solely on whether it's a varnish or lacquer or some other marketing mumbo-jumbo, it's better to pick it by resin. Below are current resins used in wood-finishing products, although a finish may contain several resin types.

Acrylic resins feature good adhesion, hardness, light stability (most don't yellow), and good rubbing qualities. These resins can be reactive or evaporative.

Alkyd resins offer toughness, adhesion, and flexibility. Alkyds wind up in many finishing products including varnishes, lacquers, conversion finishes, and water-based finishes.

Amino resins are extremely tough but too brittle to be used alone, so they're combined with alkyds and other resins to make conversion lacquers and varnishes.

Shellac has excellent adhesion and rubbing qualities, although it can be damaged by heat and doesn't offer great solvent resistance.

The finish on the right is a typical consumer-brand polyurethane, an aromatic soya oil uralkyd. The two cans on the left are the components required for an exterior-rated, nonyellowing aliphatic polyurethane.

Tung oil is lighter in color than linseed oil. Both can be used to create natural-looking "in-the-wood" finishes like those shown on the wood underneath.

Phenolic resin is a hard, brittle compound that is typically combined with tung oil to make varnishes. It has very good exterior durability and is the base for many exterior varnishes.

Urethane is a tough synthetic resin that provides excellent resistance to solvents, heat, and abrasion. There are two distinctly different versions. One is prone to yellowing and suited only to interior applications. The other is a nonyellowing, exterior-rated urethane.

Cellulose is a synthetic resin made from the cellulose in cotton or wood. There are two types used in finishing products: nitrocellulose and cellulose acetate-butyrate (CAB). Both are brittle, hard, and fast-drying. Nitrocellulose is prone to yellowing, while CAB lacquers yellow less.

Vinyl is a general term used to describe a wide class of resins used as sealers or as resins in latex paint and some conversion varnishes. They provide excellent adhesion and flexibility. When used in top-coat finishes, they're combined with other resins.

Linseed and tung oil are the two main drying oils used in finishing. These oils form the backbone of many other finishing materials like stains, sealers, and finishes.

Polyester comes in two- or three-component finishes that are mixed before application. This resin creates a very hard, tough finish that can be built up thickly without cracking or checking.

[TIP] There's some confusion between the terms "solvent" and "thinner." A solvent is a liquid that dissolves or breaks up the resin in a finish, reducing it to a liquid state, while a thinner is simply a compatible diluent liquid that reduces the viscosity of paint or varnish but is not a solvent for the resin.

Solvents and Thinners

The types of solvents that are used in finishes and finishing products can be divided into groups or "families" that share common chemical characteristics. It's important to have at least a basic working knowledge of

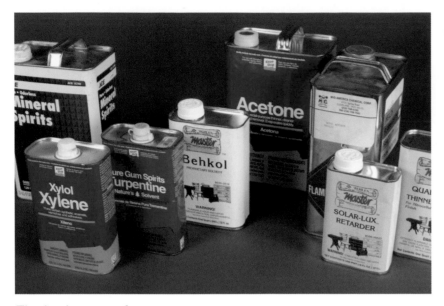

The basic types of solvents used in all finishing products are (from left) mineral sprits and xylene (hydrocarbons), terpenes (gum spirits turpentine), alcohol (denatured ethanol), ketone (acetone), esters, (butyl acetate), glycol ether (lacquer and stain retarder), and lacquer thinner (a blend of solvents).

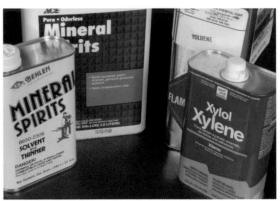

Hydrocarbons are divided into aliphatic and aromatic groups. Mineral spirits can be either "normal" or odorless. Odorless mineral spirits evaporate more slowly. Xylene and toluene evaporate much faster.

how different solvents interact with the resins in finishes.

Water dissolves dyes and many resins (such as gum arabic), but these aren't used as finishes because they're water-soluble. Water is used only as a thinner, and any finish can be commercially formulated as water-thinnable.

Hydrocarbons such as kerosene, mineral spirits, naphtha, paint thinner, toluene, and xylene serve as both solvents and thinners. They are separated into two classes: aliphatic and aromatic. Aliphatic is slower-evaporating and oilier, while aromatics evaporate faster.

Terpenes (turpentine and d-limonene) are derived from plants: turpentine from pine trees and d-limonene from citrus trees. These solvents are almost 100 percent interchangeable with the hydrocarbons listed above and are preferred by those who have adverse reactions (mostly odor-related) to petroleum-based hydrocarbons.

Denatured and methanol alcohol dissolve most natural plant and animal resins, like

shellac, as well as some synthetic resins. They also dissolve dyes. They're widely used in conjunction with other solvents for thinning synthetic finishes like lacquer.

Ketones like acetone and methyl ethyl ketone are solvents for lacquer resins and some conversion finishes, like catalyzed lacquer and polyester.

Glycol ethers are unique in that they will dissolve many natural and synthetic resins and readily mix with water. Their wide compatibility with many solvents and resins allows formulations of water-based finishes. They evaporate slowly and are used as retarder for fast-drying finishes.

Additives

Manufacturers use a variety of additives in finishes to suit a whole range of purposes. Some make a finish more viscous; some accelerate the curing; others make it less glossy or prevent the finish from forming a skin in the can. Some improve flow-out and leveling and some prevent bacteria and mold. Although you have no control over

Commonly available finish additives include (from left) retarder (solvent and water base), Japan drier, universal UVA additive, flatting agents, and fish-eye additive.

what the manufacturer puts in the can, there are a few common additives available to finishers to help solve particular problems.

Retarders are used to slow down the evaporation of certain solvents to prevent problems like blushing or poor flow-out and leveling. Common retarders include glycol ethers, as well as slow-evaporating ketones, hydrocarbons, and alcohols.

Japan drier will accelerate the cure of oil-based finishes in cold weather.

Ultraviolet light stabilizers are divided into two classes: ultraviolet light absorbers (UVAs) and hindered amine light stabilizers (HALs). The former protect stained or bare wood from fading or changing color, while HALs protect resins from deteriorating from UV exposure.

Flow-out additives solve the problem of "fisheye" and other incompatibility issues between the finish and the wood surface, often caused by silicone contamination.

Flatting agents are used to decrease the sheen of a finish. Although you can add these to a finish, it's best to simply purchase finish that's already formulated for your desired sheen, such as flat, semigloss, or satin.

[TIP] **Paint is simply a clear finish that includes enough pigment to hide the wood's grain. Because white is the most opaque and fade resistant of all the pigments, most consumer paints include it.**

Testing a Finish

If you're unsure of the particular qualities of your chosen finish, it's always wise to test it on scrap. The three primary issues of concern are adhesion, hardness, and water- and solvent resistance.

When you're applying a finish over stains, glazes, or other finishes, good adhesion is important. If you're unsure as to the compatibility of the various products, you can perform a simple adhesion test.

▶ See *"Testing for Adhesion"* on p. 213.

To test the hardness of a finish, wait until it has cured, then try to make an indentation in it using your thumbnail. Alternatively, use a ballpoint pen to write on a piece of paper placed over the finish, then check for writing impressions in the finish.

To check the fully cured finish for water and solvent resistance, place 10 drops of water, alcohol, household cleaner, or other solvents on the surface, then cover the drops with a small dish. Wait several hours, then wipe off the solvents and check for damage.

This varnished surface passed all the solvent resistance tests except from lacquer thinner, which left a visible mark after several hours.

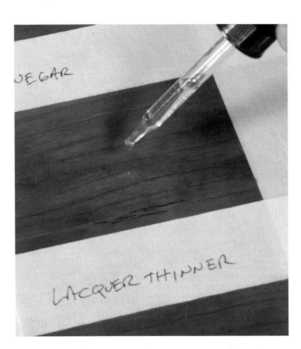

Straining the finish is the first step for a quality finish. A metal strainer stand can be purchased from safety and lab suppliers. When pouring from a full can, tip it slightly and let the finish run down the side.

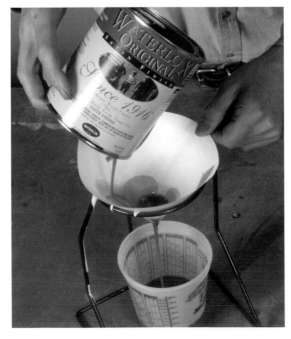

The Basics of Applying Finishes

In the remaining sections of this book, I'll discuss the best ways to apply particular finishes. However, here I'll address some basic guidelines that pertain to applying nearly all finishes.

Preparing a Finish

Instead of working directly from the finish can, it's a good idea to strain all finishes before application and dispense them into smaller containers. Thinning a finish for application is more accurately done using a viscosity cup, which is a small cup with a precisely machined hole in the bottom. To measure for proper viscosity, you time how long it takes a specific finish to drain from a specific cup (such as 16 seconds in a Ford no. 4 cup). Viscosity ratings are typically provided for various industrial coatings.

Applying Multiple Coats

With pure oil finishes and most oil/varnish blends, you can only apply a maximum number of coats before you're just wiping off what you apply. Film-forming finishes all have a minimum number of coats that should be applied for durability. Low-solids evaporative finishes like shellac and lacquer require four or five coats. With high-solids finishes like varnish, apply at least two coats.

The solids content of a finish may be listed on the can or the technical sheet. There are two references. One notes solids content by weight and the other lists solids content by volume. The volume measurement is what's most important to the finisher as you can calculate the *dry-mil* thickness from the

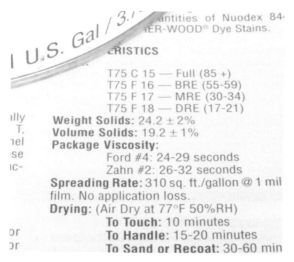

CRISTICS

...antities of Nuodex 84-
...ER-WOOD® Dye Stains.

```
              T75 C 15 — Full (85 +)
              T75 F 16 — BRE (55-59)
              T75 F 17 — MRE (30-34)
              T75 F 18 — DRE (17-21)
lly   Weight Solids: 24.2 ± 2%
T,    Volume Solids: 19.2 ± 1%
ıel   Package Viscosity:
se            Ford #4: 24-29 seconds
ıc-           Zahn #2: 26-32 seconds
      Spreading Rate: 310 sq. ft./gallon @ 1 mil
      film. No application loss.
      Drying: (Air Dry at 77°F 50%RH)
              To Touch: 10 minutes
or            To Handle: 15-20 minutes
or            To Sand or Recoat: 30-60 min
```

To calculate dry-mil thickness, you need to know the volume of the finish's solids content. If it's not listed on the can or the technical data sheet, consult the manufacturer.

wet-mil thickness. Wet-film thickness can be measured with a simple tool.

> See *"Measuring Finish Thickness"* on p. 214.

For example, if the solids content by volume is 35 percent, you'll know that three 2-mil thick wet coats will result in a dry-mil thickness of 2.1 mil (3 x 2 x .35).

Finish Sheen

Many finishes are available in various sheens, including gloss, satin, and flat. If you plan to apply more than three coats of finish on a dark wood, it's advisable to use gloss for the base coats to "build" the finish, then apply satin as the last coat. This prevents the cloudy look that sometimes results from multiple coats of a satin or flat finish. When working with nongloss finishes like semi-

gloss, satin, and flat, stir the product well to disperse the flatting agent. I use flat stir sticks because they'll scrape the flatting agent off the bottom of the can to redisperse it.

Finishing Insides

Never apply any finish made with a drying oil to the insides of drawers, chests, or armoires where food or clothes will be stored. This includes all oils, varnishes, modified oils, and oil/varnish blends. The smell of the product seems to linger forever. It's better to use shellac or lacquer. Reactive two-component finishes are also fine.

Finishing Resinous Hardwoods

Rosewood, cocobolo, and many rosewood substitutes contain natural oils that impede the ability of oxygen to enter the oil and begin the curing process. Avoid applying any drying oil products directly to the wood. If you wish to apply a varnish, seal the bare wood first with shellac or vinyl sealer.

Satin, semi-gloos, and flat sheen finishes should be stirred thoroughly to disperse the flatting agent. Use the flat edge of a paint stick to scrape the agent off the bottom of the can.

Sanding Between Coats

Sanding between coats removes blemishes, smoothes the surface, and improves intercoat adhesion of finishes. It generally isn't required unless directed by the manufacturer, provided the finishes are applied within four to six hours of each other and the prior coat is clean. Reactive finishes need a certain amount of drying time before sanding is mandatory. (Check the product label.) Because most evaporative finishes remelt the prior coat, sanding between coats is only done to correct defects, which can typically be sanded out using 240- or 320-grit sandpaper. Sanding reactive finishes requires using finer grits like 400 to avoid visible sanding scratches. If you're not sure, 400- or 600-grit sandpaper is always a safe bet for sanding a finish. When sanding complicated profiles, use a cushioned abrasive.

Finishing Parts

Dismantle large items as much as you can. Finish backs and drawer bottoms separately whenever possible. If you have a complicated project with a lot of slats, for example, consider finishing the various parts before assembly. You can dip small parts or attach them to a strip of wood for brushing. If you spray small parts, build a screen box or stabilize them by taping them to a piece of plywood.

Finishing Both Sides

It's always a good idea to finish both sides of parts at the same time.

▶ See *"Finishing Both Sides"* on p. 220.

Spraying small wooden knobs on a screen box constructed with ½-in. wire mesh allows the air pressure to pass through so the parts don't blow around.

To retain the crispness of carvings, such as on this ball-and-claw mahogany foot, the author applied two light coats of shellac with an artist's brush, followed by a gentle rubbing with 0000 steel wool.

This speeds things up and protects against warping in very low or very high humidity.

Finishing Carvings

To maintain the crispness of carvings, apply as little finish as possible and avoid sanding between coats if you can help it. Spraying is generally the best application technique. I personally like the look of low-solids lacquer or shellac on carvings.

Testing for Adhesion

If you're unsure of the adhesion properties of a finish or combination of finish products, test them on scrap first. After the test finish has cured at least four days, put a new blade in an X-Acto™ knife and cut a series of 2-in.-long cuts ⅛ in. apart. Cut all the way through the finish into the wood, then make another series of cuts at a 90-degree angle **(A)**. With your finger, lightly brush the surface to remove any detached flakes or cutting debris. Unroll enough clear packing tape to get to fresh tape, then cut off a 6-in. to 8-in.-long piece and place it over the crosshatches. Press it down firmly with the tip of your finger **(B)** or a pencil eraser. Grab one end of the tape and pull it off in a steady motion at a 180-degree angle backwards upon itself.

Examine the crosshatch area for detached flakes. Up to 20 percent pull-up represents acceptable adhesion, while anything over that is considered fair to poor. This walnut test panel—which was finished with a water-based lacquer applied over a boiled linseed oil sealer—passes with flying colors **(C)**. The lighter maple panel did not pass **(D)**.

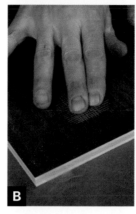

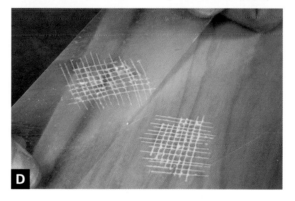

Measuring Finish Thickness

Finish manufacturers may not want you to exceed a wet-film thickness in a single application. Others may specify a certain dry-mil thickness to ensure adequate performance. To calculate any of these, you need to know how to use a simple tool called a mil gauge. A mil gauge is a piece of stamped metal with "teeth" in mil (one-thousandths-of-an-in.) increments. To use the gauge, first spray or hand apply your coating onto a test piece just as you would your project **(A)**. Press the gauge down into the wet finish at a 90-degree angle **(B)**. Withdraw the gauge and note the first tooth that isn't coated with finish and the one next to it that is coated. (For purposes of clarity in the photo, I've dragged the gauge across the coating to demonstrate that the 6-mil tooth doesn't make a mark in the film while the 5-mil tooth does.) **(C)**. This shows that this coating measures 5 mils thick.

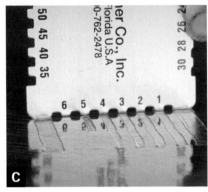

Checking Viscosity

To check the thickness of a liquid finish in preparation for application, you can buy a viscosity cup for less than $10 from many spray-gun suppliers.

Before checking the viscosity, make sure the finish is at 70° F., as viscosity is affected by temperature. Begin by submerging the cup completely in the finish **(A)**. Now lift it 6 in. from the finish **(B)** and begin timing from the moment the top rim of the cup breaks the surface of the finish to the moment the first break appears in the fluid stream **(C)**.

The number of seconds you count represents the viscosity. If your cup is different from the one referenced by the finish supplier, conversion tables are available. Clean the cup well with a small brush, as residue in the orifice can give you a false reading.

Preparing the Brush

Brushing problems, such as debris in the finish and loose hairs, can be avoided by preparing the brush before you use it. The best preventive maintenance starts with storing brushes in drawers to protect them from sawdust and other airborne particles **(A)**. Before you use a brush, flick the bristle ends back and forth to displace dust **(B)**. Remove any loose hairs if they're visible. Dunk the brush all the way up to the metal ferrule in the solvent used for thinning and cleaning the finish. Scrape the excess solvent off the brush by dragging it across the lip of the container, and then blot up the excess with a clean, dry cotton rag **(C)**. This solvent dip conditions the bristles, makes the initial coats go on more smoothly, and makes the brush easier to clean later.

The Basic Brushstroke

The basic brushstroke for tops or other flat, horizontal surfaces allows you to flow on a finish. Condition the bristles of the brush as described in the preceding essay, then dip the bristles to about half of their total length into a container filled with the finish. Gently squeeze off the excess against the sides of the container **(A)**. Starting about 3 in. in from the edge **(B)**, pull the brush lightly toward the edge and lift up at the end **(C)**.

Come back to where you started, and brush to the opposite end to complete the pass **(D)**. Duplicate the procedure, overlapping your strokes from ¼ in. to ½ in. to complete **(E)**. Try to work quickly to allow yourself enough time to "tip off" the finish afterward. This is done by holding the brush perpendicular to the board and lightly dragging it across the surface. Varnishes allow you a good deal of open time to come back and tip off, while fast-drying lacquers and shellac make it more difficult.

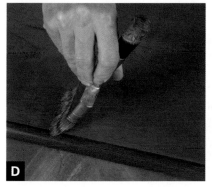

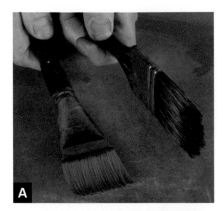

Brushing Shellac and Lacquer

To lay down fast-drying finishes like lacquer and shellac, I like to use a technique that deposits a thinner, more quickly drying coat. When applying shellac, I use a 1-lb.-cut mixture. For lacquer, I use brushing lacquer thinned one-to-one with lacquer thinner. The best brushes for this technique are artist's brushes that don't have much bristle content, so they hold less finish **(A)**. This means a smaller chance of depositing thicker amounts of finish when you start your brushstroke. Rather than flowing on a coat the width of the brush, you can work sections at a time.

Working a 4-in-by-4-in. section, begin near an edge and drag the brush off the edge of the workpiece **(B)**. Reload the brush, and work another section and then whisk back and forth quickly between the two sections to blend them together. These brushes are well suited to complicated or small areas, as you can flick whisper-thin layers of shellac or lacquer onto edges **(C)**. When brushing round or turned items, you can use a light "flicking" stroke in a round-and-round fashion to prevent drips **(D)**.

Spraying Flat Surfaces

The basic spray technique for tops and other flat surfaces is called a crosshatch, box-coat, or double-pass spray. Spray all four edges first, holding the gun perpendicular to the edge, then bring the gun up to a 45-degree angle to the surface, and spray once to get extra finish on top of the edges **(A)**. Working at a 90-degree angle to grain, start your first pass at the edge closest to you. With the gun off the edge, pull the trigger so finish is coming out before it hits the edge **(B)**. and move it across the surface, holding it perpendicular to the top and at the correct distance. (Your gun manual should provide guidelines.) Keep the trigger depressed until after you've passed the opposite edge of the workpiece, and then repeat the pass, overlapping the first one by half **(C)**. Continue until you reach the end, then rotate the workpiece 90 degrees and repeat **(D)**. (It helps to work on a turntable.) Crosshatching ensures even coverage of finish.

[TIP] **You can wipe away a drip immediately with your finger as long as you don't risk damaging a delicate toner or glaze underneath. Respray the affected area afterward.**

A

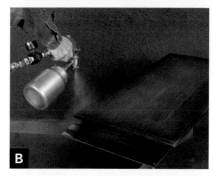

B

C

D

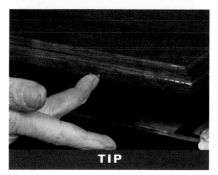

TIP

Spraying Complicated Items

Spraying complicated, three-dimensional projects like chairs requires that you work from the least visible parts first to the most visible. For a chair, turn it over to have better access to the stretchers, and then begin by spraying the bottom of the seat **(A)**. Don't forget the bottom of the crest rail or similar unseen areas that need finish **(B)**. Spray the back and crest, and the edges of the seat, but leave the top of the seat for last. To get finish into the top back of the seat where the spindles are connected, come in from the front of the seat and spray right through the spindles **(C)**. Then quickly rotate the chair 180 degrees by spinning your turntable, and spray the back of the seat top **(D)**.

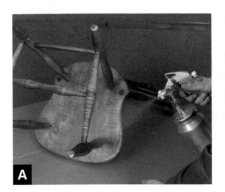

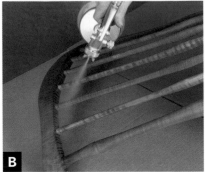

Spraying Vertical Surfaces

To efficiently spray a large vertical side like the one on this entertainment center, it helps to use a remote pressure-feed spray rig. Start at the bottom of one side and spray upward **(A)**. With a pressure-feed rig, just orient the gun 90 degrees to the side, which will lay down a horizontal pattern. If you use a gravity-feed or suction gun, you can turn the air cap to orient the pattern horizontally. Overlap each previous pass by half, as when spraying horizontal surfaces **(B)**, but make only a single pass to avoid drips. Placing items on a turntable allows you to easily spin them to spray both sides. For face frames, start from the bottom and work up. If possible, adjust the width of the gun's fan pattern to match the width of the frame members **(C)**.

Spraying Cabinet Interiors

To make a large piece like this maple entertainment center more manageable, separate the top and bottom sections and take off the back. Work from the back, spraying each of the four interior sides separately.

Start by "cutting in" all four edges of each side, doing the top first, then coming down the back of the face frame **(A)**. Note how the gun is held vertically so the spray pattern is vertical. When spraying the bottom, reorient the spray gun **(B)**. Finally, spray the center of the panel **(C)**. Do the top and two sides, but leave the bottom for last so overspray doesn't settle there and create a rough finish **(D)**. Spray toward the filters at the back of the booth. This draws the overspray away from the piece. Orienting a floor fan behind you would accomplish the same thing if you're working outdoors.

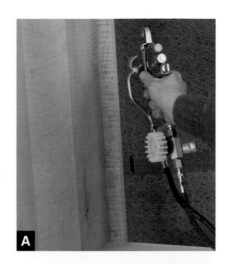

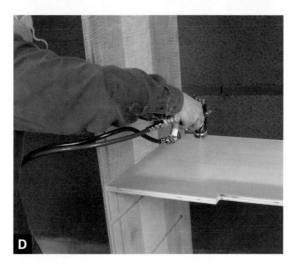

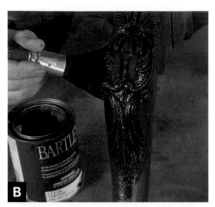

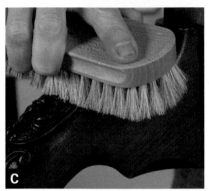

Finishing Carvings

Carvings require special attention in finishing. When I finish by hand, my favorite technique consists of applying a shellac sealer followed by gel varnish.

Seal the carving by brushing on a coat of 1-lb.-cut shellac with a small artist's brush **(A)**. After it dries, lightly smooth it with gray, ultrafine synthetic steel wool. Remove the dust, and then apply some satin gel varnish, using a stiff bristle brush to work it into the carvings **(B)**. Before it sets up, use a shoe-shine brush to remove the excess gel from the recesses. Wipe the varnish off the brush, then use it again, just as if you're shining your shoes, to burnish the surface to a soft satiny finish **(C)**.

[**VARIATION**] Use aerosol spray lacquer in flat or stain instead of gel varnish after sealing with shellac.

Finishing Both Sides

Solid wood tops, doors, and other surfaces that aren't rigidly held in place should be finished on both sides. This prevents the possibility of warping and cupping during an abrupt change in humidity. When spraying a top, place it on two lengths of pipe insulation, with iron pipe inserted to weigh them down and keep them in place. Place the pipes between the screws for your nail board, making sure the screw tips sit at least an inch below the insulation. Place the show side down on the insulation-covered pipe to support the top **(A)**, and then spray the bottom **(B)**. Don't spray the edges, so you have something unfinished to grab onto to flip it over **(C)**. After flipping it over, spray the show.

Brushing a Frame-and-Panel Assembly

When finishing frame-and-panel assemblies, use a nail board. This not only speeds up the process but prevents drips from a brushed finish from crawling around to the other side. Start by applying finish to the back side of the panel but don't do the edges yet (A). Then lift the door by the edges and flip it over on the nail board (B). For this frame-and-panel door, I generally use a small brush with no divider (like an artist's brush) to apply the varnish, since it holds less finish and is less likely to "pool" the finish in the crevices where you start your stroke. Finish up the rails and stiles and center panel, then do the edges (C). After removing excess finish from the brush with a dry rag, pull out any pooled finish from the crevices.

Prefinishing

"Prefinishing" before gluing up prevents glue squeeze-out, allows access to otherwise tight areas, and prevents finish from pooling in crevices and corners. This little cherry pipe box was finished after all glue-bearing surfaces were taped off with blue painter's tape. Mark a line for the tape by dry-fitting the pieces, then marking the joint edge with an awl (A). Also, mask off dadoes with the same tape (B).

After applying shellac finish, remove the tape and glue up the project. The glue won't stick to the shellacked surfaces, so you can easily wipe it clean (C). Alternatively, you can let the glue dry just enough so it will peel off, but don't let it dry completely, as it becomes hard to remove.

[**VARIATION**] **For mortise-and-tenon joinery, apply tape to the tenons and stuff the mortises with paper towel before prefinishing.**

VARIATION

Reactive Finishes

Oils and Varnishes

Conversion Finishes

Paint

REACTIVE FINISHES ARE THOSE that cure by reacting with another component—either oxygen in the air or a catalyst added to the finish before application. These finishes include oils, varnishes, and conversion finishes. In this section, we'll look at these finishes in more detail and how to use and troubleshoot them. I group these finishes into the categories of true oils, heat-modified oils, varnishes, and conversion finishes.

True Oils

Various natural oils are used in finishing products, including linseed oil, tung oil, soya and safflower oils, and coconut oil. Linseed oil comes from the flax plant, while tung oil comes from the nuts of the tung tree, originally indigenous to the Far East, but now cultivated in South America as well as the United States. Semidrying oils like soya and safflower oils and nondrying oils like coconut oil serve as components in varnishes and other finishes. Of all these products, linseed oil and tung oil find the most widespread use as finishes.

Drying oils like tung oil and linseed oil convert from a liquid to a rubbery solid by combining with oxygen from the air in a process called auto-oxidative polymerization. Without getting too technical, this means that when the oil is applied in a thin film, oxygen enters the oil molecule automatically, causing larger molecules to form. This

Linseed oil and tung oil represent the most common oil finishes. Of the two, tung oil (at right) is lighter in color, yellows less over time, and offers better water resistance.

chemical reaction knits the molecules together in a process called "cross-linking."

Neither of these two oils dries hard enough to form a suitable film finish on wood. What they do is penetrate the structure of the wood cells, encasing the cells in a rubbery solid that deepens color and enhances figure. However, as long as the wood is cared for and not subjected to prolonged contact with water, chemicals, or stains, these oils will create an attractive, natural-looking, easily applied finish. While raw tung oil is still widely used by finishers, raw linseed oil has fallen into disuse due to its long drying time.

Boiled and Polymerized Oils

If raw linseed oil is heated and then allowed to cool to room temperature, the oil dries faster. This heat-treated product used to be called "boiled" linseed oil. However, the stuff you buy under that name today isn't really boiled. Instead, chemical driers have been

POLYMERIZED OIL FINISHES

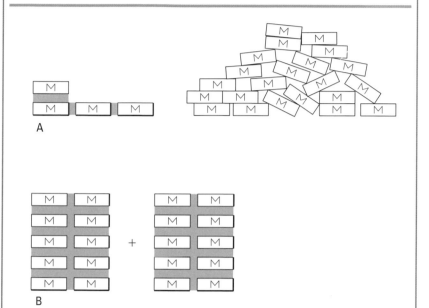

To return to our brick wall analogy from Section 13, when raw tung or linseed oil dries at ambient air temperature, it's like slowly building a wall, one brick at a time, from a large pile of bricks (A). However, heat-treating the oil pre-polymerizes it, creating larger "prefabricated" units (polymers), which can build the same size wall faster and with less cement (cross-links) (B).

added to promote faster drying. Polymerized linseed oil isn't typically marketed as a finishing product under that name, though it undoubtedly shows up in other finishes, like Danish oil.

Polymerized tung oil is produced under controlled heating conditions, resulting in a durable product that cures quickly. Because heat treating makes the oil much thicker than raw oil, thinner is typically added.

Oil Finish Basics

The purpose of oil finishes is to create a "close-to-the-wood" natural-looking finish. Oils deepen the color of wood and accen-

The more coats of oil you apply, the deeper the look and the more the figure is enhanced. The left side of this figured maple received seven coats of boiled linseed oil, while the right got only two.

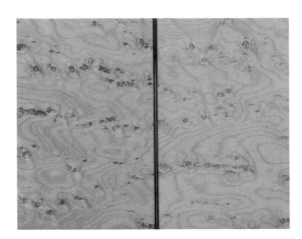

Varnishes are one of the most popular finishes for consumer use. They're available in a wide variety of formulations and consistencies, including thin wipe-on products and thick pastes called gel varnishes.

▶ OIL OR VARNISH?

The basic difference between oil and varnish is that oil will dry to be

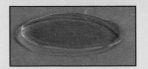 

soft, wrinkly, and gummy if applied thickly or built up as a "film" finish. For this reason it's classified as a "penetrating" finish. However, if oil is cooked with very hard natural or synthetic resins, a harder, glossier, more durable product is formed. Varnishes are film-forming finishes. The above photos show the difference between a varnish (right) and pure oil (left) when both are applied to a piece of glass.

tuate figure. Unfortunately, oil finishes don't provide much protection against liquids or abrasion. On the other hand, they're easy to repair and maintain. If the surface starts looking dull or gets scratched or banged up, simply apply more oil to it.

Oils can be applied before harder finishes like shellac and lacquer to seal the wood and to make the figure and grain "pop." The harder top coat offers the necessary resistance to scratches, liquids, and heat. Oil finishes are not the best choice over stained or glazed wood, as the oil doesn't provide a hard enough finish to protect the color. It particularly doesn't protect well against rubbing or scratching on chair arms, drawer fronts, or other areas that come in frequent contact with hands.

It's best to apply oil in thin coats so it will dry properly, especially in cold weather, which extends the cure time. Tung oil will frost, or form a whitish-looking finish, if applied too thickly. Although linseed oil has a light amber color when applied, it will yellow after a year or so. This is rarely a problem on dark woods, but on light woods like maple or birch, it can lead to an unattractive yellow color. Tung oil yellows less.

Caution: Oil-soaked rags pose a serious fire danger due to the risk of spontaneous combustion. Dispose of all rags properly, as discussed on page 20.

Varnish

A wide variety of varnishes are available to finishers today. Most modern varnishes are made using alkyd phenolic and urethane resins combined with various oils. The main difference between oil finishes and varnishes is that a varnish will dry to a hard, glossy film, while oil will not. (See the sidebar on the facing page.)

Originally, varnish was made by "cooking" natural and fossilized resins like amber, copal, or sandarac with a drying oil like linseed oil. These types of cooked varnishes are known as oleoresinous varnishes, which means the resin is dissolved or incorporated into the oil through heat. Cooked oleoresinous varnishes are still made, using both natural resins and synthetic phenolic resin.

Most modern varnishes are alkyd-based. Oils like linseed, soya, safflower, or tung are combined under heat with an acid and an alcohol compound (alcohol plus acid created the term al-kyd). If a portion of the acid used in alkyd manufacture is replaced with a chemical called an isocyanate, a urethane/alkyd (called uralkyd) is produced. This is sold as an oil-based polyurethane.

One of the main determining characteristics of a varnish is its oil-to-resin ratio, referred to as the "oil length." The amount of oil in the varnish affects its hardness and flexibility, as shown in the drawing at right. The type of resin in a varnish also determines its character.

Alkyd-based medium- and long-oil varnishes serve as standard, all-purpose interior finishes with decent general protective qualities. Linseed-based alkyds are starting to be phased out, due to the amount of solvent necessary to make them. Lighter-colored, less-yellowing soya-based alkyds are replacing them.

Phenolic long-oil varnishes are also used for interior work, but their main application is for exterior varnishes. They are usually made with tung oil.

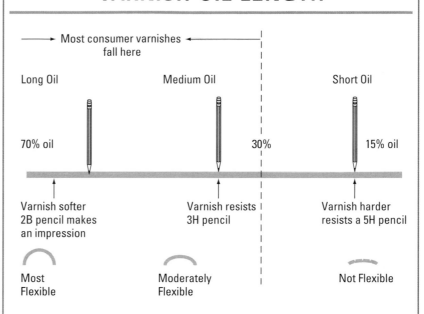

VARNISH OIL LENGTH

Most consumer varnishes fall here

Long Oil	Medium Oil	Short Oil
70% oil	30%	15% oil
Varnish softer 2B pencil makes an impression	Varnish resists 3H pencil	Varnish harder resists a 5H pencil
Most Flexible	Moderately Flexible	Not Flexible

The amount of oil used in a varnish determines the hardness and flexibility of the finish. Long-oil varnishes are typically used in outdoor applications where flexibility, but not hardness, is important. For furniture such as desks and tables, increased resin content contributes hardness for better durability. Most consumer varnishes fall between a 30-percent and 70-percent oil length. Short-oil varnishes typically require baking to cure and are used only in industrial applications.

Particular varnishes vary in their characteristics. Tung oil/phenolic resin varnishes (far left) tend to be the darkest, while soya alkyds are the lightest (far right). The Fast-Dry varnish, second from right, is a vinyl-modified alkyd.

Varnish is arguably the easiest finish to brush because you have enough open time to come back and fix any drips, brush marks, or other mishaps.

▶ WHAT "DO NOT THIN" MEANS

The label on almost every can of varnish sold today states that the product should not be thinned. This warning is a result of the Clean Air Act of 1990, which mandates that finish makers conform to federally estab-

> **Coverage/Dry Time:** One gallon co imately 350-550 sq. ft. (32-51m²). Allow to dry at least sixteen (16) hours befc or use. Drying time will vary dependir perature, humidity and film thickness. in cold or damp conditions.
>
> **Thinning/Clean-Up:** DO NOT THIN Use mineral spirits for clean-up.
>
> **Storage and Disposal:** Keep cont when not in use. Do not transfer cont

lished solvent emission standards. If you add thinner to the product, it no longer complies with these standards. While many manufacturers strive to make finishes that perform adequately without thinning, some may be pretty viscous. Nobody is going to arrest you if you add thinner to varnish, but I suggest trying to work with the product as is before thinning it. If the finish seems thick, first try warming it to room temperature.

Urethane/alkyd varnishes are generically referred to as "polyurethane." They provide the best resistance to heat, solvents, and abrasion.

Fast-dry varnishes are made with a vinyl alkyd. These dry dust-free in 15 to 30 minutes, but they're not as durable as the other three.

Varnishes can be brushed, wiped, or sprayed on. Some varnishes may be fairly thick, as a result of current air-quality regulations that mandate reduced solvent content. This means you many need to thin the varnish with either naphtha or mineral spirits if you want to wipe or spray it. (See the sidebar at left.)

> **[TIP]** When brushing varnishes, most finishers prefer using a natural-bristle brush, as it holds more varnish than a synthetic-bristle brush. Synthetics, however, are much easier to clean.

Oil/Varnish Blends

To satisfy the market demands for a finish that is somewhere between the "in-the wood" look of pure oil finishes and the "thick film" appearance of a varnish, many finish manufacturers have developed products that can best be described as extremely long-oil varnishes. The classic version of this finish is known as Danish oil, which is marketed under different names, including Nordic oil and Scandinavian oil.

These finishes behave much like oil finishes, although they may produce a marginal increase in durability over a straight oil. They are applied like oil, in that they are wiped on and allowed to sit before you wipe off the excess. They dry a bit faster than boiled linseed oil or raw tung oil and can be built up to an acceptable finish more quickly because of their small amount of resin.

There are no standard formulations for these finishes, so it's anybody's guess as to exactly what's in them. Because of this uncertainty, many finishers opt for making their own versions. I've found that a good starting recipe is to combine 1 cup interior alkyd varnish with 1 cup naphtha and ¼ cup linseed oil or tung oil. The less oil you add, the less you detract from the durability and hardness of the varnish. Adding Japan drier speeds up the longer dry time created by adding oil.

Although oil/varnish blends are applied in a manner similar to that of pure oils, there are a few differences. First, oil/varnish blends will "tack up," or start to dry, more quickly than pure oil, so you have to wipe them sooner. Second, on open-pored woods like oak, you may have problems with oil/varnish blends thinned with mineral spirits. If you flood the surface, the pores may continue to bleed oil after the excess finish is wiped off. There are three ways to deal with this problem. The first is to simply avoid flooding the surface; instead, apply the first coat or two thinly and allow them to dry. Once the pores are sealed, they won't bleed. The second approach is to monitor the workpiece and keep wiping the surface free of bleeding oil. The last approach is to seal the surface with ½-lb.-cut shellac before applying the oil.

Conversion Finishes

Conversion finishes include multiple components that must be mixed before application to start the curing process. These products may also go by names like "catalyzed," "two-part," or "two-component" finishes. They are based on a variety of resin systems, but there are three primary classes: amino, urethane, and polyester. I'll discuss these in turn.

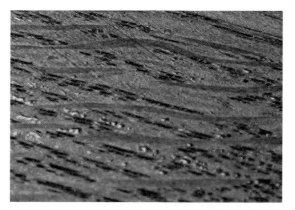

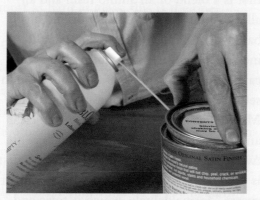

> ### PREVENTING CURE IN THE CAN

Ambient oxygen in containers can cause premature drying of oils and varnishes. To prevent this, you can displace the oxygen in the container with inert gases before closing the container.

A proprietary product like this anti-skinning gas displaces the oxygen in the varnish can with a mix of nonreactive nitrogen and carbon dioxide.

If bleeding oil is allowed to dry on the surface, it will form scabs of gummy finish that are hard to remove with a dry cloth. You can remove these with a cloth moistened with lacquer thinner, but I find using a sharp scraper the best approach.

You can use vinyl sealer under all amino-based finishes (right). Special polyurethane isolante sealers are available for use with 2K polyurethane and polyester finishes (left).

When mixing small amounts of some multipart finishes like this isolante sealer, it's best to weigh the components, which is more accurate than mixing by volume.

One way to avoid wasting finish by mixing too much is to prepare the components ahead of time in premeasured amounts for quick mixing when necessary. Use clean plastic or glass containers.

sary. However, some products are mixed by both weight and volume. The easiest finishes to prepare are the 2K urethanes, which are typically mixed in an easy two-to-one ratio of finish to hardener.

Once you mix the components, you'll have to use the product within the time frame specified on the product label. When you get used to working with a particular product, you'll be better able to judge how much to mix for a specific application. Always add the catalyst before adding thinner.

Applying the proper film thickness is very important when using catalyzed lacquers, precatalyzed lacquers, and conversion varnishes. Generally, you shouldn't exceed 4 to 5 mils dry-film thickness.

▶ See *"Measuring Finish Thickness"* on p. 214.

Polyester and 2K urethanes do not have dry-mil thickness restrictions, so you can build the finish as much as you wish.

The most common problems with all amino-based, 2K polyurethane, and polyester finishes are traced to poor adhesion, improper mixing of the product, or missing the recoat window. Adhesion problems can show up as white patches when the finish is bumped, dented, or exposed to moisture. Improper mixing and application of the product usually results in wrinkling or crazing. These problems can sometimes be corrected by sanding and recoating.

When you're ready to apply a coat of the finish, spray your test panel first and wait at least 5 to 10 minutes to see if any problems develop. Before spraying crucial jobs, it's

When you use conversion finishes, any problems like fish-eye or the wrinkling shown here will be almost immediately evident on your scrap test board.

sometimes wise to first torture your test piece by letting water sit on it for 24 hours to check water resistance. You should also test for adhesion problems.

▶ See *"Testing for Adhesion"* on p. 213.

If no problems show up on your test piece, go ahead and spray the first coat on your project. As when spraying any finish, spraying conversion finishes requires proper ventilation. However, amino-based finishes emanate formaldehyde gas when drying, so make sure to place the newly finished workpiece in a well-ventilated area to cure. Apply the second coat within the time period specified on the product label. Applying the second coat too late or without a good sanding of the prior coat can result in wrinkling or crazing.

[TIP] **When using oil-based glazes with amino-based finishes, either use a glaze specified by the manufacturer, or sandwich the glaze between coats of vinyl sealer. .**

▶ CONVERSION FINISH GLOSSARY

If you're new to conversion finishes, you may find some of the industry terms perplexing. Following are brief descriptions of terms.

Aliphatic urethane—a nonyellowing urethane with exceptional exterior qualities.

Aromatic urethane—a yellowing urethane found in oil-based polyurethane and 2K urethanes.

Catalyst—a chemical that speeds up or activates the curing of a reactive finish.

Crazing—minute fissures on the surface of the finish, usually due to excessive application of the finish.

Dry-Mil Film Thickness—The standard unit of measuring finish films. One mil equals one-thousandth of an inch.

Formaldehyde—an ingredient and toxic byproduct of amino-based finishes.

Initiator—a chemical peroxide that "initiates" the process by which a polyester finish cross-links and cures.

Melamine resin—a type of amino resin used in conversion varnishes and lacquers.

Promoter—a cobalt-based chemical in polyester finishes that speeds up the curing process.

Pot life—the amount of time that a multiple-component finish stays usable after mixing.

Recoat window—the time frame during which another coat of finish can be successfully applied.

Urea formaldehyde—a resin used in conversion varnishes and lacquers.

Wrinkling—a defect that occurs in conversion finishes when a second coat is improperly applied.

VARIATION

Applying Pure Oil Finishes

Before applying the first coat of a pure oil finish like boiled linseed oil, warm it for faster penetration. Begin by heating the oil to 150° F. in a double boiler **(A)**. Flood the first coat on liberally, replenishing any dry spots as they appear **(B)**. Allow the oil to sit for 15 to 30 minutes, and then remove all the excess from the surface with a rag.

Let the first coat dry overnight, then apply a second unheated coat, exactly the same as the first, except that you can use a piece of 600-grit wet/dry sandpaper to wet-sand the second coat into the wood **(C)**. This creates a slurry of oil and sanding dust that will make the surface smoother by helping to fill the pores. Afterward, wipe the surface clean with a rag, leaving a thin film of oil. You can apply as many additional coats as you like. Each one will increase the depth and luster of the wood. After applying the final coat, you can wax the dried finish or burnish it with a clean, dry rag to increase luster.

[VARIATION] Thinning pure tung oil one-to-one with mineral spirits will make it dry faster. Preheating the oil isn't necessary in this case.

Applying Wiping Varnish

Before applying varnish by wiping, first determine the solids content of the product you'll be using. If the solids content exceeds 30 percent—as is the case with most modern varnishes—thin the varnish one-to-one with mineral spirits **(A)**. Alternatively, you can use naphtha as the thinner, which will speed up the dry time.

Flood the first coat on and wipe it off after a few minutes **(B)**. This coat should be dry enough so you can apply a second coat in two to four hours. I usually apply subsequent coats using a folded nontextured paper towel like Viva™. Using a flip-top bottle, I dispense the varnish onto about an inch of the leading edge of the paper towel and wipe it on the workpiece **(C)**. Rather than applying the finish and wiping it away like an oil, wipe a coat of varnish on thin, then leave it to dry. You can typically apply two or three coats per day. Sanding between coats isn't necessary.

After applying three or four coats, you can lightly sand the varnish to smooth the surface. This is one of the key steps to a high-quality finish. Using 600-grit paper, sand the surface using a light touch **(D)**. Finish up by smoothing it with 0000 steel wool. You can stop here for a natural, low-luster sheen, or apply additional coats for more luster and depth.

A

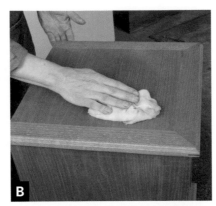

B

C

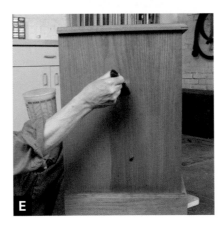

D

E

Brushing Varnish

When brushing on varnish, apply a sealer coat first. You can use a varnish sanding sealer or simply thin the first coat of varnish one-to-one with naphtha. I often use shellac instead because it dries enough to scuff-sand in 30 minutes **(A)**. After scuff- sanding, use a tack cloth to remove all the sanding debris **(B)**.

Next, brush on a coat of unthinned varnish using the "flow-on" technique.

➤ See *"Brushing Shellac and Lacquer"* on p. 216.

Tip off the varnish to level it out afterward **(C)**. Apply a minimum of two coats—more if you want a thicker build. You do not have to sand after every coat as long as the coats are applied within a day of each other. However, you may want to scuff-sand between coats to flatten out brushstrokes or remove bits of debris. You can use wet/dry sandpaper lubricated with mineral spirits, or dry sandpaper, as shown here. Some varnishes gum up sandpaper, but you can remove the gummy "corns" by swiping the sandpaper on a piece of synthetic abrasive pad **(D)**.

To brush vertical surfaces, apply the varnish by first brushing from side to side. Then smooth it out by tipping it off, moving from top to bottom **(E)**.

Conversion Varnish and Catalyzed Lacquer

Conversion varnish and catalyzed lacquer are both applied in the same manner. In this particular case, catalyzed lacquer was applied over a stain and glaze on this curly maple tabletop. (I stained and glazed a test panel for previewing the results before finishing the tabletop.)

After dyeing the top with "maple" water-soluble dye, I allowed it to dry for eight hours. Next, I applied a coat of vinyl sealer to the tabletop and to my test piece. After letting it dry 30 minutes, I sanded the surface smooth with 320-grit sandpaper **(A)**. Next, I glazed the top and my test piece with oil-based glaze **(B, C)**. After the glaze dried for two hours, I applied another coat of vinyl sealer, let it dry for an hour, then lightly sanded it.

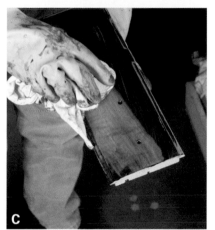

Although most manufacturers suggest using catalyzed lacquer unthinned, I added 10 percent thinner to make it spray better. Then I applied my first coat **(D)**. This first coat often creates an extremely attractive appearance because of its minimal build, but two coats are recommended for maximum durability. After the first coat dried for two hours, I scuff-sanded with 600-grit paper to remove imperfections and dust, then applied the second coat. If there will be wrinkling or any other application problems, they'll usually show up with this second coat, so make sure you spray your test panel first.

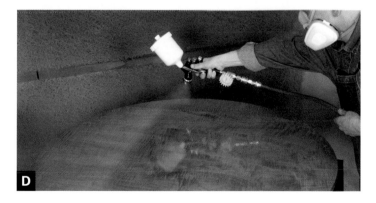

A

D

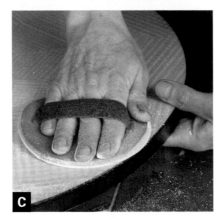

B

C

2K Urethane with Polyester

Here the system is demonstrated using polyester as the build/grain fill base and 2K urethane as the top coat. Since this ash tabletop has a tropical wood edge of padauk, an isolante sealer which must be used whenever you spray polyester or 2K polyurethane finish over tropical woods, oil-based stains, or glazes, was used first. Use a scale to better measure the small amounts for mixing. Spray the isolante sealer **(A)** and let it dry for two hours.

When mixing polyester, use very clean equipment. Try plastic quart mixing containers, wiping the inside first with acetone to remove any possible contaminant. When thinning polyester, use the acetone thinner recommended by the manufacturer. The generic acetone you see in the photo here is used only for cleanup **(B)**.

Spray the polyester base coat. To get a good grain fill on this curly ash, two double-pass crosshatch coats were applied at one-hour intervals. These were allowed to dry for 12 hours, then sanded level, using 320-grit through 600-grit paper **(C)**. Polyester sanding dust is very powdery and hazardous, so I work in the spray booth to evacuate the dust. If you sand in the main shop area, use a down-draft table or sander connected to a shop vac. After removing all the sanding dust, apply the 2K urethane top coat **(D)**. I used gloss, which I buffed out later to a mirror finish.

Caution—2K urethanes contain isocyanate, which requires special handling and safety gear. Always wear gloves when mixing. I prefer an air-supplied respirator, as seen in the photos. It's okay to use cartridge-style respirators, but they should be the full mask type to protect your eyes. Make sure you change the cartridges regularly.

Brushing Oil Paint

Prepare for painting by sanding the surface to 180 grit, then wiping it clean with denatured alcohol **(A)**. Next, apply a good primer, which is key to a good paint job. You may want to consult with your paint dealer to select the best primer for your purposes. Some primers are better suited to stain blocking, while some work better when applied over an existing finish. Others may offer better sanding qualities. Shellac-based primer works well for all these purposes and dries very fast, so I used it here **(B)**.

Apply one coat of the primer, let it dry one hour, then sand with 220-grit paper. Check for surface imperfections like small dents, which are much easier to see after priming. Use latex wood filler to fill any dents, then sand the filler level with 220-grit paper. Apply another coat of primer, let it dry one to two hours, then sand it with 320-grit paper to smooth out the brush marks.

I recommend adding a paint conditioner to the paint to increase its flow-out **(C)**. Apply the paint with a good-quality bristle brush, using the same techniques as when you brush. When painting complicated edges, try to wrap the brush around the entire molding if you can **(D)**. Place a light behind the workpiece, then inspect the surface for missed spots. Finally, tip off the surface by dragging the tips of the bristles over the paint.

[TIP] **To ease brush cleanup, first press out as much of the paint as possible onto a piece of newspaper before washing the brush with solvent.**

A

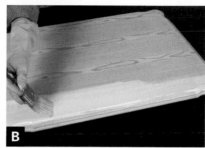

B

C

D

TIP

Spraying Paint or Tinted Conversion Varnish

Oil and other solvent-based paint is best applied with a spray gun. For this project, I made my own off-white paint by adding 15 percent white tint by volume, and three drops of burnt umber, to a clear satin conversion varnish (**A**). In preparation for painting, first ease all sharp edges with 150-grit sandpaper.

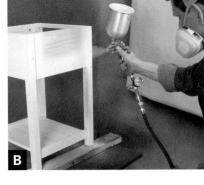

First apply a primer (**B**). A catalyzed primer formulated to provide the same tough durability as the conversion varnish itself was used here. For dark-colored paint, it's wise to use a darker-colored primer, as a light one may peek through the top coat. You can sometimes buy different-colored primers, but adding a concentrated tint to a white primer works just as well (**C**). Typically one or two coats of primer will do the job. After applying the primer, let it dry, then sand it with 320-grit paper to smooth it.

Before applying the finish coats, first remove every trace of dust from the workpiece to prevent contamination of the paint. I used compressed air for cleaning, blowing the dust toward my spray booth filters. If you don't have a similar way to exhaust the dust, remove it by wiping with a tack cloth or rag dampened with naphtha. Otherwise, the dust floats up in the air only to land in the paint later. After cleaning the work, spray the top coats of paint. I typically apply one coat, then wait two hours before sanding away any imperfections with 600-grit paper. Then I apply my final coat (**D**).

When spraying oil-based paint follow the above procedure, but substitute an oil-compatible primer or shellac as a sealer. The oil-based primer provides more overall durability. Instead of using mineral spirits to thin the paint, use naphtha to speed up the dry time and prevent sagging (**E**).

Evaporative Finishes

Shellac

Lacquer

EVAPORATIVE FINISHES cure by releasing the solvents in the finish into the air, leaving behind the resin. The resin is essentially unchanged, or nonconverted, by the process. The two most common evaporative finishes are shellac and solvent-based lacquers. Many water-based finishes are evaporative too, but since some are also reactive, I'll discuss water-based finishes in Section 16.

Shellac

Shellac is a natural resin that's derived from the secretions of the Lac bug—an insect that feeds off trees indigenous to India and Thailand. The secretions—in the form of cocoons—are gathered from the trees and refined into dry flakes or buttons, which are dissolved in alcohol for application. Cans of premixed shellac are commonly available, but you can also purchase "dry shellac" in flake or button form to mix yourself.

Depending on the region it comes from, the time of year it is harvested and other environmental factors, raw shellac (called seed-lac) may be a dark garnet color (top, left) or a lighter caramel color (top, right). Further refining produces the buttonlac (bottom).

Machine processing filters out the wax and the color to produce grades of shellac ranging from dark garnet (right) to lighter grades called "orange" (middle) and "super blond" (left). The color of each type of shellac is seen on the wood below it.

Premixed shellacs are available in both waxed (left three) and dewaxed (right three) form. The product at far right is a padding lacquer made with shellac and the solvents used for lacquer.

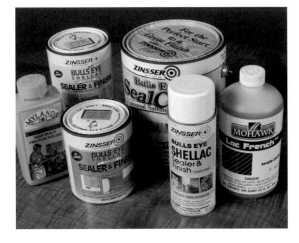

The most important characteristics of shellac are its color, the methods used for removing some or all of its color, and whether the natural wax has been removed. Shellac ranges in color from a light straw to a dark brown. The color has no affect on the working characteristics of the finish. When you buy it in dry form, you have more color choice than when you buy premixed shellac.

The color of the natural product can be removed either by chemical bleaching or by a filtration process. It is generally agreed that chemical bleaching causes molecular changes that render the shellac less stable in dry form than shellac decolorized by the gentler filtration process. Chemically bleached shellac is a granular white powder instead of flakes. Liquid chemically bleached shellac is sold as "white" or clear shellac, but when it's in liquid form you have no way of telling whether it's been chemically bleached.

The natural wax in the resin decreases shellac's moisture resistance and can cause adhesion problems with polyurethanes and water-based finishes. Because of this, it's wise to use dewaxed shellac when applying a shellac sealer coat for use with these finishes. The product label should identify it as dewaxed shellac.

Shelf Life

Shellac is available in many premixed formulations. However, you can also mix your own by dissolving shellac flakes or buttons in alcohol. Using a premixed formulation is certainly convenient, but many finishers prefer to mix their own to ensure that it is fresh. Freshness is important because shellac starts changing chemically as soon as it's mixed with alcohol. Although some finishers get by just fine with shellac that is years old, my testing indicates that solutions made from dewaxed flakes less than six months old have the best overall moisture resistance. Shellac that is past its shelf life does one of two things: It either won't dry hard or will cause another finishing material applied over it to wrinkle. User-mixed shellac typically has a shelf life of about six months to a year.

Dry flakes or buttons can safely be stored in a cool, dry place indefinitely without compromising their quality.

I suggest that when you're using shellac for your total finishing system—that is, including top coats—you mix it fresh from dewaxed flakes. Otherwise, I think it's fine to use premixed shellac for general sealing and washcoating, and as a toner base. When you're using premixed shellac, I suggest buying a brand that lists a manufacturing date. Make sure you'll be using it within its stated shelf life. Store all shellac—whether premixed or in flake form—in a cool, dry place.

Mixing Shellac

Dry shellac is mixed with denatured alcohol in a particular ratio called a *cut*, which refers to the amount of shellac in pounds dissolved in a gallon of alcohol. A 2-lb. cut of shellac is 2 lb. of shellac resin dissolved in a gallon of alcohol. A 5-lb. cut would be 5 lb. of resin dissolved in a gallon, etc.

When mixing shellac from flakes or buttons, you can scale down the ratio of cut to make a suitable amount. Premixed shellac is typically sold in a 2-, 3-, or 4-lb. cut, which may need to be diluted for certain applications. For converting premixed shellac to a different cut, refer to the chart on p. 242.

[TIP] **When mixing shellac, use a name-brand denatured alcohol that states "for use as shellac thinner."**

Denatured alcohol is ethanol, which is the same alcohol used in alcoholic beverages. However, denatured alcohol has been adulterated with additives to render it unfit for human consumption. A typical denatured formula consists of 190-proof ethanol, 4 percent

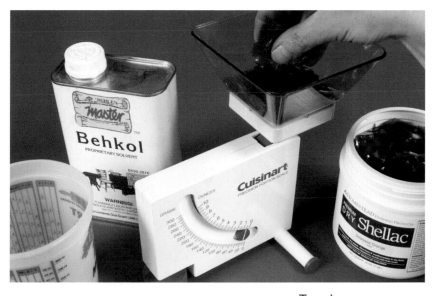

Shellac Solids

The chart below lists the percentage of solids in a given "cut" of shellac. This will help in calculating dry-film thickness.

CUT	SOLIDS % WT.
¼ lb.	3.5%
½ lb.	7%
1 lb.	14%
1.5 lb.	18%
2 lb.	22%
3 lb.	31%
4 lb.	37.5%
5 lb.	42%

To mix a manageable amount of a specific "cut" of shellac, simply scale down the ratio of flakes to alcohol. For example, adding 2 oz. of flakes to 8 oz. of alcohol produces a half-pint of 2-lb.-cut shellac.

methanol, and 1 percent MIBK. The proof refers to the amount of pure ethanol as a percentage divided by 2 (e.g.: 200 proof equals 100 percent ethanol, 190 proof equals 95 percent ethanol). Some finishing purists insist on using 200-proof ethanol, which dissolves the flakes a bit faster. However, using this as opposed to commercial denatured alcohol hasn't proven to increase the durability or other properties.

Although there are various ways to eyeball a given weight of shellac, it's best to weigh it on a scale. Measure the amounts of alcohol and shellac you want to use and mix them in a glass or plastic jar. Shake the solution every

30 minutes to prevent a large mass of partially dissolved shellac from forming at the bottom. Once the shellac is mixed, date the jar. I suggest using the mixture within a year.

Lacquer

Lacquer is fast drying and imparts depth and richness to wood. Depending on the type used, lacquer has moderate to excellent durability and rubs out well. There are several different types of lacquers, all with different performance characteristics.

Nitrocellulose lacquer is the most commonly available lacquer. It has moderate water resistance but is sensitive to heat and certain solvents. The biggest drawback to nitrocellulose lacquer is its tendency to yellow over time, which can be undesirable on light-colored woods and white finishes. Some nitrocellulose lacquers are a rich amber color, others are pale, and some are clear enough to be termed "water white,"

Mix and store shellac in glass jars with plastic lids if possible. To keep the lid from sticking, wrap the neck of the jar with Teflon plumber's tape or smear the jar threads with petroleum jelly.

Shellac Conversion Ratios

To convert remixed shellac to a dilute cut, add the appropriate amount of alcohol, as shown in the chart. For example, to convert a 2-lb. cut to a 1-lb. cut, add ⅔ of 1 part alcohol to 1 part existing 2-lb.-cut shellac solution.

	PARTS ALCOHOL: PARTS EXISTING CUT					
EXISTING CUT	**¼ LB.**	**½ LB.**	**1 LB.**	**1.5 LB.**	**2 LB.**	**3 LB.**
½ lb.	1:1					
1 lb.	3:1	⅞:1				
1.5 lb.	4½:1	1⅔:1	⅓:1			
2 lb.	5:1	2:1	⅔:1	¼:1		
3 lb.	8¾:1	3¾:1	1½:1	¾:1	⅓:1	
4 lb.	11:1	5:1	2:1	1¼:1	¾:1	¼:1
5 lb.	12¾:1	5¾:1	2¾:1	1½:1	1:1	⅞:1

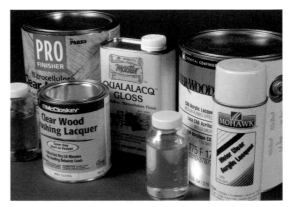

Lacquer is still considered by many professionals the best all-around finish for wood. Nitrocellulose lacquer (left) is a pale yellow liquid that yellows more over time. Acrylic lacquer (right) is water-clear and nonyellowing.

although these are not as optically neutral as the acrylic lacquers discussed next. Most nitrocellulose lacquers sold today fall into the pale amber class.

Acrylic-modified lacquers are usually based on a mix of acrylic and a nonyellowing cellulose resin called cellulose acetate butyrate (CAB). They have the general properties of nitrocellulose lacquers with the exception of being absolutely water white—meaning they will not impart an amber shift when applied to light woods and will not yellow over time.

Lacquer is formulated with approximately 20 percent solids, which means that only one-fifth of what you apply to the surface remains as a film after the solvents evaporate. Lacquer is typically thinned even further by the user for spraying. You can add as little or as much thinner as you wish without causing problems. However, if you want the lacquer to build quickly, try to add as little thinner as possible.

Using Shellac and Lacquer

Shellac and lacquer are both applied in a fairly similar manner using a brush or spray gun. (The main exception is the technique of French polishing, which is discussed on page 248.) The primary advantages of both products are that they dry very quickly and that each subsequent coat "burns in" to the

► See *"Evaporative and Reactive Finishes"* on p. 202.

previous coat by melting it. Because these finishes dry so quickly, dust doesn't have much time to settle into the finish. The resin does not have to undergo any chemical

---

► MODIFYING LACQUER

Lacquer thinners are formulated to provide different evaporation rates to aid spraying under various weather conditions. "Fast" thinner is best for use in temperatures ranging from 50° F. to 60° F. "Medium" thinner works well in 60° F.-to-80° F. temperatures. Use "slow" thinner for temperatures above 80° F. If the can of thinner doesn't state the evaporation rate, it's probably medium thinner.

Acetone can be added to a medium thinner in a one-to-one ratio to accelerate the evaporation in cold weather. To slow down the evaporation of a medium thinner on hot and humid days, you can add 1 or 2 oz. of lacquer retarder per qt. of thinner. Other potential lacquer additives include silicone to eliminate fisheye and flow additives to reduce orange peel.

---

change, so the piece can be rubbed out and recoated quickly, allowing you to apply several coats in a day. When sanding between coats you can use 240-grit sandpaper, as any sanding scratches will be melted away by subsequent coats.

Most problems with shellac and lacquer are weather-induced. Hot and humid conditions may impart a whitish appearance to the finish shortly after you apply it. Called blushing, this problem is caused by moisture being drawn into the finish from the ambient air, causing the resins to "kick out," or come out of solution. If the blush doesn't go away on its own as the finish dries, it can be fixed by spraying a slower-evaporating thinner on the surface to remelt the finish. Alternatively, you can sand away the blushed areas before apply-

A slow-evaporating alcohol like isobutanol can be added in amounts of up to 10 percent by volume to make shellac easier to brush or spray. Lacquer retarder can also be used if you can't get isobutanol.

ing another coat. In hot and humid weather, many finishers add lacquer retarder or a slow-evaporating thinner to their lacquer.

Another common problem with lacquer is pin-holing, which shows up as small holes, typically over pores. It's caused by incompletely evaporated solvents from a prior finishing product, or by applying too thick a coat in humid weather. This problem is very difficult to fix, but you correct it to some degree by sanding away as much of the finish as possible, then recoating during drier weather.

Brushed or sprayed shellac can sometimes form a thick ridge on sharp workpiece corners. Called fat-edge, this problem is caused by surface-tension disparities that occur as the shellac is drying. It can be remedied by adding a silicone-based wetting agent to the finish. Another problem related to surface tension is fisheye in lacquer, as discussed on p. 197. Fisheye can't simply be wiped away. You have to either let it dry, then sand the finish off, or else immediately mix some fisheye additive into the lacquer and respray the surface before the original coat dries.

When brushing shellac or lacquer, it's best to apply multiple thin coats rather than fewer thick coats. Thinner coats dry faster and are easier to sand because of the minimal brush marks.

Brushing Shellac and Lacquer

Both shellac and lacquer can be brushed on using either a natural or synthetic brush. For shellac, I prefer to use a 1- or 1½ lb.-cut mixture. Brushing lacquer is formulated the same way as spraying lacquer, except that it includes slower-evaporating solvents to allow for better flow-out before it dries. The proprietary thinner designed for a particular brand of brushing lacquer is usually a slow-dry thinner, but you could also use a commercial medium-dry lacquer thinner. When brushing shellac and lacquer I prefer to apply multiple thin coats, particularly on complicated surfaces. It's best when brushing to apply at least two coats before sanding out brush marks or dust nibs.

When brushing either finish, you may find that the solvents and the friction from the brush pull up dye stains that were applied without a binder. You can remedy this by using a very light touch with the brush, or by sealing the dyes in with an oil-based product like Danish oil, boiled linseed oil, or tung oil. Let the sealer coat dry at least overnight before brushing. An alternative is to spray aerosol shellac over the dye.

> [TIP] Aerosol shellac is convenient to use and doesn't contain wax, ensuring compatibility with other finishes.

Spraying Shellac and Lacquer
Shellac and lacquer both spray well, but this requires safety precautions, as the overspray is flammable. You'll have to either spray outdoors or in a properly equipped spray booth.

▶ See *"Spraying Finishes"* on p. 13.

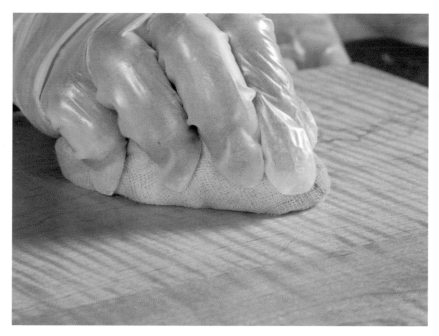

A thin coat of boiled linseed oil or tung oil rubbed into the wood before you apply shellac or lacquer "pops" the figure, giving the surface of the wood a three-dimensional quality.

Because the first few coats of lacquer tend to absorb unevenly, a sealer coat of shellac, sanding sealer, or vinyl sealer is usually applied first. Using a sealer coat isn't mandatory, but it speeds up the finishing process. Use vinyl sealer when the piece will be subjected to moisture. Prior to applying the sealer, you may want to rub a thin coat of boiled linseed or tung oil into the wood to make the figure "pop" and give the surface of the wood a three-dimensional quality.

When you spray either finish, use a setup for light-viscosity finishes unless you're planning on spraying a high-solids lacquer with no thinner added. For spraying, I typically work with 2-lb.-cut shellac or 21-percent-solids lacquer, cut 50 to 100 percent with thinner. If spraying on a humid day, you can use a slow thinner or add lacquer retarder to your normal thinner. When you're spraying shellac with a turbine-powered gun, the hot air prematurely flashes the fast-evaporating

denatured alcohol, so adding retarder may help when using these guns.

Shellac dries better when applied in thin coats. It should not be sprayed on in layers thicker than 2 or 3 mils, and no more than two coats should be applied in a single day. For lacquer, three coats can usually be applied in a single day. For both finishes, waiting one to two hours between applications should be fine on a 70° F. day with 50 percent relative humidity. On more humid days, extend the time between coats. It's not necessary to sand between coats of either finish unless you need to remove imbedded dust or debris. However, many finishers do sand after three or four applications to ensure as smooth a final finish as possible.

Specialty Shellac Applications

Shellac can be applied using a couple of techniques that aren't possible with lacquer. Both involve wiping the shellac on with a cloth. The techniques are called *French polishing* and *padding*.

French Polishing

French polishing is an age-old process in which multiple coats of shellac are applied by hand to create a very smooth, defect-free gloss finish. Performed properly, the technique involves building up thin layers of shellac to produce a deep, lustrous finish without the heavy build you often get with lacquer or varnish. The finish is rubbed to a high gloss at the same time it is applied, meaning you don't have to wait until a coat dries to rub it out, as you would with varnish or lacquer.

Though a bit more labor-intensive than simply brushing or spraying a finish, French polishing doesn't really deserve its reputation as a laborious skill that's difficult to master. Although sprayed lacquer has largely replaced it these days, French polishing still has its advantages. The finish dries fast, doesn't have an unpleasant smell, and doesn't require expensive application equipment. It's still in demand as a finish for musical instruments and period furniture reproductions.

The application sequence involves three stages: filling the pores, "bodying" the shellac, and clearing the shellac.

Filling the pores is done to create a smooth, flat surface for applying the shellac. You only need to fill the pores of open-pored woods. For French polishing, the pores are filled with rottenstone or 4F pumice instead of paste wood filler. Because filling the pores of open-pored woods can be problematic, I suggest first practicing French polishing on a close-grained wood like cherry or maple that doesn't require filling.

Bodying the shellac involves applying whisper-thin coats over an oiled-wood surface. The shellac is applied using a two-part pad made from an outer muslin cover and an absorbent inner cotton or wool core. Because the shellac tends to dry quickly as it's being rubbed on, a bit of baby oil is added occasionally to the pad to prevent the finish from sticking to it.

The final step of clearing the shellac is necessary to remove the residual baby oil introduced by the process.

[TIP] When coloring open-grained woods that will be French polished, avoid using a pigment stain, because the friction from the pad and abrasive filler will easily cut through it. French polishing works best over dye stains or chemical stains.

A properly executed French polish produces a high-gloss finish of incredible depth, using only a very thin film of shellac.

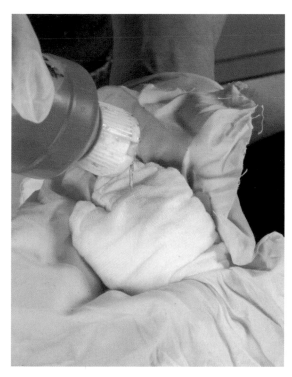

The traditional pad for French polishing consists of wool wrapped with a linen cloth. However, a cotton cloth wrapped with muslin will also work. A plastic container with a nozzle makes a great dispenser for the shellac.

Pads for French polishing and padding shellac can be stored indefinitely in an airtight jar for reuse later.

Padding Shellac

Padding shellac refers to the method of wiping on thin coats of shellac using a cloth pad. This technique differs from French polishing in that no oil is used for lubrication. Also, the shellac is wiped on with a single piece of absorbent cloth instead of a two-part pad. As with wiping varnish, the shellac is applied in very thin coats. However, because shellac dries so quickly, you can apply additional coats in a matter of minutes, as opposed to the hours or days of dry time required with varnish. A padded-shellac finish can easily be accomplished in a day, then rubbed out and waxed the next.

The pad used to apply shellac should be soft, absorbent, and as lint-free as possible. I use a product called padding cloth or trace cloth. During the finishing process, the pad can be stored in an airtight jar. A squeeze-type bottle with a nozzle does a good job of dispensing the shellac onto the pad.

Note: While a product called "padding lacquer" is available, it is simply shellac to which solvents for lacquer are added, along with lubricating additives. It was formulated for on-site repair of lacquered furniture. For finishing I prefer straight shellac.

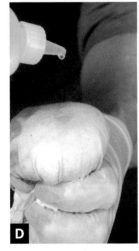

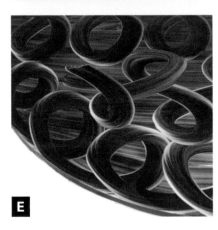

French Polishing

Begin by applying a coat of boiled linseed oil to the surface, rubbing it in with a clean cotton rag **(A)**. When you're working with open-pored woods, the next step is to fill the pores. To do this, sprinkle some rottenstone over the surface and work it into the grain using a circular motion. (You can use 4F pumice on unstained wood.) As the rottenstone mixes with the oil on the surface, it should become dark and less chalky looking **(B)**. If it stays chalky looking, add more oil. Examine the surface in backlighting to make sure all the grain is filled, then wipe it with a clean cloth to remove the excess. Apply more oil and rottenstone the next day, and then let the piece sit for at least three days.

Next, apply a coat of shellac using a two-part pad made by wrapping a 14-in.-square of 80 thread-per-inch unbleached muslin around a golf ball–sized wad of cotton or wool **(C)**. Pour an ounce of denatured alcohol into the core and twist the ends of the muslin over, leaving no seams or wrinkles on the bottom. Flatten the pad by pressing it down gently down on a clean surface. Then open the cover again and "charge" the core with 1 oz. of dewaxed 1-lb.-cut shellac. Wipe the shellac onto the workpiece in straight strokes, moving from one edge to the other three times. When the shellac dries out, recharge the core with more.

When the shellac starts becoming too tacky to wipe, apply a few drops of baby oil to the bottom of the pad to lubricate it **(D)**. Then start rubbing in circles and figure eights. Make 6-in. to 8-in.-wide curlycues at the perimeter and rub the center area, moving in a figure-eight pattern **(E)**. (Note that the rubbing pattern shown in the photo was made using white polishing compound simply to show the process.) After 15 to 20 minutes, the surface should start to shine. Your goal here is to "body" the shellac enough to completely fill the grain. This bodying process will go faster if you switch to a 2-lb.-cut shellac. When the grain appears filled and the surface is covered with a "lens" of shellac, stop and let the finish dry overnight.

The next day, sand the shellac lightly with P600-grit sandpaper lubricated with mineral spirits or naphtha **(F)**. Afterward, smooth the surface further with 0000 steel wool or gray abrasive pads. Then remove the sanding residue and continue the bodying process using 2-lb.-cut shellac, lubricating the pad with baby oil and moving it in curlycues and figure eights to build the shellac evenly. When the pad starts to dry out, instead of charging it with more shellac, simply bear down harder using 30 to 40 lbs. of pressure **(G)**. (You can test your pressure using a bathroom scale.) You're finished with the bodying process when the pores are no longer visible after an overnight drying. This process may take three days for open-pored woods, while close-pored woods might require only a day.

After the surface dries for a day or so, you're ready to clear the residual oil from it. To do this, wipe the surface with a clean, soft cloth dampened with naphtha. Then, in preparation for bringing up the final brilliant shine, first pour 1 oz. of denatured alcohol into a clean absorbent cotton cloth **(H)**. Work the cloth between your hands to distribute the alcohol until it feels as moist as a dog's nose. Then gently sweep the rag across the finished surface, working more quickly as the alcohol dries out, until you're buffing it as though shining shoes with a brush **(I)**. As the rag loads up with oil, change its position to present fresh material to the workpiece.

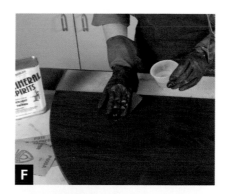

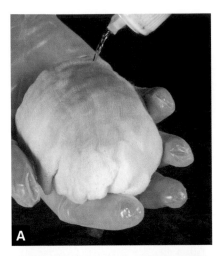

Padding Shellac

Padding shellac is a technique, not a product. The procedure differs from French polishing in that no lubricating oil is used. Also, the application pad is made and used differently.

Make an applicator pad by wadding up a lint-free absorbent cloth so there are no seams or wrinkles on the bottom. Squirt about 1 oz. of denatured alcohol into the pad, squeezing the cloth to distribute the alcohol throughout and to wring out the excess. Next, squirt 1 to 2 oz. of 2-lb.-cut shellac onto the bottom **(A)**. Apply the first coat to the workpiece, flooding the surface, then wiping off the excess **(B)**. After 30 minutes, scuff-sand with P600-grit sandpaper and remove the dust.

To apply the next coat, load the pad with shellac again. Beginning at the edge nearest you, swoop down onto one end of the workpiece, dragging the pad fully across it **(C)**, then swooping up off the opposite end, like an airplane landing and immediately taking off again **(D)**. Next, reverse the stroke you just made, making a swooping pass over the same area but from the opposite direction. Continue across the full width of the workpiece in this same fashion, always moving in the direction of the grain. After you've covered the entire workpiece, it should be dry enough to repeat the process again from the beginning. Afterward, finish the edges of the workpiece in the same manner.

As the pad starts to dry out, reload it with more shellac. A dry pad can leave streaks or fibers in the sticky shellac. After the surface dries, rub out any application marks using fine sandpaper followed by 0000 steel wool. Build the finish to any thickness you wish.

Padding is best suited to flat surfaces. When finishing corners and tight areas where the pad can't easily reach, begin by applying several coats of shellac with a brush to create an initial build.

Brushing Shellac

To brush shellac, first condition the brush by dipping it into denatured alcohol, then wringing out the excess. Dip the brush halfway up the bristle length into 1-lb.-cut shellac, then scrape off the excess on the edge of the jar **(A)**.

With a complicated surface such as this piecrust top, you can't drag your brush fully off the edge of the workpiece as usual, so you'll have to modify your technique. With the brush lightly loaded with shellac, begin your stroke where the top meets the carved profile, then pull the brush toward the center **(B)**. Work your way to the opposite end of the workpiece, lightly reloading the brush as necessary. Whenever you start a new section with a reloaded brush, whisk it backward into the adjacent fresh finish to blend the two areas together **(C)**. Use the edge of the brush to reach into fluted areas and other three-dimensional profiles **(D)**. A smaller brush works well for carvings. Use a gentle, up-and-down slapping motion for edges **(E)**.

Try to work quickly and rhythmically in order to blend sections together before the shellac starts setting up. If partially set-up shellac starts to "tear" under the brushstrokes, stop working that area, as trying to fix it at this point will only make it worse. You can sand rough areas smooth after the finish dries.

The beauty of shellac is that by the time you've completed a full coat, the finish is usually dry enough to begin the next coat immediately. However, don't apply more than three coats in a session before letting the workpiece dry for six to eight hours.

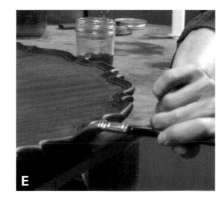

A

B

C

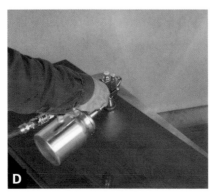

D

Basic Sprayed Lacquer Finish

This unstained walnut table with sculptural legs is a great candidate for a sprayed lacquer finish. I applied two coats of sanding sealer followed by two coats of gloss lacquer, then a coat of satin lacquer. I worked on a turntable for quick, easy access to all parts of the chair.

Start by applying two light coats of sanding sealer thinned with an equal amount of lacquer thinner. Beginning with the base, spray quickly and evenly while rotating the turntable to avoid stopping and starting the spray. Work from the inside out, starting with the insides of the legs and working toward their outside surfaces **(A)**. To spray the tabletop, set the gun up for a 6-in.-wide spray pattern and make sure the atomization is consistent across its width.

► See *"Adjusting a Spray Gun"* on p. 55.

Let the sealer dry for a couple of hours, sand it lightly with P600-grit paper, and blow off the dust. Then apply two coats of gloss lacquer thinned with equal parts of lacquer thinner. After this dries overnight, sand with P320-grit paper followed by a gray synthetic abrasive pad. The finish will be thin, so go easy near edges and corners. Use abrasive pads on the curves. Blow or vacuum all the dust off, and wipe the entire piece with a tack rag **(B)**.

To prepare for spraying the final coat, thoroughly vacuum your spray area and clean off your clothes with compressed air **(C)**. Stir the satin lacquer well and strain it through a fine-mesh filter before pouring it into the spray gun. Apply the satin lacquer in a double-pass pattern **(D)**.

► See *"Spraying Flat Surfaces"* on p. 217.

Filled-Pore Lacquer Finish

Lacquer applied over pore-filled mahogany creates one of the most elegant finishes. To prepare it for lacquering, first dye it with a water-soluble dye, sealed the surface with a sanding sealer, then apply dark oil-based paste wood filler to the pores.

Begin by spraying on a washcoat of sanding sealer thinned with equal parts lacquer thinner **(A)**. To add interest, shade the edges and perimeter of the top very slightly with a dark brown dye toner. Let this dry for an hour, then prepare a mix of two parts lacquer with one part thinner for the next step. Using the mix, next apply three double-pass coats, allowing two hours of dry time between each.

After allowing the finish to dry overnight, sand the finish to level out any pore craters. It's best to initially sand by hand. If it then appears that the finish is thick enough, you can carefully power sand large, flat surfaces **(B)**. Use synthetic abrasive pads on profiled edges **(C)**. After removing the sanding dust, I wiped the surface clean with a tack rag, then sprayed four more coats of lacquer.

To minimize excess buildup, which creates a "plastic" look on profiled edges, try to spray the lacquer toward the inside of the perimeter, avoiding the profiled edges **(D)**. Let the piece dry at least a week before rubbing it out to create the desired sheen.

Lacquering over Paint

The deep, lustrous finish often seen on pianos, high-end musical instruments, and furniture is created by applying multiple coats of clear lacquer over an opaque paint, then polishing the cured finish. On this painted table, I used nitro-cellulose lacquer, polishing the finish afterward.

The first step in the process is to sand the surfaces to 220 grit, then raise the grain with water and sand again to ensure a smooth surface. Next, apply a coat of primer colored to match your desired top coats. If you like, you can simply add tint to a sanding or vinyl sealer for this first coat **(A)**.

When the primer coat is dry, examine the surface carefully for defects, which should be clearly apparent because of the solid-colored primer. Apply filler to any defects **(B)**. After the filler dries, sand everything again with 220-grit paper, then apply another coat of primer. After this second coat dries, sand it smooth with P320 paper, and then apply your paint.

Colored lacquers can be hard to find, so I make my own from clear lacquer, adding 15-20 percent colorants by volume. I made up a mix of black for the table base and red for the tabletop **(C)**. I applied two coats, sanded the surface with P600 sandpaper, then applied two more coats.

Let the paint dry overnight, then sand one final time with P600 paper, followed by a gray synthetic abrasive pad. Remove all the sanding dust and start applying your clear lacquer coats **(D)**. When mixing the lacquer for spraying, use as little thinner as possible to minimize the chance of drips on vertical surfaces. I typically apply three or four coats one hour apart, sanding the dried finish smooth with 320-grit paper afterward. Apply three or four more coats, then let the finish cure for two weeks before rubbing out to the desired sheen.

Brushing Lacquer

Brushing lacquer isn't as easy as brushing shel-lac. Lacquer starts to set up so quickly that you don't have the luxury of tipping off the finish to remove brush marks. These shortcomings are offset by lacquer's quick dry time, clarity, and rubbing qualities.

When brushing large, flat areas, it's best to "flow on" a thick coat and let it level out under its own weight. Use a thick natural-bristle brush, which will hold a lot of finish. Begin the first stroke about 3 in. in from one edge, and brush a path of finish all the way to the opposite edge of the workpiece. Then lay down another path of finish adjacent to the first one, but ½ in. away **(A)**. At the end of each path, drag the brush off the edge, then immediately come back and feather out the pool of lacquer created at the beginning of the stroke. Feather out the ½-in. gap with the brush before you start a new stroke **(B)**.

For more complicated items like this mahogany display cabinet, I thin brushing lacquer 10 percent with lacquer thinner and work the surface quickly **(C)**. To finish two sides of a workpiece immedi-ately, use a staple board **(D)**. I applied four coats, sanding after the second coat with P320-grit paper to remove any defects such as small bub-bles, brush marks, or drips. I used gray abrasive pads to smooth contours. If you want a satin fin-ish, you can either apply gloss lacquer and rub it to a satin sheen afterward, or simply apply satin lacquer for the final coats.

A

B

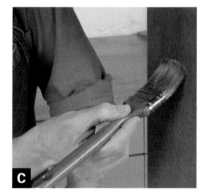

C

D

Crackle Lacquer

When a painted finish develops cracks as a result of aging it's called it a "crazed" finish. This look can be deliberately accomplished in a new finish by using a special lacquer called "crackle" lacquer. When this extremely brittle lacquer is applied over a standard lacquer base, the top layer will crack as it dries, revealing the contrasting base coat beneath.

Crackle lacquer can be opaque or clear. For this project, I'm using opaque crackle. Start by spraying the base coat with a standard colored lacquer **(A)**. After the paint dries, sand the base coat smooth, let it dry overnight, then apply the crackle coat. It takes some practice to get the hang of this technique. You must apply the proper amount as evenly and quickly as you can. You cannot spray with the double-pass technique or respray after the crackling effect begins, or you'll destroy the effect. Heavy, wet passes produce large cracks while lighter coats produce smaller cracks **(B)**. You can see the effect plainly on the back, where the cracks increase in size. Note the practice panel at the bottom right. I particularly like the effect of the smaller cracks on the case top **(C)**.

Water-Based Finishes

Hand Application

Spray Application

WATER-BASED FINISHES provide an attractive alternative for finishers concerned with the fire and health hazards presented by solvent-based finishes. Water-based finishes dry fast, clean up easily, and don't emit unpleasant odors. This makes them perfect for finishers who work out of small shops that aren't outfitted with facilities for spraying solvent-based finishes.

A Little History

In the 1980s, manufacturers started introducing water-based clear finishes as an alternative to flammable, toxic, environmentally unfriendly solvent-based finishes. Because the purpose of any solvent is basically to act as a carrier that evaporates after application, it made sense to the manufacturers to replace the solvent with something else. Water was the logical choice because it is nontoxic and nonflammable.

Water-based finishes dry quickly with minimal odor and are well suited to both hand and spray application. Our quality-control inspector, who is checking for any missed areas, seems to agree.

➤ WHAT "WATER-BASED" MEANS

"Water-based" is a generic term that applies to finishes that use water as a primary thinning solvent. However, the water is not a true solvent for the resin. Although many people in the manufacturing side of the industry use the terms "water-borne" or "water-reducible" to differentiate between finish chemistries, "water-based" works for a general description.

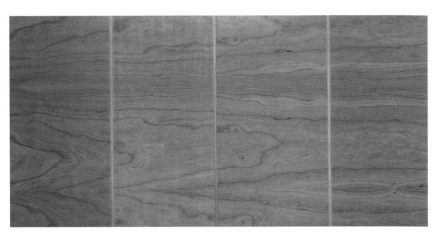

Water-based finishes do not share the same general properties with regard to clarity, warmth, color, grain raising, and flow-out. From left, an exterior-grade water-based spar varnish; an acrylic urethane blend; an acrylic co-polymer; and an oil-modified urethane.

The first water-based finishes could best be described as latex paint without the pigment. They looked pasty, didn't apply well, and generally disappointed their users. Since then, however (and particularly in the last 10 years), vast improvements have been made in these products, especially in the types of resins and additives that manufacturers use. Unfortunately some of the original bad impressions still linger today, and there is a lot of erroneous information floating around, which I'll try to dispel in this section.

The Composition of Water-Based Finishes

Just like solvent-based finishes, water-based finishes are composed of resin, solvents, and additives. To get the normally hydrophobic ("fears water") resin to mix with water in the finish, formulators create an emulsion or dispersion. In both cases, sticky particles of polymerized resin are dispersed in a matrix of water, surfactants, solvents, and additives.

In fact, as many as 20 separate components may be necessary to make a water-based finish perform properly. The specific composition of a given water-based product determines its clarity, warmth, and color, as well as its grain-raising and flow-out properties.

The process of getting these components to work together under a variety of conditions is extremely challenging. For example, defoamers are added to counteract the foaming caused by surfactants, whose job is to lower the surface tension of the finish for better leveling. To aid in flow-out and coalescence, special slow-evaporating ingredients (called tail solvents) and other additives are necessary. And because the emulsion takes on the viscosity of the water, thickeners may be added to prevent the finish from dripping down vertical surfaces.

Acrylics and urethanes are the two primary resins used in water-based finishes. They both provide good clarity, gloss, adhe-

Water-based finishes are formulated from acrylics, urethanes, or a combination of the two. Available in interior or exterior grades, they all have a milky look before and during application, but they dry clear.

Using Water-Based Finishes

If you've tried water-based finishes, you've noticed that they don't look or behave like solvent-based products. It's worth working past any frustrations with this to gain the advantages that water-based products offer in terms of their clarity and minimal odor, as well as their nonyellowing, fast-drying characteristics. To help you adjust to using water-based finishes, I've distilled the most common differences down to the following: appearance, grain raising, flow-out and leveling, equipment cleaning, and weather-induced problems.

sion, and rubbing qualities, and most of them are nonyellowing. These resins can cure through either a reactive or evaporative process. The reactive-curing acrylics and urethanes are sometimes referred to as "self-cross-linking" and use oxygen to establish cross-links between the molecules, yielding a tougher finish.

As with their solvent-based cousins, the urethanes in water-based finishes are either aromatic or aliphatic. Both types possess many of the same scratch, mar, heat, and solvent resistance as the solvent-based versions. Many manufacturers blend the two resins to enhance certain characteristics. For example, an acrylic may be blended with a urethane to make the latter more heat and solvent resistant. Or a urethane may be blended with an acrylic to make the finish rub out or adhere better, to make it harder, or simply to reduce the cost. Some of the newer-generation resins used in water-based finishes are actually produced as acrylic-urethane molecules.

Appearance

One objection to early water-based finishes was the pale look they imparted to wood. They didn't deepen the color of the wood as solvent-based finishes do. These days, however, different resins and additives have resolved many of these problems. Still, many water-based finishes are optically different from solvent-based finishes like lacquer, shellac, and varnish. On woods like cherry, walnut, and mahogany, water-based finishes

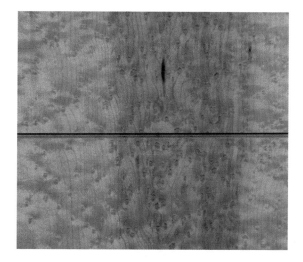

Modern water-based finishes compare very favorably in appearance to their solvent-based counterparts. The top section of this board was finished with a current-generation acrylic urethane, while the bottom was coated with nitrocellulose lacquer.

Ways to "warm up" a water-based finish include adding a yellow-orange dye to the finish (bottom), sealing the wood with dewaxed shellac (second from bottom), and applying a honey-colored dye to the wood prior to finishing (second from top). The top shows the finish on untreated wood.

can lack the warm, pleasant amber color that solvent-based finishes impart. This isn't necessarily a problem on pickled or light-colored woods. In fact, the neutral color and nonyellowing characteristics may be seen as a benefit. However, there are situations where you'll want to warm up the color of a water-based finish. There are several ways to do this.

- Dye the wood an amber color before applying the finish. Use a diluted dye stain to approximate the color of the yellow naturally imparted by varnish or lacquer.
- Seal the bare wood with shellac. This adds a warm amber color under the water-based finish while preventing grain raising at the same time.
- Add a small amount of a compatible stain color to the finish itself. Some manufacturers offer this color as an additive, but you could simply mix up a honey-colored stain

yourself. If you use dry dye powder, predissolve it in a small amount of water before adding it to the finish.

Grain Raising

Unlike solvent-based finishes, water-based finishes raise the fibers of the wood, creating a very rough surface. Many manufacturers of water-based finishes have formulated special sealers that minimize this grain raising but it can still be a problem, in which case you'll need to take one of the following approaches:

- Sand the wood to 320 grit instead of stopping at 180 or 220 grit.
- Sand the wood to 180 grit, then preraise the grain by wiping water onto the surface. After the water dries, sand with 220-grit paper.
- Apply a shellac sealer coat, which will minimize grain raising. The shellac will also help warm up the color of darker woods like walnut and cherry.
- Stain the bare wood first with an oil-based stain. Just make sure the stain is compati-

Applying a sealer coat of dewaxed shellac will minimize grain raising and deepen the color of the wood if your water-based finish otherwise creates a pasty look.

ble with your water-based finish. If necessary, test the adhesion.

► See *"Testing for Adhesion"* on p. 213.

Flow-Out and Foaming

Some brands of water-based finishes foam quite a bit when brushed. If this happens, first try a different brush. The best brushes I've used for water-based finishes are fine-bristled golden Taklon brushes. If you continue to get bubbles, try a different brand of finish.

Poor flow-out—the result of incomplete coalescence—usually shows up as a pebbly looking surface. This can be caused by the finish drying too fast during hot weather or by the hot air generated by a turbine. The best solution is to make sure that the finish is at 70° F. and that your project and environment are at least at 65° F. Failing that, you can try adding a retarder available from the manufacturer to slow down the drying. However, I recommend always trying to correct problems without adding anything to a water-based finish.

A water-based finish may look terrible right after it is applied. It may not flow out and level quickly, like solvent-based lacquer or shellac. But be patient; coalescing takes time. Let the solvents in the finish do their job. It's not unusual to leave a hopeless-looking finish at night only to find a perfectly level, clear finish the next morning.

[TIP] **Don't use water as a retarder, as is sometimes mistakenly recommended. When you add water to a water-based finish, you are actually speeding up the dry time, not slowing it down.**

► ADDITIVES FOR WATER-BASED FINISHES

Because of the complex nature of water-based formulations, it's not easy to compensate for problems by introducing additives, as you might for solvent-based finishes. I always recommend changing equipment setup or technique before putting anything into a water-based finish. The only "additive" you can safely add without causing problems is distilled water, usually up to 20 percent for clear finish and 10 percent for paint. If that doesn't solve the problem, try a different technique or a different brand of finish.

When you add too much water, you change the chemistry of the finish, increasing its surface tension. This can result in beading or poor flow-out. If you need to slow down the dry time to improve flow-out and leveling, use a retarder specified by the manufacturer. You may encounter "tips" in various magazines that recommend adding things like lacquer thinner, mineral spirits, or half-and-half to solve particular problems. This is bad advice, and I don't know of a single manufacturer that suggests it.

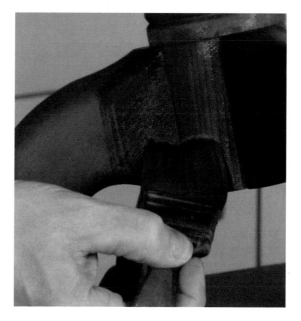

Fine-bristled Taklon brushes work best for all water-based finishes. The sharp chiseled edge on this 2-in. brush nicely handles the intricate details on this turned table base.

Many finish manufacturers make a water-based cleaner that works better than acetone or lacquer thinner to strip dried water-based finish from your equipment.

Spray blow-back can clog the fluid nozzle and air orifices in a gun's air cap. You can easily scrape dried finish from the nozzle using your fingernail or a toothpick. (The X-Acto knife shown here is used only for photographic clarity.)

In hot and humid conditions, you can help drive the water out of the finish by positioning a fan to blow across the workpiece after you've applied the finish.

Equipment Cleaning

Water-based finish cleans up with water but only before it dries. Be sure to clean your brushes immediately with water and soap before hanging them up. Spray equipment can be cleaned with water to purge most of the water-based finish, but it has a remarkable tendency to adhere to metal components in a gun and cup. A better choice is to use a plastic gravity cup fitted to a gravity gun that has stainless-steel parts along its fluid path.

You can remove dried water-based finish using lacquer thinner, acetone, or special water-based cleaners. When spraying intermittently throughout the day, you can safely leave the finish in the gun for up to four hours. During this time, the only thing you may have to do is occasionally flick dried finish from the nozzle area. After four hours, the gun may need a more thorough cleaning. If you find a lot of finish residue on the air cap, reduce the air pressure or hold the gun a little farther away from the workpiece.

Coping with the Weather

Try to avoid finishing in temperatures below 55° F. or during days when the relative humidity exceeds 90 percent. It's possible to finish during extremely high humidity, but you typically cannot apply as thick a coat as you normally would. During cold weather, heat your shop if possible, and make sure the finish is also warm before applying it. If you still have problems after changing your techniques or controlling temperature or air movement, consult the finish manufacturer regarding an additive to solve your specific problem.

Always strain water-based finishes through a fine- or medium-mesh strainer before applying them.

Applying Water-Based Finishes

Prepare for finishing by sanding the wood to 180 or 220 grit. Avoid stearated sandpapers for this, as they can cause fisheye in subsequent coats. After sanding, clean up your finishing area. Because water-based finishes dry quickly, dust settling in the finish is not as much of a problem as with varnish, but you'll still want to minimize the problem. Also, try to have fresh air moving through the finishing area if possible.

If you like, you can begin by applying a coat of compatible sanding sealer, which will "powder" more easily than straight finish when sanded. However, this isn't always necessary, as most water-based finishes are "self-sealing" and don't require a special sealer. Water-based finishes can be used straight from the can or thinned with as

much as 10 percent to 20 percent water (check with the manufacturer for amounts over 10 percent) to ease application. Always strain the finish through a fine- or medium-mesh strainer before applying it.

[TIP] **Don't punch holes through the metal can lid of water-based finishes as you might with solvent-based products. The holes will pierce the liner, exposing the steel and causing rust.**

Brushing

When brushing water-based finishes, use a fine, soft, synthetic-bristle brush. Avoid cheap, blunt-bristle brushes made for latex paint, as they'll leave brush marks in the finish. Taklon brushes, Chinex™, Tynex™, or Orel™ filament with scored ends all work well. Combinations of both natural and synthetic bristles are also very good and hold more finish than purely synthetic bristles. Before using the brush, dip it in water to condition the bristles. Wring out the excess before dipping it in the finish. When coating floors or other large surfaces, use a synthetic applicator pad. To condition the pad, mist it with water before loading it with finish.

Spraying

The basic process of spraying water-based finishes is exactly the same as spraying solvent-based lacquer or shellac. However, there are two exceptions: You may need to change the setup of your gun and vary your technique slightly. Check with the manufacturer for the recommended setup.

Most brands of water-based finishes require a setup for light-to-medium-viscosity liquids. Many finish manufacturers recom-

Step-Down Cleaning of a Spray Gun

Before spraying with a gun that is used to apply both solvents and water-based finishes, clean the gun, using the appropriate solvents in the proper sequence.

CONDITION	CLEANING STEP 1	CLEANING STEP 2	CLEANING STEP 3
To switch from oil-based finishes or lacquer to water-based	Lacquer thinner	Denatured alcohol	Water
To switch from water-based to oil-based finishes or lacquer	Water	Denatured alcohol	Lacquer thinner
To switch from water-based to shellac	Water	Denatured alcohol	
To switch from shellac to water-based	Denatured alcohol	Water	

For low-tech spraying of water-based finishes, set a fan on low and place it behind you to drive the overspray away from the workpiece. Protect nearby machinery and benches with plastic drop cloths.

mend spraying thin, light coats 1 to 2 mils thick. However, some recent formulations can be sprayed more heavily. Water-based finishes will easily run and drip on vertical surfaces, so you may have to apply numerous lighter coats. When spraying water-based finishes with an HVLP turbine system, you'll need at least a three-stage turbine, as smaller units are too underpowered for proper atomization.

When scuff-sanding between coats of water-based finish, avoid using stearated paper as the antiloading compounds will cause fisheye in subsequent coats. Manufacturers have addressed this by offering newer-generation sandpaper made with modified antiload compounds. These include 3M Fre-Cut® Gold and Mirka® Royal Gold. For scuff-sanding water-based finishes, I prefer dry sanding with these papers

Conventional rosin-treated tack cloths will cause problems with water-based finishes. Instead, clean up sanding dust with a lint-free damp rag or with a special tack cloth made specifically for these finishes.

rather than using lubricated wet/dry silicon carbide paper.

For cleaning up the sanding dust, use water-based-tolerant tack cloths instead of conventional rosin-treated tack cloths. Alternatively, you can use a damp, lint-free cloth. Don't use steel wool when working with water-based finishes, as it can rust. Use synthetic steel wool pads instead.

Hybrid Water-Based Finishing

Many solvent-based products like stains and glazes have longer open times and a natural oily quality that makes them easy to manipulate. Because of these qualities, many finishers prefer to use solvent-based grain fillers, stains, glazes, and toners to color the wood before

applying clear water-based top coats. This approach is called "hybrid" finishing.

Water-based finishes can be applied over most solvent-based stains and glazes as long as a "tie coat" of dewaxed shellac is applied on top of the solvent-based products. In some cases water-based finishes can be applied over solvent-based products without the tie coat. Before attempting this, though, check with the finish manufacturer or perform an adhesion test.

➤ See *"Testing for Adhesion"* on p. 213.

After applying the solvent-based products, wait at least a week for them to cure thoroughly before applying the top coat for the adhesion test.

Water-Based Paint

One area of finishing where water based products dominate is in the field of decorative paints. Although oil-based paint is preferred by many professionals due to its superior leveling characteristics, it's more usual to find finishers using water-based (latex) paint for interior walls and trim.

Water-based paints use a wide variety of resins, but two of the most common are vinyl and acrylic. Vinyl latex paints are used primarily on drywall and other surfaces that do not need heat, chemical, and abrasion resistance. For furniture, however, you're better off with the protective qualities offered by acrylic and urethane resins. Water-based acrylic and urethane paints are among the best choices for furniture, but these aren't commonly available. A second choice would be acrylic paint that's sold in major paint stores for trim and other hard-wearing sur-

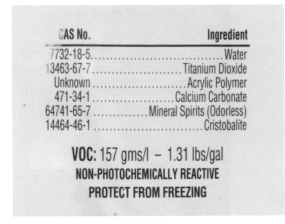

CAS No.	Ingredient
7732-18-5	Water
13463-67-7	Titanium Dioxide
Unknown	Acrylic Polymer
471-34-1	Calcium Carbonate
64741-65-7	Mineral Spirits (Odorless)
14464-46-1	Cristobalite

VOC: 157 gms/l – 1.31 lbs/gal
NON-PHOTOCHEMICALLY REACTIVE
PROTECT FROM FREEZING

This label is an example from a 100 percent acrylic paint (acrylic polymer) suitable for furniture. If the list of ingredients has vinyl, vinyl latex, or acrylic-styrene (styrene is a type of vinyl), it's a latex paint. The other ingredients are the solvents (water, mineral spirits), pigments (titanium dioxide, calcium carbonate), and a flatting agent (cristobalite).

Premixed milk paint is sold in bags as a powder to which water is added right before use.

faces. "Acrylic"—not "vinyl"—should show up on the list of ingredients for a suitable furniture paint.

Most latex paint produced in this country is meant to be brushed on or applied with a roller, so it's purposely thickened to prevent dripping and spattering. Unfortunately, thick paints don't spray well with air-powered guns. Therefore, professionals use airless equipment to spray unthinned latex paint. However, if you use conventional or HVLP spray equipment, you'll have to thin the paint. Alternatively, you can buy water-based paint that hasn't been thickened, but you'll probably need to get it from a specialty supplier. (See Resources on p. 287.)

One particular water-based paint that's popular for furniture finishing is milk, or casein, paint. It owes its origin to old-fashioned paint recipes based on casein, which is the principal protein found in milk. Casein—an extremely durable binder—is dissolved in water along with lime. This creates a colloidal dispersion similar to the chemistry of other water-based finishes. Colored pigment is then added, typically in the form of natural earth colors like umbers and ochres. Premixed milk paint is sold in bags as a powder to which water is added right before use.

Brushing Water-Based Finish

If you wish, you can use dewaxed shellac as a sealer under water-based finish. On this cherry table it will eliminate grain raising and seal in any residual sodium hydroxide used as a chemical stain **(A)**. If you don't wish to use shellac, instead sponge the wood with distilled water after sanding it to 220 grit to raise the grain. After the wood feels dry to the touch, resand it with 320-grit paper.

Dip a synthetic bristle brush into water to condition it, then wring out the excess. Strain the finish through a fine or medium strainer into a cup, and dip the brush halfway up the bristles into the finish. Press the bristles against the side of the cup to remove excess finish **(B)**. Apply the finish in smooth, wet strokes with the tip of the brush **(C)**. Try to flow the finish off the tip of the brush without pressing down too hard on the bristles. While the finish is still wet, level it off by lightly dragging the tip of the bristles fully across the surface while holding the brush vertically. To brush edges, corners, and nonflat areas, lightly load just the very tip of the brush for more precise control **(D)**. Work in a warm room with plenty of air circulation to help the finish dry properly, but don't blow air across the finish as you're brushing it.

After the first coat dries, it may feel rough. If the wood is unstained, you can scuff-sand it at this point. With stained wood, though, you may want to apply an additional coat before scuff-sanding to avoid cutting through the stain. On complicated areas use a cushioned abrasive pad **(E)**. Two coats suffice for the base of this table, but three were applied to the top, which will see a bit more wear.

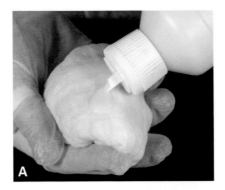

Wiping Water-Based Finish

Wiping on water-based finish eliminates bubbling, which is one of the most common problems encountered when brushing. To prepare the finish for wiping, add between 10 percent and 20 percent water by volume. To avoid pulling up dyes that were applied with no binder, seal them in with dewaxed shellac first. This unstained table was sealed with a 1-lb.-cut of dewaxed shellac, followed by a scuff-sanding with P400-grit paper.

To apply the finish, first work about an ounce of water into a soft, absorbent, lint-free cloth that's wadded to fit comfortably in your hand with no seams or creases on the bottom. Then dispense ½ oz. to 1 oz. of thinned finish onto the pad **(A)**. Apply the finish in a smooth, consistent manner, moving from one edge to the other **(B)**. Overlap each previous stroke by about 1 in. Replenish the finish on the rag when the workpiece surface starts to streak. After covering the surface, you can reduce the dry time to almost nothing by blow-drying the finish to drive off the water **(C)**. At this point, you're ready for the next application. Apply no more than four applications in an hour.

Wiping is well suited to finishing complicated parts like this base, which would tend to produce bubbles if finished with a brush. To finish the legs, wrap the pad around them as shown **(D)**.

Wiping will produce a streaky finish with a gloss product, so it will need to be rubbed out. If you use satin or flat, you can get a very acceptable surface without rubbing out. In the case of this tabletop, I sanded with 400-grit paper, followed by scuff-sanding with a gray synthetic pad after four applications.

Milk Paint

Milk paint is well suited to this utilitarian pine coatrack purchased at an unfinished furniture store. Prepare the workpiece by filling any nail or staple holes with wood putty, then sanding with 150-grit paper, rounding over any sharp edges **(A)**. Seal any knots using dewaxed shellac.

Powdered milk paint sold in bags is mixed one-to-one with water by the user. Stir the mixture well, then let it sit 15 minutes. Brush the paint on using a synthetic bristle brush **(B)**. The first coat will raise the grain quite a bit, so lightly sand it smooth while wearing a dust mask. Remove the dust with a damp cloth, and then apply a second, final coat.

To create an antiqued effect, I began by applying a light buttermilk color over the red **(C)**. After it dried, I used steel wool to cut through the dried buttermilk color on the edges to lend it a lightly distressed look.

Milk paint is prone to water spots, so it's best to protect it with a coat of clear finish. Oil-based finishes deepen the color of the paint, while water-based finishes have the least effect on it **(D)**.

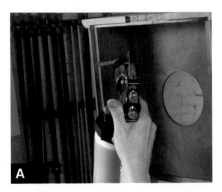

A

B

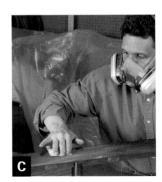

C

D

Spraying Water-Based Finishes

To set up for spraying a water-based finish, first strain the finish into the gun cup, then adjust the gun for low fluid delivery. To get the feel of the operation, begin by spraying on a nonshow surface on your project, such as the underside of a table or the inside of a cabinet **(A)**. Move the gun in a slow, steady motion, maintaining a consistent distance from the workpiece. After completing a section, check the surface for drips or runs, particularly on perpendicular surfaces. If you see them, you're applying too heavy a coat, and you'll need to adjust the gun's fluid delivery, move it faster across the workpiece, or back it up a bit as you spray. Once the gun is adjusted properly and you get the feel for how fast to move the gun, spray the outside of your project **(B)**. Use a nail board for finishing the doors.

The first coat should be hard enough to sand in about an hour. However, if your workpiece was stained, it's better to apply two coats of finish before sanding to minimize the chance of cutting through the stain. Use 400-grit or finer sandpaper **(C)**. Remove the sanding dust by wiping the surface with a damp rag, then with a tack cloth suited for water-based finishes. Apply the final coats lightly, about an hour or two apart **(D)**. I wanted a flat finish for this clock, so I applied two coats of gloss topped by a coat of flat to avoid a hazy look on the dark wood from three coats of flat finish.

Hybrid Water-Based Finishing

You can take a hybrid approach that combines the use of solvent-based products under water-based top coats as shown on this guitar.

Begin by filling the grain with a blue-tinted oil-based paste filler. Then apply an alcohol-based dye to the entire body. Next, a coat of dewaxed shellac is sprayed on as a sealer **(A)**. The shellac also builds a base that makes it easier to see the effect of a black shading toner to be applied next. The toner was made by mixing black dye into dewaxed clear shellac **(B)** and then applying it to the back and sides, shading it into the maple front with a sunburst technique **(C)**. After the

► See *"Spraying a Sunburst Pattern"* on p. 139.

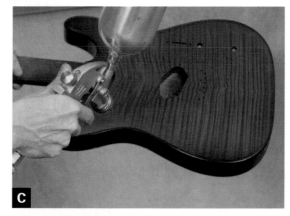

toner thoroughly dries overnight, apply a water-based sealer designed to fill in any pore cavities that weren't completely filled by the oil-based paste filler. The sealer is then sanded until no pore outline is visible **(D)**.

The final step is to spray clear 100 percent acrylic lacquer on the whole body, applying three coats one hour apart. After this dries overnight, three more coats are applied **(E)**. Let the piece cure for at least two weeks before buffing the finish out to a high gloss.

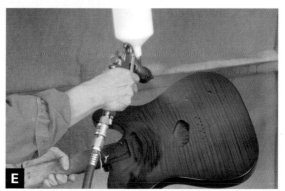

A

B

C

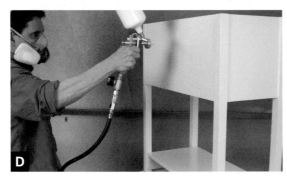

D

Spraying Water-Based Paint

Unless you use an airless spray gun, you'll have to thin latex paint to spray it. Although a special nonthickened water-based paint is made for compressor- and turbine-driven guns, it's hard to find at paint stores. Instead, the next best thing to use is 100% acrylic paint. It's commonly available in just about any color imaginable and is suitable for hard-wearing surfaces like those on this microwave cart.

Acrylic paint for brushing or rolling is thick and must be thinned for spraying by adding 10 percent water by volume **(A)**. The resulting thinner viscosity allows spraying with a conventional gun or a turbine-driven gun, provided you use the larger nozzle setups required. I prefer to use an inexpensive gravity-feed gun with a 2.2mm nozzle. These guns are easy to clean, and I can run the air pressure higher than normal to get good atomization.

Start by applying a primer and filling any cracks or splits with putty **(B)**. Sand the dried putty and the primer, then clean off the dust. Begin spraying the first coat with the air pressure turned down to allow easy spraying into all the nooks and corners **(C)**. For the final passes on large areas, turn up the pressure to produce the best atomization, practicing the setup on a test panel first **(D)**.

Rubbing Out Finishes

Rubbing Out by Hand

➤ Rubbing Out a Thin Finish (p. 280)

➤ Rubbing and Waxing Combined (p. 281)

➤ Rubbing to Gloss by Hand (p. 282)

➤ Rubbing to Satin by Hand (p. 283)

Rubbing with Power

➤ Wet Sanding with Power Tools (p. 284)

➤ Power-Buffing to Gloss (p. 285)

➤ Rubbing to Satin with Abralon (p. 286)

RUBBING OUT a finish is the last step in finishing. Its purpose is to remove any imperfections, to smooth the surface, and to establish the desired finish sheen. However, rubbing out a finish is optional, and you don't have to do it if you're satisfied with the way the finish looks without it. That said, knowing how to rub out a finish is a potent weapon in your arsenal of problem-solving and special-effects skills.

Rubbing Out Finishes

Rubbing out a finish involves using abrasives to create a fine, consistent pattern of scratches in the finish. By using successively finer abrasives, you can create any sheen ranging from a nonreflective flat to a highly reflective gloss finish.

Rubbing out is typically done in two stages. The first stage involves removing imperfections and flattening the finish, which is done with coated abrasive papers.

A wet-sanded and buffed gloss finish is just about the most elegant finish you can achieve. This rubbed-out finish is receiving a final hand-glazing treatment to make it perfect.

The second stage—polishing to the desired sheen—is done with steel wool, synthetic abrasive pads, and abrasive powders.

Any film-forming finish can be rubbed out, but some are easier than others. Evaporative finishes such as shellac, solvent-based lacquer, and many water-based lacquers are thermoplastic, hard, and brittle. These rub out easily and buff quickly to a uniform gloss. Because coats of an evaporative finish melt together to form a single, contiguous film, rubbing the finish does not expose the individual finish layers. On the other hand, rubbing out reactive finishes can result in "witness lines" that appear at the edges of a layer of finish that has been abraded through to expose the adjacent layer of finish underneath.

Reactive thermosetting finishes, such as most oil-based varnishes, catalyzed varnish, and polyester, are tough and flexible enough to be rubbed out, but they don't always take a uniform sheen and can be difficult to polish to a gloss sheen. Hard, tough thermosetting finishes like 2K urethane and catalyzed lacquers can be buffed to a brilliant gloss, but typically not as quickly as a solvent-based lacquer or acrylic.

Soft finishes like tung oil, linseed oil, Danish oils, and oil/varnish blends can be waxed or maybe burnished with a cloth, but they aren't rubbed out.

Some finishes are formulated with fine light-scattering silica to produce a flat, satin, or semigloss sheen that is less than glossy. Although these finishes can be rubbed out to remove defects, it's best to leave them unrubbed if possible, as rubbing can destroy the effect of their intended sheen.

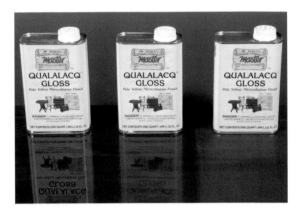

The degree of sheen in a finish is indicated by its reflectivity. From left, gloss reflects a distinct outline of the can with an easily readable label; satin blurs the image and makes reading the label difficult; a flat finish shows almost no reflection.

Creating Sheen

A smooth, scratch-free gloss surface reflects light perfectly. But a glossy surface may not suit your project, so you may prefer a duller sheen. Nonglossy sheens can be produced by either abrading a gloss finish with fine scratches or by using a finish that includes flatting agents.

You can abrade a finish to create varying degrees of sheen. Scratches left by 400-grit sandpaper will result in a very dull surface, while grits ranging from 400 to 1000 will create sheens ranging from flat to satin. A semigloss sheen results from using 1200 grit. When you start getting into fine polishing, the surface begins to take on a gloss.

Flatting agents are small transparent particles (typically silica-based) that diffuse light in the same manner as scratches. Because generic descriptions of sheen vary among manufacturers, industrial finishes are more precisely defined by their "degree of

Sheen Classifications

GENERIC SHEEN DESCRIPTION	DEGREE OF SHEEN	IMAGE DISTINCTION
Flat	10	No reflection
Eggshell	10-20	Slight sheen; like the surface of an egg
Satin	20-35	Fuzzy image; indistinct letters
Semigloss	35-70	Lines of image somewhat distinct; blurry letters
Gloss	70-85	Glossy but not wet looking; readable letters
High-gloss	85+	Wet looking; mirrorlike; crisp outline with detail

sheen." This measurement is determined with an optical instrument called a glossmeter, which measures reflected light at a specific angle (usually 60 degrees), and which allows architects and others to more accurately specify a particular sheen.

[TIP] **A disadvantage of a high-gloss finish is that any surface imperfection will be glaringly apparent.**

Materials for Rubbing Out

Various abrasives are used for rubbing out finishes. As discussed earlier, coated abrasive papers are used for the initial smoothing and flattening of the finished surface. Afterward, steel wool, synthetic abrasive pads, and abrasive powders are used to bring the finish to the desired sheen.

Abrasive Papers

Wet/dry silicon carbide sandpaper is the traditional favorite for sanding finishes. It is usually lubricated with rubbing oil, mineral spirits, naphtha, or water with a dash of dishwashing soap added to prevent the paper from clogging up during use. To avoid this

Various abrasives are used for rubbing out finishes. From left, dry pumice and rottenstone powders; compounding pastes and liquid polishes; synthetic and regular steel wool; foam-backed abrasive pads and wet/dry sandpaper; and rubbing lubricants.

clogging, modern nonloading aluminum oxide or silicon carbide papers can be used for dry sanding some finishes. The advantage to dry sanding is that you can more clearly gauge your progress to prevent sanding through the finish. When you're wet sanding, the lubricant makes bare wood appear finished.

Steel Wool, Synthetic Steel Wool, and Flexible Sanding Pads

Steel wool is graded using the aught system, which ranges from 3 (very coarse) to 0000 (finest). Typically, 000 or 0000 is used for rubbing out finishes. An alternative to steel wool is synthetic steel wool, which is a non-woven synthetic fiber pad with abrasive particles. Both regular and synthetic steel wool can be used dry or with a lubricant.

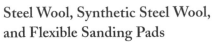

▶ See *"Steel Wool"* on p. 28.

A third choice is to use flexible sanding pads, which are basically foam-backed versions of silicon carbide wet/dry paper that have a grip backing. Because they're cushioned, they don't do a very good job of shearing off high spots like dust pimples, and they won't level irregularities in the finish. Instead, these pads are typically used to establish a consistent scratch pattern to create a flat or satin sheen. They're best lubricated for use, just like silicon carbide paper.

Abrasive Powders, Pastes, and Sticks

Abrasive powders are used to polish the finish to the desired sheen after sanding and steel-wooling. The powders traditionally used for polishing include pumice (powdered volcanic glass) and rottenstone (powdered decomposed limestone). Pumice is sold in various grades ranging from 1F (coarse) to 4F (fine). Rottenstone is finer than pumice and is sold in only one grade, which is fine enough to polish a surface to gloss. Pumice and rottenstone are typically used in conjunction with a liquid like soapy water or rubbing oil to make a paste.

When using stationary buffing machines, you use silica abrasive in stick form to "charge" the buffing wheel by holding the stick to the spinning wheel.

A modern silica abrasive is also available for polishing. Precisely manufactured to ensure uniform particle size, this silica abrasive is sold in the form of a liquid suspension, a paste, or as a hard stick. The liquid and paste are rubbed in by hand or with hand-held power buffers, while the sticks are used with stationary buffing equipment. The paste and liquid forms can be found at automotive supply shops, while the sticks are available from specialty suppliers.

Silica abrasive is usually sold under a generic name like "compounding or polishing material." You use the compounding material first, then the polishing compound. The sequence may be designated as something like coarse no. 1, medium no. 2, fine no. 3. Try to stick with one particular brand of product since the grit designations may differ from one manufacturer to another.

Some thin finishes like this wiping varnish may require only a light scuffing with fine sandpaper, followed by a light rubbing with steel wool.

Film Thickness and Rubbing Out

Rubbing out removes some of the finish, so the thickness of a given finish determines how aggressively it can be leveled and smoothed. Many finishes don't need to be rubbed out very aggressively. Thin finishes like wiping varnish, for example, may need only a light sanding with fine sandpaper followed by a light rubbing with steel wool. On the other hand, if you want to sand a finish dead level, you'll want to start with a relatively thick finish to avoid sanding through it to the wood or underlying stain. A dead-level surface is particularly critical if it will be rubbed to a high gloss, which will clearly reflect any surface imperfections.

If you plan on a gloss finish, make sure to fill the pores of open-pored woods like mahogany, walnut, and oak. For hand-rubbed satin finishes, it doesn't make any difference whether the pores are open or filled. If you rub out to gloss any open-pored dark woods, use dark-colored pastes called "ebony" and dark waxes. Otherwise,

residual compound caught in the pores shows up white.

As mentioned earlier, coats of reactive finishes (varnishes, catalyzed lacquers, and two-part finishes) do not fuse into each other as coats of evaporative finishes do. This can pose a problem if you rub too aggressively because you can abrade through one coat of finish into the underlying one, exposing "witness lines" at the edges of the sand-through. To prevent this problem with reactive finishes, I begin by applying three coats to seal in any stain or paste-wood filler. After the finish dries for a day, I sand it level using P600 paper. Then I apply one full, wet final coat.

For evaporative finishes like lacquers, shellac, and water-based products, I also apply three initial coats, then let them dry for a day. Afterward, I level the surface with 320-grit wet/dry paper. I finish up by applying three full, wet coats of finish in preparation for rubbing out.

[TIP] Finishes may shrink away from edges as they dry, leaving these areas vulnerable to sand-throughs during rubbing out. You can compensate for this by spraying extra finish on the edges, although that won't help with hand-applied finishes.

Whatever finish you use, it's important to let it cure as much as possible before rubbing it out. Cured finishes sand and buff better and faster than incompletely cured finishes, so the longer you wait the better. Shellac, solvent- and water-based lacquers, and two-part finishes should cure at least a week. Oil-based varnishes and polyurethane should cure at least two weeks. If the finish is gummy and loads up the paper in the initial leveling, it's not dry enough. Let it cure longer.

Thin Finish Rub-Out

There are two situations where you might rub out a thin finish. The first is when you have a minimal film build on the wood because you're going after a more natural appearance. The second is when you apply thin finish coats with a reactive finish like varnish or some water-based lacquers. These coats do not fuse together, and aggressive rubbing may break through the final coat, creating witness lines at the edges of the sand-through.

I prefer to dry sand thin finishes with antiloading paper. Dry sanding allows you to see what you're doing and to get a better feel for how much finish you're removing,

For dry sanding, always use sandpaper with antiloading additives. This stearated sandpaper reduces the formation of little bumps, or "corns," of dried finish on the sandpaper.

An in-line pneumatic sander like this Stuhr model makes short work of wet sanding large flat surfaces, like dining table tops and piano lids.

because you can see the finish powder up as you sand. Once the dry sanding is done, you can proceed to rubbing with steel wool.

Because a thin finish rub-out is the easiest and least invasive rubbing procedure, it's a great practice technique to use on various finishes to get a feel for the basics of rubbing out.

Thick Finish Rub-Out

You can level thick finishes more aggressively to get a perfectly flat surface when viewed in backlighting. Once the finish is leveled, you can bring it up to the desired luster by creating a pattern of progressively finer scratches. This is done with steel wool, abrasive powders, or liquid pastes.

Start by sanding with the finest grit of wet/dry paper that will efficiently remove the imperfections. I usually begin with 400 or 600 grit (P800-P1000) but I'll use a coarser grit if the surface has orange peel. You can perform this process by hand, but if you do large surfaces like dining tables on a regular basis, consider getting an in-line pneumatic sander. Not only do these tools speed things up, but they produce a consistent scratch pattern that matches the factory finishes you see on high-end furniture. A finish is typically wet sanded to a certain grit, then either rubbed by hand to create a satin sheen or buffed to gloss.

Rubbing to Satin

Rubbing to satin begins after the surface has been level-sanded to 600 grit (P1200). You can do this by hand or machine. The classic hand-rubbed effect is done with 0000 steel wool, rubbing the finish in straight lines. This creates a very unique look, but in certain lighting situations, the distinguishable

Abralon is silicon carbide paper bonded to a soft foam pad that can be attached to a grip-type random orbit sander.

This hand-held buffer is sold as a sander-polisher. The best models include variable speed control and large handles that allow you to grip them from the top or side. The grip-style wool bonnets can be attached and removed easily. Use separate bonnets for compounding and polishing.

scratch pattern left by the steel wool may be objectionable. Instead, you can use a flexible sanding pad, which is simply extremely fine silicon carbide sandpaper bonded to a foam pad. It can be used with a random orbit sander or by hand.

Rubbing to Gloss

The difference between a rubbed satin sheen and a gloss is simply a pattern of finer scratches on the latter. To polish a satin sheen to gloss, continue wet-sanding up to 1000 grit (P2000) after leveling with coarser grits. You then have the choice of proceeding through the traditional polishing compounds of pumice, Tripoli, and rottenstone, or you can substitute prepared liquid or paste polishing compounds.

Rubbing to gloss by hand is a lot of work. If you often rub out large surfaces, you can save a lot of time by investing in a power buffer. The best hand-held buffers are right-angle variable-speed models. These are used with a wool bonnet or a foam pad. If you buff a lot of small, three-dimensional pieces, consider getting a pedestal buffer that

is fitted with sewn cotton pads. Small, decorative objects can be buffed with slow-speed grinder attachments.

Many finishers escape the extra work of rubbing out and buffing a finish to gloss by using a technique called "flow-coating." This works best with evaporative finishes like lacquer. To flow-coat, sand your last coat with 400 grit to remove any defects, then abrade the whole surface with gray synthetic pads. Remove all the dust and apply a final wet coat consisting of one-third lacquer and two-thirds thinner, with 2 to 3 oz., of lacquer retarder added per quart.

This table is the surface you get "off the gun" by flow-coating. Though not the dead-flat, perfect gloss that abrading and rubbing produces, it's a good technique for production situations or when you want to save time.

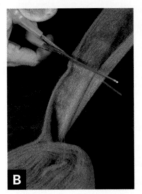

Rubbing Out a Thin Finish

Cut a sheet of 600-grit (P1200) sandpaper into quarters. Tuck one of the corners of the short edge between your pinky and ring finger, then fold the paper across your palm, grasping the opposite end between your thumb and fore-finger **(A)**. Use this abrasive "pad" to lightly shear the pimples and other defects from the surface. (If the finish doesn't powder easily, let it cure longer before sanding.) Hold the paper flat at the edges of the workpiece to avoid cut-ting through the finish there. Afterward, wipe off the dust with a solvent-dampened cloth. Do not sand intricate moldings, turnings, or carvings.

Unravel a 0000 steel wool pad or cut a 12- to 14-in. length from a roll **(B)**. Fold it twice, then rub the perimeter of the workpiece, moving in short, quick strokes about 3 in. in from each edge **(C)**. A dull scratch pattern will be apparent in rak-ing light. As you continue to rub, you'll notice shiny spots at the bottom of pores and low areas. To make these disappear, bear down a bit more on the steel wool. Then rub out the rest of the piece, blending all the areas together afterward with a few quick passes over the entire surface.

To bring up the shine further, apply some paste wax and buff it when it's dry **(D)**. On open-pored finishes, use a dark wax or polishing compound if the light color of the wax or compound in the pores is objectionable. To rub moldings, turnings, and carved areas, apply just enough pressure on the steel wool to knock the gloss down a bit. You can tear off small pieces of steel wool to make pads that conform to the shape of moldings.

Rubbing and Waxing Combined

If you're after a semigloss sheen, you can combine steel-wooling and waxing at the same time. The high gloss left by the water-based finish on this cherry brandy stand needed both smoothing and a bit of deglossing. For cherry and other dark woods, use a dark-colored wax. Natural wax is fine on lighter-colored woods like ash, birch, and maple.

After lightly shearing away any pimples with 600-grit paper (P1200), make a 0000 wool pad, as described on the facing page. Squirt an ounce of naphtha or mineral spirits into it (**A**). (Mineral spirits will extend the dry, or "flash," time of the wax.) Dunk the pad into the wax to pull up a teaspoonful or more, and start rubbing the wood with the solvent/wax mix (**B**). If you wish, deliberately leave excess wax in any molded edges or other crannies to simulate an aged look (**C**). When the wax starts to haze, use a shoe brush to buff it to a soft luster. Compare the garish gloss on the unrubbed right side of this cherry base with the left side, which was rubbed with the wax (**D**).

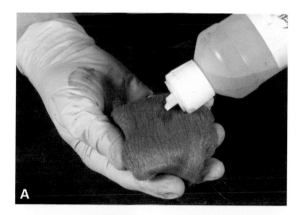

Rubbing to Gloss by Hand

Start by sanding with 320-grit (P600) paper lubricated with soapy water made by adding a capful of dishwashing detergent to a quart of water. Wrap a quarter-sheet of sandpaper around a cork block and wet sand the finish to remove brush marks and other defects **(A)**. The surface should have a dull sheen after you wipe away the slurry. On narrow pieces like frames, sand by hand to avoid cutting through the edges **(B)**.

Continue wet-sanding to 1000 grit (P2000). Traditionally, abrasive powders have been used after wet sanding to bring the surface sheen up higher. Use 4F pumice first, which removes the scratches left by the fine sandpaper. Rub the pumice with a damp rag in circular motion **(C)**. To bring the finish up to gloss, rub with rottenstone next. The pumice and rottenstone will leave a slight residue in the open pores of woods like mahogany, so in those cases, finish up by applying dark wax **(D)**. If you want a slightly less glossy surface, rub with 0000 steel wool after applying the wax.

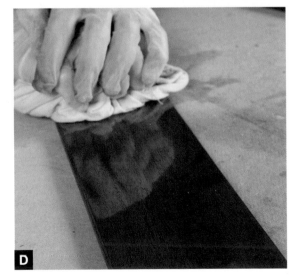

Rubbing to Satin by Hand

The perfectly flat and silky finish often seen on high-end furniture is likely a rubbed satin finish. This is best done on evaporative finishes, but you can do it on reactive finishes as long as your final coat is at least 2 to 3 mils thick when dry.

Start by wet sanding to level the finish. Use rubbing oil, which is messier than soapy water but makes the sandpaper cut faster and last longer. Start with 400-grit (P600-800) paper wrapped around a cork block, and continue up to 600 grit (P1200) **(A)**. Here, I sand right up to the edges where the raised profiled edge starts, and switch to a gray synthetic pad for the molded edge. Wipe away the slurry and make sure the surface has an even pattern of scratches with no low spots **(B)**. If just a few isolated imperfections remain, it may be prudent to live with them rather than risk cutting through the finish with continued sanding.

If you would like the steel wool to cut a little less aggressively, you can use a steel wool lubricant called wool lube or wool wax, which is a thick, syrupy soap. Do not use this product on shellac or water-based finishes because its alkalinity may harm them. For these finishes use rubbing oil. After dribbling some on the surface, use a cork block wrapped with steel wool to rub the surface, moving in the direction of the grain to create a "brushed-metal" effect **(C)**. Go over the whole surface from one edge to the other at least six times. Rub the molded edges by hand **(D)**.

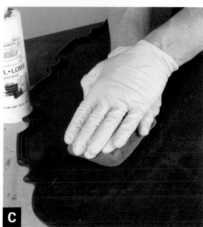

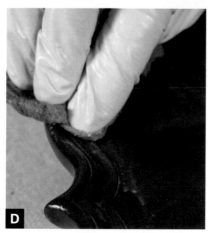

Wet Sanding with Power Tools

If you work on a lot of large, flat surfaces like dining-table tops or pianos, it can pay to invest in an in-line pneumatic sander. These monsters have two opposing pads that move back and forth in an in-line pattern. The weight of the machine (the larger models weigh 32 lbs.) simply requires that the operator guide it. The model I'm using here (see Resources on p. 287) takes two one-third sheets of sandpaper, allowing you to quickly cover a fair amount of surface area. Start the machine on the surface and use both hands to guide it (**A**). When you get up to an edge, make sure at least one-half of the over-hanging pad is still on the table surface to prevent tipping (**B**).

Abralon, produced by Mirka abrasives, works extremely well for wet sanding a complex three-dimensional object like a guitar body (**C**). Abralon is a silicon carbide abrasive attached to an open-cell foam pad with a grip backing on the opposite face. You can attach it directly to a random orbit sander pad or provide an extra measure of deflection and "cushion" by including a ½-in.-thick interface pad (**D**).

Power-Buffing to Gloss

To rub to gloss with a power buffer, level-sand the surface starting with the finest grit capable of leveling the surface efficiently. I began with 400-grit (P600) sandpaper for this demilune table, then sanded up to 1000 (P2000).

Use two pads—one for the compounding paste and the other for the finer polishing paste. Condition the spinning pad by holding a stick against it to remove loose fiber and old compound **(A)**. Apply one tablespoon of compound paste per square foot of surface, and smear it around evenly with the buffer turned off **(B)**. With the buffer resting on the surface, start it up on its lowest-speed setting and start moving it immediately. Tilt it 3 to 5 degrees so that only half the pad is in contact with the surface **(C)**. When buffing the edges of the workpiece, tilt the buffer so that the part of the pad contacting the surface is rotating away from the edge, to prevent catching **(D)**. Buff the edges first, then come back and blend in the center with the compounding pad. All the wet-sanding scratches should now be replaced by a dull pattern of scratches from the compound.

Switch to the polishing pad and repeat the process using the polishing paste. The gloss should come up quickly as the paste breaks down **(E)**. Finish up the gloss buffing by misting some water on the surface to keep it cool while polishing lightly with the dry pad. To achieve a wet-gloss look, the final step is to apply a superfine polish or glaze by hand to the surface.

VARIATION

[VARIATION] **A Surbuf® pad is a smaller bonnet with a grip back that attaches to a random orbit sander. Though not as fast as a power buffer, these pads are used with compounds and pastes in the same manner.**

A

B

C

D

Rubbing to Satin with Abralon®

If you want a satin finish without the brushed-metal effect achieved with steel wool, try using Abralon cushioned abrasives on a random orbit sander. This abrasive material is sold in grits from 180 to 4000 and is used extensively by production furniture shops to eliminate the tedious process of hand-rubbing with steel wool.

Start by using fine sandpaper to remove finish defects like pimples, brush marks, or orange peel **(A)**. Soapy water can be used as a lubricant with a random orbit sander **(B)** as long as you're plugged into a ground fault circuit interrupt (GFCI) outlet. Otherwise, use rubbing oil, which doesn't present an electrical shock hazard.

Center the disk on your sander pad, then start the sander up while it's resting on your workpiece. Move it over the surface slowly at first, then speed up your movement. If the sander stops spinning, use more lubricant. The extra ½-in.-thick interface pad should be installed when you're doing legs and aprons **(C)**.

Personally, I think using an air-powered palm sander is much less fatiguing than holding an electric palm sander. Its lower profile also allows easier access into tighter areas **(D)**.

Resources

Many of the products used in this book can be found in hardware stores and home centers. Specialized wood-finishing products such as dyes, shellac, grain fillers, lacquers, and varnishes can be found at the following:

Homestead Finishing Products
(216) 631-5309
www.homesteadfinishing.com

Woodcraft
(800) 225-1153
www.woodcraft.com

Rockler Woodworking and Hardware
(800) 279-4441
www.rockler.com

Klingspor's Woodworking Shop
(800) 228-0000
www.woodworkingshop.com

Touch Up Depot
(866) 883-3768
www.touchupdepot.com

Section 1

Temperature/ Hygrometer gauge

Model # 63-1032
Radio Shack
(800) 843-7422
www.radioshack.com

Plastic containers

U.S. Plastic Corp.
(800) 537-9724
www.usplastic.com

Section 2

Premium Sandpaper

Klingspor's Woodworking Shop
(800) 228-0000
www.woodworkingshop.com

*Mirka Abrasives
(800) 843-3904
www.mirka-usa.com

*3M Corporation
(888) 364-3577
www.3M.com

Section 3

Safety Suppliers

Conney Safety Products
(800) 356-9100
www.conney.com

Spray Gun Cleaning Suppliers

Spray Gun Solutions
(303) 424-3741

Section 5

Flexible and contour sanding blocks

Klingspor's Woodworking Shop
(800) 228-0000
www.woodworkingshop.com

Section 6

Inlay kit

Woodcraft
(800) 225-1153
www.woodcraft.com

Section 9

Natural Dyes

Kremer Pigment
(800) 995-5501
www.kremer-pigmente.com

Earth Guild
(800) 327-8448
www.earthguild.com

Chemicals

Olde Mill Cabinet Shop
www.oldemill.com
(717) 755-8884

Section 9

Glue Size

Custom Pak Adhesives
(800) 454-4583
www.custompak.com

Section 11

Polyester Grain Filler

IC&S
(800) 220-4035

Section 13

Viscosity and Mil Gauges

Homestead Finishing Products
(216) 631-5309
www.homesteadfinishing.com

Section 14

Polyester, 2K polyurethanes

IC&S
(800) 220-4035

Conversion Lacquers and Varnishes

Sherwin Williams
(800) 474-3794
www.sherwin-williams.com

ML Campbell
(800) 364-1359
www.mlcampbell.com

Mohawk Finishing Products
(800) 545-0047
www.mohawk-finishes.com

Section 16

Water-Based Finishes

*Fuhr International
(800) 558-7437
www.fuhrinternational.com

Compliant Spray Systems
(800) 696-0615
www.compliantspraysystems.com

Target Coatings
(800) 752-9922
www.targetcoatings.com

Section 17

Stuhr Sander

Cooper Power Tools*
(800) 845-5629
www.cooperpowertools.com

* Manufacturer; they may direct you to a retailer

Index

W

Walnut, 23, 104, 144, 152, 252
Walnut hull dye, 140, 141, 142, 143, 148
Washcoats, 155, 156-58, 165, 166-67, 173, 174
Waste disposal, 20
Water, 87, 96, 208
Water-based fillers, 182-83, 184, 187
Water-based finishes, 257-72
   additives for, 261
   appearance of, 259-60
   brushes for, 43, 261, 262
   brushing, 262, 267
   coloring, 131, 260-61
   composition of, 258-59
   hybrid, 265, 271
   over fillers, 181-82
   safety of, 205
   as sealers, 189-90
   sealers for, 192, 260, 267
   spraying, 13, 177, 262-65, 266, 270-72
   thinning, 46
   washcoats, 158
   weather and, 262
   wiping, 268
Water-based paint, 265-66, 269
Water-based polyurethanes, 204
Water-based stains
   characteristics of, 104, 105-6, 110, 111
   glazes, 125
   hand application of, 112, 115
   for splotching control, 156, 158
   spraying, 117
   for toners, 130, 131
Water spots, 89
Waterstone, 38
Wax, 204, 281
Wax crayons, 93-94
Wet-mil thickness, 210-11, 214, 231
Wet sanding, 29, 121, 284
White oak, 143, 145, 184
Whitewashing, 152
Wide-belt sanders, 32
Wiping stains, 111, 112, 114, 165
Wiping varnish, 233
Wood
   closed-pore, 176
   defects, 86-101
   dense, 105
   diffuse-porous, 104
   inexpensive, 173
   moisture content of, 10

   natural color of, 204
   open-pore, 92, 104, 176, 177, 226
   patches, 89-90
   types of, 61
Wood fillers. See Fillers
Workbenches, 17
Workshop environment, 8-21, 201-2
   heating, 11
   humidity, 9-10
   for spraying, 13-15
   temperature, 9-10, 11
   ventilation, 11-12
Wrinkling, 231

Y

Yellowing, 113, 201, 205

Z

Zinc stearate, 191-92
Zirconia aluminum grit, 25